THE TENDING INSTINCT

TIMES BOOKS | Henry Holt and Company New York

| THE |

TENDING

INSTINCT

*How Nurturing Is Essential for
Who We Are and How We Live*

Shelley E. Taylor

Times Books
Henry Holt and Company, LLC
Publishers since 1866
115 West 18th Street
New York, New York 10011

Library of Congress Cataloging-in-Publication Data
Taylor, Shelley, E.
The tending instinct : how nurturing is essential to who we are and how we live /
Shelley E. Taylor.—1st ed.
p. cm.
Includes bibliographical references and index.
ISBN 0-8050-6837-6 (hbk.)
1. Sociobiology. 2. Sex differences. 3. Nurturing behavior.
4. Stress (Psychology) I. Title.
HM628 .T38 2002
304.5—dc21   2002019879

First Edition 2002

Designed by Paula Russell Szafranski

Printed in the United States of America

1   3   5   7   9   10   8   6   4   2

Contents

THE TENDING INSTINCT

Preface

I could have begun this book in 1981, but instead I decided to have children. The trade-off is not what you might imagine. At the time, the personal message was clearer than the professional one. I was interviewing people with cancer about the aspects of their lives that had helped them cope with their illness and the debilitating treatments it imposed. One especially articulate woman led me to change the course of my life. She and her husband had raised four children who were now, as she put it, her sustenance through the long months of radiation and chemotherapy. I have rarely met anyone so satisfied with the life choices she had made. I returned home and said to my husband, "I think we're making a mistake."

Until that moment, we had decided to remain childless, so we could devote ourselves to our admittedly exciting careers. During the more than ten years that we held to this resolve, I published a lot of scientific papers, and he designed a lot of buildings. We continued our work after the children came, of course, but our lives now seemed to be linked backward and forward in time to our ancestors and to future generations, and outward, to our community, its schools, and our neighborhood, in ways that we had never before experienced. The sustaining relationships I had been writing about in my papers were now a more immediate part of my life.

Over the years, my scientific interests broadened from a social-psychological focus to include a biological perspective: first, as an interest in health—who stays well, who gets sick?—and then further back to the underlying neuroendocrine processes that get a person from good health to bad or from bad health to well again. I began to see how the social and biological pieces of a human life fall into place, complementing, influencing, and sometimes disturbing one another.

Like many people, I originally assumed that biology largely determines behavior, and so it was a tantalizing surprise to see how clearly social relationships forge our underlying biology, even at the level of gene expression. Chief among these social forces are the ways in which people take care of one another and tend to one another's needs. An early warm and nurturant relationship, such as mothers often enjoy with their children, is as vital to development as calcium is to bones. Even in adult relationships, we tend to each other's needs in ways that sustain long and healthy lives. My story, then, is about giving care—not the necessity or obligation of caregiving, but its potency.

My story is also about women and men and the differences between them. It did not set out to be so, but this has become an insistent theme in ways that are surprising and perhaps controversial. Women play a more central role in tending to others than do men. Tending abilities are, by no means, unique to women, but when we tell the story of "man" from the perspective of woman, we necessarily see different things—less about power and aggression, more about caring and nurturance, and, perhaps most surprising, a fair amount about how caring and nurturance shape the expression of power and aggression.

This view is somewhat at odds with the prevailing account traditionally offered by sociobiologists or evolutionary psychologists. Writers from these traditions often represent the human social landscape as a battleground, where the successful outmaneuver the weak through a competitive edge, deception, or sheer blunt force. Even relations between the sexes are said to be a battle. I find this characterization to be a baffling half-truth at best. It leaves out so much of human nature—how we love, nurture, and care for one another in manifold ways.

My own field—the study of stress—also reflects these competing viewpoints. The dominant metaphor, "fight or flight," represents the threatening social landscape as a solitary kill-or-be-killed world. My work suggests instead that the human response to stress is characterized at least as much by tending to and befriending others, a pattern that is especially true of women.

When I first challenged the idea that "fight or flight" is a universal characterization of stress, I was concerned about how it might be received. The response was very gratifying. I received letters and e-mails from all over the world, many of which posed questions, others of which expressed appreciation. But most of them had a common theme, which is reflected in the comments of one woman who wrote, "I've been reading popular accounts of science for years, and finally, here is something I recognize." This is one of my goals in this book, namely to add balance to our view of human nature. After some debate, I decided to call this book *The Tending Instinct*, because I want you to recognize that the caregiving we provide to others is as fundamental to human nature as our selfishness or aggression, themes on which scientists more commonly, though perhaps overzealously, reflect.

"Instinct" is a loaded word, and I choose it with cautious deliberation. Some scientific accounts will claim that, to be instinctive, a behavior must be automatic and invariant, destined to emerge, regardless of the environment in which it will be expressed. But, in fact, environmental conditions—intense stress, for example—can upset, derail, and change the form of much biologically driven behavior, and this is true of tending as well. Tending is not invariant or inevitable, but it is insistent in ways that justify the term instinct. We have neurocircuitries for tending as surely as we have biological circuitry for obtaining food and reproducing ourselves. Brain development has been driven by our tending, as we'll see. And how others fare in times of stress—from how calm they are to their likelihood of becoming ill—depends on the quality of the tending they receive.

But instinct is a loaded word for reasons that have political significance as well. When instinct is combined with the idea of tending, especially in women, it is a slippery slope to mothering instinct, women's destiny, and other terms that have so often been used to box women into roles they may not choose to play. In the years that I trained as a scientist, we solved this political dilemma by arguing that men and women were the same. Cultural and social expectations led us to assume different roles, of course, but if we could magically eliminate these sources of influence, the mythology went, our natures would be human, not distinctively male or female. How did we sustain such a fiction during the decades of research attesting to the contrary? That is a rhetorical question I will not attempt to answer. But probably the saddest fallout of our efforts to squeeze men and women into the same psychological mold was our intense embarrassment over anything inconveniently female in nature, and this included motherhood.

So squeamish have we been about the role of mothers that we've often sidelined and marginalized it, referring delicately to the "caregiver," as if any rather nice person might step in and do the job. Let me hasten to add that I am not arguing against nannies, day care, or any of the cobbled-together arrangements that beleaguered working parents make so they can simultaneously raise and support their families. What I am saying is that tending is a vitally important task that shapes the health and character of children (and adults), and it should be recognized as such. I hope you will finish reading this book with a renewed respect for it.

This point highlights a second theme, namely the fact that a primary product of our evolution is a large, magnificent brain with the capacity for planning, decision making, and choice. There are few "shoulds" or "musts" in the human social environment. We are the most flexible species on earth, and we have the ability to play almost any role we choose. Women can take on roles that traditionally fell to men, as surely as men can take on what traditionally have been thought of as women's roles. Both genders have the capacity for tending.

Let me now scramble down from my high horse and tell you what else I hope you will get from this book. I hope to leave you with a respectful but clear-eyed view of biology. Sometimes we reify it, and especially when we think a behavior may have a genetic basis, as tending no doubt does, we can unthinkingly exaggerate biology's importance. This viewpoint has been fueled by the excitement surrounding the mapping of the genome and the anticipation that we will soon understand the genetic bases for medical and psychological problems and their cures.

If I've done my job correctly, by the end of this book you will see that the genome is like an architect's first plan, a rough projection of how a person may turn out. But like most such efforts, this plan is revised during the course of the building process. The kitchen is rotated ninety degrees, the living room is extended a few feet. Later, the owner adds a bathroom, perhaps even a whole second story. This is what happens when genes meet the environment in which they find expression, and tending is a large part of this environment.

From life in the womb to the surprisingly resilient brain of old age, the social environment molds and shapes the expression of our genetic heritage until the genetic contribution is sometimes barely evident. We will see how mothering can forestall the potential effects of a gene, how a risk for disease can fail to materialize with nurturing, and why a genetic propensity may lead to one outcome for one person and the opposite for another, based on the tending they received.

Nonetheless, I give you fair warning: The biology of tending will be only roughly sketched out. Most readers, alas, do not want to wade through puddles of acetylcholine and cortisol to get to the "good stuff," and so those readers who think the synapses and neurotransmitters *are* the good stuff will need to go to the Notes and the References to chase these points further. I hope you do. The thrill is in the chase.

We're entering a new period in science, in which the rewards will come less from the breakthrough investigations of individual scientists than from fitting together the pieces of research to see what it all means. E. O. Wilson recently gave this viewpoint eloquent expression in his 1998 book, *Consilience*, in which he argued that social and biological insights are leaping together, part of a large and complex jigsaw puzzle to which the contributions of many sciences are essential. This book is in the spirit of what will, I hope, be a consilient era of collaboration.

I would like to have been the person who discovered this story and conducted the major studies that form its plot. In fact, I did little more than pick up pieces that were lying around in different but related fields and try to fit them together. In that effort, I have been well served by the MacArthur Foundation's SES and Health Network, under the direction of Nancy Adler, especially by my associations with Bruce McEwen and Teresa Seeman. Rena Repetti has been involved in many aspects of this thinking, and I owe her a great debt and thanks. Michael Meaney and John Cacioppo have also had a major impact on my thinking. None of these people bear any responsibility for any analytic or evidentiary shortcomings, however. The National Science Foundation and the National Institute of Mental Health have supported my work for many years, for which I am extremely grateful. I thank Rob McQuilkin, my agent, for his confidence, his Herculean efforts on my behalf, and his unflagging good nature, and my editors, David Sobel and Heather Rodino, for their many helpful insights. Many colleagues and friends collaborated with me on the research that forms the basis of this book or made valuable suggestions on early drafts, and they include Naomi Eisenberger, Tara Gruenewald, Regan Gurung, Laura Klein, Brian Lewis, John Updegraff, Rebecca Sage, David Sherman, Sally Dickerson, Jun Xu, Amy Goldring, and Johanna Jarcho. I thank Anne Peplau and Carol Tavris especially for their perspectives on this work. I am thankful to Nina McDowell, Regan Roby, and Melissa Dunagan for their tireless involvement in all aspects of the project. My deepest debt goes to my husband, Mervyn, and to my children, Sara and Charlie, for their confidence, love, and support. Their tending is my sustenance and inspiration.

| CHAPTER 1 |

The Power of Tending

E lsie Widdowson was a remarkable woman. A medical researcher at Cambridge University in the 1940s, she was a prominent scientist at a time when women scientists were quite rare. In 1948, Widdowson worked in a unit in Germany that was responsible for monitoring the nutrition of children orphaned by the war. The children she studied were raised in two group homes, each of which housed about fifty orphans ranging in age from four to fourteen. All of the children had suffered from poor nutrition toward the end of the war, and so they were all well below the heights and weights that were expected for their ages. And although the rations at the orphanages were a considerable improvement over their wartime fare, they were still barely adequate to meet these growing children's nutritional needs.

Widdowson and her colleagues wanted to see what would happen if the rations were improved even a little bit. Would the orphans catch up to their peers in height and weight or remain far behind? One of the orphanages, Bienenhaus, was given extra bread, jam, and orange juice for six months, while the other, Vogelnest, acted as a comparison that received no supplements. To the astonishment of the research team, the children at Vogelnest, the orphanage not receiving the extra food, grew nicely, whereas the children at Bienenhaus, the orphanage where extra food was plentiful, grew hardly at all.

During the next six months, the researchers reversed the conditions, and Bienenhaus reverted to standard rations, with Vogelnest now receiving the supplementary food. To the amazement of the research staff, the children at Bienenhaus, who were no longer receiving supplements, began to grow quickly, while the growth of those at Vogelnest tapered off. This, of course, is exactly the opposite of what extra food should do for children, and so Widdowson stepped in to see what was going on. Pretty quickly, she realized that the important story was not about food. It was about Fraulein Schwarz.

At the outset of 1948, Fraulein Schwarz was in charge of Bienenhaus. A stern, forbidding woman, Schwarz ruled her roost with an iron will and a quixotic bad temper. One day she might sharply reprimand a child for wearing gloves and the next day, scold that same child for not wearing them. To instill discipline, she had them sit in silence with their food in front of them until it grew cold. The children lived in constant fear of her anger, and outbursts of tears were commonplace. Even the lucky addition of food supplements could not offset the devastating effects of Fraulein Schwarz's cold tyranny on the growth of the Bienenhaus orphans.

Vogelnest, by contrast, was directed by Fraulein Grun, a bright sunny woman who genuinely loved the children in her charge and who was loved in return. Even without extra rations, the children of Vogelnest thrived under her nurturant care. But unhappily for her charges, Fraulein Grun left Vogelnest for another position, leaving a vacancy that was filled by none other than Fraulein Schwarz. Coincidentally, this switch in leadership occurred at precisely the moment that the supplements were withdrawn at Bienenhaus and introduced at Vogelnest.

Fraulein Schwarz was herself replaced at Bienenhaus by Fraulein Weiss, a woman much like Fraulein Grun in disposition, who was soon cherished by her new charges. At Bienenhaus, then, even though the food supplements had been withdrawn, the children grew under the loving attention of Fraulein Weiss. The children of Vogelnest, in contrast, now had to deal with the dreaded Fraulein Schwarz.

Fraulein Schwarz had her favorites, however—eight children on whom she bestowed nothing but praise and favoritism, and she took these children with her when she moved from Bienenhaus to Vogelnest. These eight children, then, had not only the praise and attentiveness of the otherwise cold and uncaring Fraulein Schwarz; they also received the food supplements for an entire year, first at Bienenhaus and then at Vogelnest. When their growth rates were measured, they were by far the tallest and heaviest of all the children.[1]

It is astonishing what a little affection and love can do. It must have been just a little—each orphanage had fifty children after all. But the share that each child got from a warm and loving caregiver did more for that child's growth than expensive food supplements. Through accounts such as these, you begin to recognize just how potent tending can be. And when you see that cruelty overrode even the effects of food supplements on physical growth, you begin to understand just how powerful a force fear can be as well. In this amazing story lie the twin sides of our human nature, which largely determine whether we thrive under the nurturant companionship of others or shrivel in body and spirit from fear and neglect.

When scientists have written about the nature of people—often referred to as the nature of man—they frequently portray a selfish, aggressive individual striving to maximize his outcomes, cooperating with others only if, over the long term, it will further his personal advancement. This perspective has been shaped directly or inadvertently by popular as well as scientific writings that focus heavily on the experience of men. Perhaps you were raised, as I was, on Lionel Tiger's *Men in Groups*, Konrad Lorenz's *On Aggression*, Richard Dawkins's *The Selfish Gene*, or Robert Ardrey's *African Genesis*—big, chest-thumping books that touted our selfish, individualistic, aggressive nature, the inevitability of male domination, and the success of the clever, deceptive man who turned every situation to suit his personal end. If these books are unfamiliar to you, the theme probably is not: each person is to others as little more than an opportunity for manipulation or exploitation.

While these books may not be wrong, they are most assuredly incomplete. On reading these accounts, one would have to conclude that their authors had either forgotten about women altogether or deeply misunderstood them. In their myopic focus on the aggressive experience of men, they ignore a very rich aspect of both women's and men's lives, namely the caring, nurturant side of human nature. When we look instead to women's lives for clues about human nature, the significance of nurturance snaps into place with such clarity that you wonder how its centrality could possibly have eluded scientific concern for so long.[2]

A mere glimpse at women's experience reveals that tending to others and caring for their needs is as vital a product of our evolution and as wired into our genes as our aggression and competitive nature. And, as we'll see, looking at human nature from the perspective of women's experience highlights the more nurturant aspects of men's lives as well. Nor is tending merely something nice that we do to ensure that babies will survive, men and women will stay together (at least for a while), and the sick, the infirm, and the elderly will not be abandoned. The tending instinct is every bit as tenacious as our more aggressive, selfish side. Yes, it is possible to carve out self-interested explanations for the caring we do. People give to charity for the tax breaks, mothers nurture babies to pass on their genes, we donate our time to humanitarian causes because it make us feel good about ourselves. But these explanations are strained, failing to capture either the impetus for tending or the joy it often brings. Base selfishness is not the source of our caring. Tending to others is as natural, as biologically based, as searching for food or sleeping, and its origins lie deep in our social nature.

AT FIRST GLANCE, a crowd of cladocerans, a type of microscopic aquatic zooplankton, would seem to have little in common with human beings. But like many species, including our own, the cladocerans have discovered that traveling in a pack is the best way to confuse and evade a natural predator, in their case the bladderwort plant. On their own, incautious zooplankton wander next to the sensitive hairs on the outside of the bladderwort's leaves, which, when they sense the presence of potential food, open a trap and capture the zooplankton for a later meal. But in response to a signal that alerts them to the bladderwort's presence, the zooplankton swarm, creating a density that makes it much harder for the bladderwort to do its hunting. Swarming slows the individual cladocerans down, allowing them to avoid the bladderwort's trapping mechanism; the bladderwort, in turn, finds that what seemed to have been a wonderful opportunity for dinner has resulted in empty traps instead.[3]

Human beings are much the same. During the long period of human prehistory, the million or so years when much of our evolutionary development is thought to have occurred, our social nature was honed to a degree only now being appreciated. In early societies, the social group kept potential predators at bay, and vital tasks such as hunting, some forms of gathering, and warfare were also aided by cooperation among individuals.

As the insistence of day-to-day survival needs has subsided, the deeper significance of group life has assumed clarity. The cooperative tasks of hunting and warfare represent the least of what the social group can accomplish. Group living is intrinsically soothing and comforting. We enjoy not only a happier but also a longer life in the company of others because the social groups that envelop us literally promote growth and regulate our stress systems. We are, of course, the source of one another's stress as well, but, as will become evident, the biological environment that is fostered by close relationships permits us to flourish in good health and recover from poor health quickly.[4]

As was true for the microscopic cladocerans, an impending threat especially activates social ties. A tragic or intensely stressful event rapidly evokes bonding with others, as recent threats to our nation have made painfully clear. We turn to our families for comfort, bond with our neighbors, donate dozens, even thousands of hours to the welfare of strangers who gladly return the favor. We keep one another from breaking down in fear, from turning in on ourselves, from getting sick, as our stress systems work overtime, trying unsuccessfully to battle an elusive enemy. These are the true triumphs of our social nature—the tending and healing powers that few of us knew we had.

Scientific evidence suggests that we have been caregivers since the outset of our existence. Skeletal remains indicate that many people with congenital disorders or horrific injuries nonetheless lived long lives for their era. Someone must have taken care of them. And one can only guess at the extent of injury and illness that left no enduring traces. Hunting and, to a lesser extent, foraging were risky jobs. For injured people to have survived, someone must have brought home food and water, lit fires, and driven off the inevitable predators attracted to those who had inadvertently stumbled into harm's way.[5] Anyone who has spent days home from work caring for a sick youngster or a spouse with back trouble knows that tending is part of the human condition and probably always has been.

Given the overwhelming evidence for tending, I'm going to start with the observation that we are fundamentally a nurturant species and show how it reveals a fundamental truth about human nature: The brain and body are crafted to tend, not indiscriminately so, but in order to attract, maintain, and nurture relationships with others across the life span. Beginning in the womb and extending into adulthood, who we are—our character, even our physical health—depends upon the people who tend to us and how well we get along with them—our mothers, fathers, friends, and lovers. Far from being mere social conventions, these relationships influence and are fundamentally influenced by biology throughout our lives in ways that can protect or hinder our health and well-being.

Does our legacy of tending to one another's needs truly merit consideration as an instinct? Can we argue with any confidence that there is a biologically driven program that underlies the many relationships in which we nurture one another? As we explore the nature of our social ties, first in the mother-infant relationship, then in relations within a social group, and between women and men, some of the same hormones will appear repeatedly—oxytocin, vasopressin, endogenous opioid peptides, growth hormone—among other suggestive commonalities. These hormones appear to be implicated in social behaviors of many kinds and are part of what scientists have called the affiliative neurocircuitry, an intricate pattern of co-occurring and interacting pathways that influence many aspects of social behavior, ranging from whether people are receptive to social relationships at all to how strong their relationships will be.[6]

All of these relationships are also marked by feelings of bonding (which may in part reflect this underlying biology), ranging from the intense attachment between mother and child to the surprisingly strong ties we can feel with strangers. As we'll also see, threatening situations especially evoke tending of all kinds. Signs of real or potential dangers alert us to join forces and watch out for one another.

Social ties echo each other in another way. All these relationships have the capacity to control stress responses. When supportive social ties are in evidence, the physiological and neuroendocrine arousal that we usually experience in response to stress is lessened. Nurturant contact with parents in early childhood, social support during times of stress, good friends (especially if they are female), and a strong relationship with a partner (especially if she is a wife) all protect against the psychological and health problems that stress otherwise promotes. These benefits, then, are evident at all levels, from the earliest bonds that begin in the womb to those experienced in our social institutions when people play, go to work, or go to war.

Before we continue this story of biology and behavior, we need to get a few myths out of the way. Our biological nature is often endowed with so much significance that exploring the biological origins of our nature can feel like dancing with a two-ton gorilla. You'd better let him lead, because you certainly don't want him to step on your feet. To many people, scientists and nonscientists alike, biology is the leader, and the environment just follows along, like an obedient Ginger Rogers. This casting of biology has several mythological components: biology is destiny; biology affects everyone the same way; biology is "natural" and, therefore, good. I will try to puncture these myths, not so we can ignore our biological origins, but so we can embrace them with understanding.

One dominant myth is that biology is inevitable, plowing right through environmental influences on behavior and tossing them to the sidelines. But looking at something that's fairly heritable—hypertension—reveals that its genetic expression is remarkably susceptible to tending.

In order to study disease, scientists often breed animals (usually rats) to have a susceptibility to a particular disorder, so they can then test drugs and other treatments to see if these interventions improve the rat's course of illness or longevity. Two neuroscientists, Brian Sanders and Matthew Gray, took a group of rat pups who had been bred to have a genetic risk for hypertension, and they then did something very simple. They fostered half the little soon-to-be-hypertensive pups to adoptive mothers from the same strain (who were therefore also hypertensive) and fostered the other half of the pups to mother rats of a different strain who were not hypertensive. They then looked to see how the baby rats managed stress as adults. Those who grew up with hypertensive foster mothers showed strong blood pressure responses to stressors, as expected, but those who grew up with foster mothers who were not hypertensive, for the most part, did not. The genetic risk was less evident when the rats were raised by normal mothers.[7]

What should this tell you? One conclusion you might draw is that mothers with a risk of hypertension have what might loosely be called a hypertensive mothering style—edgy, perhaps? It is hard to say with rats. But the second thing it should tell you is that genes are definitely not destiny. The hypertension we so commonly see running in families may be due in part to a genetic risk, but it is also likely to be heavily influenced by the family environment—affected, in part, by those very same genes, to be sure, but modifiable to such a degree that, in the right environment, the propensity to overreact to stress can seemingly disappear.

This simple study makes a very important point. The environment heavily influences the way in which many genes will be expressed. In later chapters, we'll see examples of children with a risky genetic heritage who nonetheless developed quite normally; in each case, the attentive tending of a caregiver, usually the mother, kept this "risky" heritage from emerging. What a powerful message this is: A mother's tending can completely eliminate the expression of a genetic heritage.

A second myth maintains that if the origins of some behavior are biological, then the behavior is natural and therefore meant to be. Some uses of this myth are that men are "meant to" go to war while women are "meant to" care for children. This is nonsense. Knowing the biological origins of behavior says nothing about its intrinsic goodness. By this criterion, infanticide, which has clear biological origins, is natural, right, and good.[8]

Consider the fact that women are often the caregivers of men in marriage. In Chapter 8, I will argue that this caregiving may have built on the ancient maternal caregiving system and developed because of a woman's needs to attract and hold a male partner to ensure protection and sufficient food for her offspring. But instead of concluding from such an argument, "Ah, women taking care of men—it is meant to be," why isn't it at least as reasonable for a woman to conclude, "I don't need his extra food anymore. Let him run his own errands"? My point here is not to encourage a widespread rebellion among women, as much as to show the absurdity of trying to construe what is natural or good or right from the simple fact of biological origins. Biological myths are simply stereotypes that reflect the wonder we feel about our genetic heritage. Stripping away those myths need not undermine that awe. The story of how genes interact with the environment is more exciting still.

I'm going to start the story of tending with a personal account of how I came to understand its force. It's a personal tale in another way as well, because it offers a peek into the joy of scientific discovery. And it provides the beginnings of an answer to the question, What is our human nature? We are people who tend to one another's needs, especially during stressful times. And through these actions, we have the capacity to shape one another's biology and temperament to a degree previously unimagined.

CHAPTER 2

The Origins of Tending

F ight or flight is the metaphor for how we respond to our stressful lives, or so scientists have believed for decades. The images of this coordinated stress response are familiar to all, chronicled daily in scenes of wildlife on television. One animal stalks another, the ears of the potential prey go up, and soon it is running for its life. Two animals, an elephant and a rhinoceros, perhaps, have a chance encounter at a water hole, and, in short order, they are locked in a life-and-death struggle.

Just as these images characterize our thoughts about animal behavior, so we have believed that fight or flight explains most of what is important about human responses to stress as well. Walter Cannon, an eminent scientist and physician in the 1930s, may be credited with giving us these early insights. Cannon had a patient named Tom, who, because of a medical disorder, had to be fitted with a gastric fistula, permitting Cannon a rare glimpse into the mucosa that line the stomach. When Tom was angry, Cannon observed, the mucosa became engorged with blood, readying Tom for a brisk, decisive response to the threat—fight or flight, as Cannon came to call it.

As a stress researcher, I have subscribed to the fight-or-flight meta-phor for much of my career, even as my own work told me it was incom-plete. For many years, I have studied how people cope with stress both biologically and through their actions. I've interviewed hundreds of people trying to come to terms with unexpected setbacks or losses and listened to accounts of how their lives had changed as a result. Fight or flight responses, such as anger over the injustice of their plight, frantic efforts to restore a loss such as good health, and, sometimes, depressed withdrawal as the inevitability of the setback became clear, were cer-tainly a part of these coping efforts, but they left a great deal out. Fight or flight represents each of us as solitary figures in our battles with threat, a portrait that belies what human beings actually do. In interviews with women who had breast cancer, for example, I heard how they came to value the relationships in their lives, tending to others even when they needed tending themselves, and drawing sustenance from their friends and relatives. I repeatedly heard accounts from women who had reordered their priorities and values to make time for grown children and women friends. Yet for years, I ignored the centrality of social ties for managing stress, accepting instead the conventional wisdom.[1]

In science, as in other aspects of life, you can know something with-out realizing that you know it, and only when some jarring incongruity forces a contradiction to the forefront of your mind do you recognize what your previously implicit knowledge really means. So it was with my understanding of human responses to stress.

On a Thursday in March 1998, my students and I attended a lecture on the amygdala, a portion of the brain believed to be critical to the experience of fear. The amygdala is also involved in some of our quickest responses to threat, and so how it works is critical to the study of stress—hence, my interest.

As the speaker described his very able research program, he inter-jected some observations about the rat participants in his studies that gave me pause. "Of course we had to house all the rats separately, so they wouldn't attack each other," he explained. Attack each other? I study people under stress, and attack is not what you typically see. In fact, quite the opposite—people often turn to one another for solace and support. He went on in this vein for an hour, describing rats who aggressed against their cage mates, the victims who cowered in the corners of their cages, all of them facing a short, brutal life, the fallout of continuous fighting or unsuccessful efforts to flee.

After the talk, I assembled my research group, and during our discussion I mentioned some of these anomalous comments. "You know animal researchers study only male rats," offered one of my postdoctoral students. I had known this, of course, but it had never seemed to be a potential insight until now. She went on: "Female rats have such rapid hormonal changes that you can't get a clear picture of their stress responses." "Most of the biological studies of human stress use only men, too," added a neuroscience student.

An epiphany in science is fairly rare, but when it happens, there is no sensation like it. The sudden recognition that all of the classic theories of stress were based almost entirely on males was a stunning revelation. I remember thinking, I didn't know there were any big mistakes left in science. We stared at one another as the opportunity that lay before us became clear: a chance to start over and discover what females do in response to stress.

Over the next few months, we ransacked the scientific literature and discovered that, indeed, most of the science of stress is based on males. So common is the convention of studying only male rats in animal research that many scientists do not even bother to mention the sex of their rats in their scientific papers, which is one of the reasons why the male bias was such a well-kept secret.

The research on humans was even more surprising. Women's hormones cycle just as female rats' hormones do, of course, but they do so quite predictably and over twenty-eight days, so there is no particular reason to exclude women from studies of stress. Yet prior to the mid-1990s, only about 17 percent of the participants in studies of biological responses to stress were women.

In 1995, the federal government acted on the systematic exclusion of women from research of all kinds. Their interest wasn't engaged by the biased representation of men in stress research but rather by the problems this bias creates for our understanding of heart disease, an illness believed to be heavily influenced by stress and by poor ways of managing it. The overwhelming majority of studies on the causes and course of heart disease have been conducted with men, and many of our medications and recovery programs for treating heart disease have been tested only on men as well. This bias is especially unnerving when you realize that more women than men actually die of heart disease, albeit later in life. Responding to pressure from women scientists and women's groups, the government mandated that research studies had to include both sexes.

Since this ruling, about 200 studies of stress have been published that have included about 15,000 people. Nearly 43 percent of the participants have been women, which, of course, is much better.[2] Unfortunately, though, few of these studies have compared men's and women's responses to stress, and so we still know relatively little about the differences in how men and women manage stress. Moreover, many studies of responses to particular stressors remain perversely based on either men or women, but not both. For example, studies of how people react to physical stress such as exercise include mostly men, and studies of social behavior during stress rely heavily on women, which makes it hard to piece together what men and women do that is different. Accordingly, armed with this background, we set some daunting tasks for ourselves: to ascertain how ignoring the experience of women might have biased the scientific understanding of stress and to see in what ways men and women might differ in their responses to stress.

As a point of departure, we turned to evolutionary theory. Evolutionary theory guides the study of biology and increasingly the study of psychology as well. As one scientist friend put it, "Evolution isn't just the best game in town, it's the only game in town." If you can't square your ideas with evolution, your scientific battles will be uphill.

Evolutionary theory provides good reasons for believing that many of men's and women's reactions to stress will be similar. Human beings' stress responses most likely evolved during the million or so years that we were hunters and gatherers, during the Pleistocene era. Natural selection heavily shaped these responses, since people without effective responses to stress would have died young without passing on their genetic heritage to any offspring. Predators, natural disasters, and skirmishes with outsiders were among the formidable threats that our human ancestors faced. And as these threats were common to both men and women, it follows that our stress responses would have evolved in much the same way.

What are these responses? Most commonly you experience arousal—your heart races, your blood pressure goes up, you sweat, and your hands tremble a little. The chemicals epinephrine and norepinephrine surge through the body, getting you ready to take action against the threat or get out of the way. These are the biological origins of the fight-or-flight response; if you are a scientist, you call it sympathetic activation.

The second stress system is the hypothalamic-pituitary-adrenocortical system (HPA). You don't feel the HPA response as clearly as you feel sympathetic arousal, but those sensations of anxious worrying, that feeling of lurking menace during times of stress, may be part of it. When stress activates the HPA, hormones are released that shut down nonessential bodily activities in favor of activities that promote timely and effective responses to stress, such as mental alertness and the release of energy. These stress systems get the body ready to cope with a stressor, and so in this sense they are vital to staving off threats. Men and women experience these aspects of stress fundamentally the same way. At the sight of a potential predator, arousal goes up for men and women alike.

But men and women faced some different challenges, too. Females of all species, including humans, have been the primary caretakers of offspring, and females' responses to stress would have evolved so as to include some measure of protection for their children. Otherwise, how could women have passed on their genes? If, as a mother, you flee from a menacing predator but leave your bewildered toddler unprotected, that child's chances of survival are clearly very poor. Consequently, responses to stress that favored both the mother's and the child's survival would most likely be passed on.[3]

What would those responses be? After our scientific epiphany, a group of us, three men and three women with expertise in neuroscience, evolution, stress, and social support, started meeting regularly to formulate an answer to this question. We began the way a lot of science begins, with brainstorming sessions filled with uncensored hunches and speculation. We started with images: the brightly colored male drawing away a predator while the more drab female quietly covers the offspring, evading detection. We looked for human evidence of tending in females, the ability to calm down offspring and fade into the surroundings without attracting attention. From our research with humans, we knew that women turn to the social group in times of stress, and so we looked for patterns of "befriending." We constructed our theory around these two pivotal observations about female responses to stress—protecting offspring and turning to others—and accordingly called it "tend and befriend."

Our basic points are these: In times of stress, a mother's "tending"—that is, quieting and caring for offspring and blending into the environment—is effective for meeting a broad array of threats. Calming the young and getting them out of harm's way can ensure that their lives will continue. But protecting both yourself and your offspring is a formidable task, and so women who drew effectively on the social group for help may have more successfully dealt with threats than those who did not—hence, the befriending response. Turning to the social group in times of stress protects both men and women, of course, but the social group especially aids women and children since it provides others who can watch out for the safety of youngsters and protect them, if the need arises.

What about the fight-or-flight response? Wouldn't we expect women to show this reaction to stress, just as men do? Certainly women experience the arousal that accompanies threat, just as men do, but fighting and fleeing may not always be among the most adaptive ways for them to respond. Flight by a mother can be impractical with young, immature offspring in tow, and should the mother flee without her young, they could be left fatally unprotected. Fight, likewise, is risky. Unless a mother and her young are attacked by a predator, giving the mother no choice but to defend them, attempting to fight a foe may well be fatal to mother and offspring alike.

Indeed, the fight-or-flight response to stress may be a more viable response to stress for males than for females. Male hormones, especially testosterone, appear to fuel the fight response, and a lot of evidence, ranging from boys fighting on the playground to violent crime statistics, suggests that physical aggression in response to stress is much more often the province of males than females. Flight, too, may be easier for males, if they are unencumbered by the demands of others.

From an evolutionary standpoint, tend and befriend is a plausible account of female responses to stress. Volumes of scientific work attest to animals' maternal behavior under stress, and research on humans shows some of the same patterns. What is some of this evidence? Many people would argue that we need little proof that women tend to offspring, that it's so self-evident as to scarcely require evidence. Certainly, it is the case that throughout history, and across cultures, women have been the tenders of children. And, rhetoric aside, even in countries where traditional sex roles have encountered their greatest challenges, as in the United States, women continue to be the mainstay of caring for children by a large margin. (By these observations, I do not mean that women should or must care for children or that only women can care for children, only that they are more likely to do so.) The notion of tending, however, includes something more than child care, namely a propensity to turn to offspring and to nurture them when conditions grow more stressful.

An example of what I mean by tending can be found in the fascinating research of Rena Repetti, a developmental and clinical psychologist at UCLA. Since the beginning of her career, Repetti has been interested in how men and women manage the stress of work life while simultaneously juggling the demands of a family. As a talented and busy scientist and the mother of two spirited daughters, Repetti also has a personal stake in answering this question: How *do* parents manage it? The approach she takes to this issue is straightforward. She locates working parents and has them complete questionnaires about the events of specific workdays and their subsequent activities at home. She also asks their children to fill out questionnaires about their day's experiences, particularly their parents' behavior toward them, and then Repetti compares the parents' and children's responses.

Stressful days take a toll on family relationships; that much is clear. Some days are just busy, filled with too much to do, while other days are acrimonious, producing conflict with coworkers and other interpersonal unpleasantness. Exactly how the day was unpleasant—merely busy or filled with conflict—makes a difference in how fathers behave with their families. When fathers come home at the end of a busy day, they often want to be left alone. They turn on the TV, go into the den and close the door, busy themselves with household chores, or otherwise go off by themselves for a while to unwind. This is what fathers say they do after a busy day, and their children confirm it: "Don't bother Dad right now. He's tired."

After a day filled with conflict, these same men are more likely to pick at their wives and children: "Who left the garage door open?" "Why haven't you started your homework?" "Does the kitchen always have to be such a mess?" Whether these fathers are aware that they are taking out their frustrations on their families is unclear; they may believe they are justified in their criticisms, unaware that the residue of a bad day is what has actually provoked them. But the evidence is clear. When a father's day is filled with conflict, his children say he is impatient and crabby: "Dad's in a bad mood. Stay out of his way."

The mothers in Repetti's studies behave quite differently, at least according to their children. When mothers have had a bad day, they are more affectionate with their children. They hug them more, spend more time with them, and tell them they love them. In other words, they "tend" to them. The children in Repetti's research don't know what kind of workdays their mothers had; they're just telling Repetti what their mothers did. Mothers don't seem to realize that they've grown more affectionate, but hugging and loving their children seems to work well for mothers ready to shed a bad day.[4]

WHAT ABOUT THE "befriending" aspect of the theory? Although studies of biological stress responses have largely excluded women, those that look at behavior under stress have not. Moreover, men and women themselves have very clear ideas about how they cope. When asked what they do when they're feeling stressed, women say they talk to their friends, share their problems, or call someone on the phone; men say they do this only rarely. Women ask for directions when they're lost; men often don't, at least not until they've driven around for a while. Women say they clear the air and talk through their concerns with others; men are more likely to say that they put their worries behind them.

When you listen to men and women talk about the different ways they cope with stress, as I have done for over two decades, it doesn't take long to realize that women's responses are profoundly more social. These informal accounts are backed up by scientific evidence. About thirty scientific studies have looked at what men and women do in response to stress: Do they turn to others for help or go it alone? All thirty studies show that women draw on their friends, neighbors, and relatives more than men do, whether the stress results from unemployment, cancer, fear of crime, a death in the family, or simple sadness.[5]

From a scientific standpoint, this is an amazing consistency. In the social sciences, you rarely see thirty studies all showing the same thing. The difference between women's and men's inclination to turn to the social group in times of stress ranks with "giving birth" as among the most reliable sex differences there are.

At this point, we began to formalize our evidence into a theory. The criterion we set for ourselves was a stiff one. For every point in our theory, we had to be able to show parallel evidence in both biology and behavior. In other words, we wanted to see evidence that females tend and befriend in response to stress and evidence that biological processes back it up. We plunged into the biology of stress, and this is what we found.

TENDING TO OFFSPRING is central to how animals respond to stress. One of the foremost researchers to show this is Michael Meaney, a biological psychologist with a talent for noticing important things that others have overlooked. For years, scientists have known that if you take baby rats out of their mother's nest, stroke them, put them back, and do this several times, the rats develop better physically than if you just leave them in the nest. Interpretations of this pattern varied, because it is not immediately clear what the biological benefits of stroking might be. Meaney began looking at what mothers do when their pups are returned to them. After one of these stroking sessions, mothers head over to the newly returned pup and begin a vigorous session of licking and grooming and nursing. It's the mother rat's equivalent of, "Oh, you're home! I was *so* worried! I love you so much." Rat pups thrive with this attention, and as Meaney and his colleagues' research subsequently showed, it's the maternal attention, not the stress, that causes these little pups to develop better.[6]

What is at the heart of this tending neurocircuitry? In other words, what prompts mothers to behave like this? The hormone oxytocin may play a role. Oxytocin is probably best known for what it contributes to birth, prompting labor itself and milk production. The sensations that accompany the release of oxytocin hold special interest. Right after birth, an intense calm sets in for most mothers. You've just completed one of the most vigorous and painful experiences of your life, which lasted for perhaps ten or fifteen hours, and it really is nice to have it over. But the calm is more than what comes from relief at the end of a painful experience. It has an otherworldly quality. When you look at paintings of the Madonna, you get the sense that some artists have crept into the new mother's soul and sensed what those feelings are really like. Certainly love for the newborn is part of it, but the intensity is greater and more visceral than love connotes. This is the beginning of bonding.

Being on oxytocin is a bit like being sedated, and, in fact, a lot of research on animals finds that injecting animals with oxytocin calms them down, makes them less anxious, and induces a mild state of sedation. These clues suggest that there may be a broader biological role for oxytocin. Oxytocin is not only released during labor and nursing. It is also a stress hormone that is released in smaller amounts during at least some stressful events.[7]

When we developed our theory of tend and befriend, we reasoned that there must be a biological basis for the fact that females calm down enough to avoid fighting or fleeing, tending to their offspring instead. With oxytocin, we identified one potential candidate. Not only does oxytocin reliably produce a state of calm, it is also a social hormone. Among its other effects, it leads mothers to tend to their offspring. For example, Cambridge University researchers Keith Kendrick and Eric Keverne injected female sheep with oxytocin and found that their maternal behavior increased greatly. The mother sheep groomed and touched their infants more after the oxytocin injection, behaviors that both reflected the mother's calm, nurturant state of mind and induced a similar soothed state in the offspring.[8] Herein lies a plausible mechanism for how and why mothers tend to their young in stressful times in ways that calm the infants, letting them be lulled into a warm and comforting place, despite the risks that surround them. Oxytocin may be one of nature's important ways of ensuring that mothers take to their infants, love them, care for them, and make the sacrifices that will be needed to bring them to maturity, especially during times of stress.

Oxytocin appears to get some help in this process. Among the other hormones implicated in maternal behavior are endogenous opioid peptides (EOPs). EOPs are the natural pain relievers of the body; among other functions, they have been credited with causing "runner's high," the euphoric, pain-free state that many experienced runners feel in the wake of a long, satisfying run. EOPs also seem to play a role in social behavior.

Scientists study the effects of EOPs primarily by blocking them. If you give someone a pill or an injection that keeps EOPs from coursing through the body and you subsequently see some behavior reliably change, you can fairly confidently infer that EOPs are involved in the behavior. So it is with mothering. In one study, rhesus monkeys were given an EOP blocking agent, and their caregiving and protection of their infants plummeted. A similar study found the same effects in sheep. When EOPs were blocked from flowing naturally, these normally attentive mother sheep barely acknowledged their own offspring. Since blocking EOPs effectively eliminates maternal behavior, it is a reasonable hypothesis that EOPs normally contribute to it.[9]

Other hormones may be implicated in maternal behavior. Estrogen and progesterone work together to enhance maternal responsiveness during pregnancy, priming mothers for motherhood after birth. Noradrenaline, serotonin, and cortisol go up as well. Why are there so many hormones to prompt mothering? Do we need them all?

Nature has a way of backstopping important processes, and mothering may be one of them. If you look at the human body, you'll notice a lot of redundancy—two eyes, two kidneys, two nostrils. Probably the best example is digestion. There are three ways that the stomach can produce the acids needed for digesting food, some of which work together, each of which can take over should one process shut down. As a process vital to survival, mothering may be much the same. If you raise levels of oxytocin, mothering in animals will go up, but raising EOPs will achieve a similar effect. The hormone prolactin goes up when you take care of someone else's children, but it may also go up when you care for your own children. Once scientists understand the maternal neuro-circuitry better, it would not be a surprise to discover that there are several different ways to engage maternal behavior. The survival of the species depends on nurturance, and if one hormone isn't helping to engage maternal behavior, others may well be in line to take its place.[10]

The befriending aspect of our theory, which I cover more fully in Chapter 6, appears to be regulated by some of these same hormones. When female animals are given an injection of oxytocin, for example, they behave as if a social switch has been turned on: they seek out more social contact with their friends and relatives. EOPs also influence social behavior, making women (but perhaps not men) more social.[11]

But what about human mothers? Unfortunately, we have a lot less information about the role that oxytocin may play in the behavior of human mothers because much of its work is done in the brain and cannot be directly observed. As a result, scientists have not been able to determine exactly where in the brain the oxytocin receptors are and how oxytocin flows to them in times of stress and during maternal bonding. In humans, we have to look at other evidence instead.

One type of evidence comes from observing the behavior and emotions of women who are known to have high levels of oxytocin—mothers who are nursing, for example—and comparing them with women who don't. Kerstin Uvnas-Moberg, a Swedish endocrinologist, has done exactly this. Women who are breast-feeding, she found, are calmer and more sociable than women of the same age who aren't breast-feeding. Moreover, the amounts of oxytocin these women had in their bloodstreams predicted just how calm and sociable they were. More important are the links that Uvnas-Moberg made to biological stress responses. She showed that women who are breast-feeding show less sympathetic arousal than women who are not, and they show suppressed HPA responses as well. Other scientists have now made the same connections.[12] This is an important set of findings: in humans, as in animals, oxytocin is associated with reduced neuroendocrine responses to stress—that is, with a reduction in the biological underpinnings of fight or flight.

Don't men (or male animals) have these same responses to stress, you may wonder? It doesn't appear that they do. As we'll see, men certainly respond protectively toward others during times of stress, but probably not because of the same hormonal influences. Oxytocin's effects are enhanced by estrogen, which means that, in a woman, its effects on stress responses and social behavior will be magnified by the simultaneous presence of estrogen. But the impact of men's hormones on oxytocin may be exactly the opposite. Androgens appear to antagonize oxytocin's effects, which means that whatever effects oxytocin may have on men may be reduced by the presence of male hormones. Since male hormones like testosterone often increase in response to stress, the impact of oxytocin on men's biology and behavior under stress may be quite minimal.[13]

During the course of our work, we had demanded that our theory account for several puzzles in stress research. We had predicted, for example, that something calms women, reducing the arousal that is usually seen in response to stress. We found a viable answer in oxytocin and endogenous opioid peptides. We demanded that the theory account for why women show these tend-and-befriend patterns more than men do, and the fact that estrogen amplifies the effects of oxytocin provided a viable answer. We wanted our theory to explain why women's responses to stress are so social, and we found that in animals, oxytocin and EOPs are known to be part of the "affiliative neurocircuitry," providing a biological basis for turning to others.

We published our paper on tend and befriend and awaited the response. The first to weigh in were a feminist scholar, who said it wasn't true, and humorist Dave Barry, who said that of course it was true—it was completely obvious. Shortly thereafter, a New York columnist predicted that Hillary Clinton would tend-and-befriend the election right out from under then-candidate Rudolph Giuliani, and a London-based reporter asked, apparently seriously, what women had done to cope with stress before the telephone was invented.

As the commentary continues, our thinking on these issues has expanded as well, ranging from what men do in response to stress to whether the caregiving seen in women may extend well beyond the caring for children. Does the same affiliative neurocircuitry underlie why women take care of others as well—their husbands, friends, or aging parents? And are there comparable responses in men? These are the issues I explore in this book.

Do MEN TEND in response to stress? This was a question we considered repeatedly throughout our research, and the answer always came up no or, at least, not really. Much of our reasoning came from the fact that in animal studies, oxytocin seems to be antagonized by some of the hormones that increase in men in response to stress, namely the androgens. Our analysis was lent more urgency and the need for clarification when two scientists, David Geary and Mark Flinn, argued, in response to our work, that tend and befriend applies to men as well as women. Is this true?

In recent years, we've heard a lot about fatherhood. On the one hand, committed fathers are asserting their parental rights as never before, insisting on having access to their children following a divorce and demanding joint or even sole custody. At the same time, we hear much about deadbeat dads who fail to provide for their offspring and seldom see them. Where does the truth lie?

If you look around the animal kingdom, you will rapidly come to the conclusion that human fathers are just about the best fathers on earth. They're outshined by a few birds and by titi monkeys (whose offspring would die of neglect were it not for attentive fathers), but otherwise, there are few rivals. Even chimpanzees, bonobos, gorillas, and baboons are in a different league. Compared to our primate relatives, human fathers are models of caring and attentiveness by a very large margin—indeed, in some species, not killing young is considered a sign of good fathering. Beyond dutifully providing for their offspring, human fathers offer love, caring, and pride. They invest time in children's activities. They make a commitment to children's learning and development, and allow children to assume a central position in their lives. What makes human fathers so caring?

The human father's very distinctiveness is what makes this question so hard to answer. The reason we know a lot about mothers, especially the biology of motherhood, is that, to paraphrase Tolstoy, all good mothers are essentially the same. Certainly what you need to do to be a good mother becomes much more challenging the more complex the species, but attentiveness, nurturance, and warmth are fundamental to rat and monkey mothering as well as to human mothering, and most mothers in nearly every species do it. Thus, we can look at rats and monkeys (and sheep, apes, birds, etc.) and learn something about mothering.

But with fathering, it's very different. If there aren't a lot of good fathers around in other species, it's difficult to identify the universal components of good fathering or to understand the neurocircuitry that underlies it. What hormones guide fathering? Why are some fathers so much better than others? Scientists do not yet know. Fathers have gotten little attention in both the biological and the psychological work on caring for children. The paternal role has been viewed as largely indirect—mainly as support for the mother, the primary caregiver—but clearly fathers do more.

On the one hand, fathering is a lot like mothering. Fathers explore their new babies the same way that mothers do, beginning with the fingers and limbs, and on seeing their newborns, they describe feelings of elation similar to the mothers'. Fathers talk to babies in much the same way as mothers do—their voices go up, they slow down their speech, and they enunciate each syllable with care. Fathers respond much as mothers do to infant cries, with distress and attention to babies' needs.

Babies, in turn, develop attachments to their fathers, seeking to be with them and protesting when they leave, just as they do with their mothers. The more the father cares for and plays with the baby, the more evident is this attachment.[14]

But is there a paternal neurocircuitry that is comparable to the maternal neurocircuitry? Is there a biologically based tending response in fathers? There are a few tantalizing clues. One conspicuous fact about fathering is that the male hormones that are usually associated with aggression subside somewhat when men respond to children in a nurturant way. In essence, the neurocircuitry for aggression is at least partly disengaged. But surely good fathering isn't merely the absence of aggression. When male hormones are lower, other hormones may come into play.[15]

The hormone vasopressin is attracting attention as a potential basis for men's tending responses under stress. What makes vasopressin so interesting is that, in terms of molecular structure, it looks very much like oxytocin. This suggests that both hormones may owe their origins to a simpler version of oxytocin and vasopressin. At some point, the one hormone became two, and, with its division, came somewhat different functions. Vasopressin, which both men and women have, is known primarily for regulating blood pressure and kidney functioning, but, like oxytocin, it is also a stress hormone.

This is where things get really interesting and, alas, rather speculative as well. Both men and women release vasopressin in response to stress, but unlike oxytocin, which is subdued by male hormones, the effects of vasopressin may be enhanced by them, making vasopressin a potential influence on men's stress responses. If oxytocin is associated with calm, nurturant, affiliative behavior, what does vasopressin do?

Again, because much of this action goes on in the brain, the source of our knowledge about vasopressin is from animal studies. One animal in particular, the prairie vole, has provided a lot of knowledge. Why the prairie vole and not rats, rhesus monkeys, and sheep, which provided help in understanding the effects of oxytocin in women? Unlike most male mammals, the prairie vole is a monogamous little creature who picks a mate and stays with her for life. He guards and protects her and generally keeps things safe. Since humans are fairly monogamous, too, the prairie vole provides a potential animal model for understanding what men do in response to stress. The little bit of research that has been done suggests that vasopressin may well be implicated in male responses to stress. When stress occurs, levels of vasopressin go up, and the male prairie vole becomes a protective sentinel, guarding and patrolling his territory, keeping his female partner and the young from harm.[16]

Whether vasopressin is implicated in men's responses to stress is not yet known, but there are intriguing commonalities in behavior between men and male prairie voles. Men protect and guard women and children in times of stress, for example. As Lionel Tiger pointed out in *Men in Groups*, men band together with other men to defend against threats, forming armies, neighborhood patrols, and vigilante groups. They are still by a large margin the world's police, firefighters, and soldiers. Certainly the evidence that ties vasopressin to the protective defense of others is intriguing, but whether this provides a key to understanding men's responses to stress remains unknown.

We're at the frustrating point that scientists reach when the evidence falls short of what we want to know. Eventually, we will learn more about the neurocircuitry of human fathering, but at the moment it is still, to our dismay, out of reach. One thing is fairly clear, however. Compared to motherhood, fatherhood is more variable and perhaps less biologically guided. Consequently, we could tentatively conclude that many men are good fathers because they choose to be. Mothers exercise substantial choice about their mothering, too, of course, but nature provides some firm biological nudges as well, just in case nursing and singing lullabies aren't sufficiently compelling in their own right.

To pursue this idea a bit further, fathering may be an inherently flexible behavioral system, perhaps less hardwired than mothering. As such, it may involve a lot of learning and sensitivity to cues in the environment, especially cues from the mother. This idea gets some surprising support from studies with rats. Mother rats are fairly good mothers, but before they get engaged in mothering, they have to overcome a built-in aversion to pups. No one is quite sure why, but female rats are none too smitten with babies. Immediately after the babies are born, fathers attend to their offspring, eyeing the female nervously, waiting for her to start feeling maternal. Once she does, he's gone, and for all practical purposes, his fatherhood is over. But during that little hiatus, when everyone is waiting for the mother rat to feel maternal, he watches out for the babies.

Unlike female rats, women don't usually feel an aversion to babies. Many women find babies to be quite wonderful and can't get enough of them, so fathers aren't usually needed to stem any gap in maternal attentiveness. Nonetheless, babies are a lot of work, and the enduring ties between men and women evolved in large part because two parents have more success than one in bringing children to maturity. Good fathering tends to go hand in hand with monogamy. When men are there for women, they are usually there for children as well.

But like the father rat, human fathers often take their cues from mothers and from the social context of the family. Mothers can be ferocious gatekeepers when it comes to children, and so unless they are single parents, fathers often follow the mother's lead. When mothers set rules and guidelines, fathers often back off. When mothers are less restrictive, fathers become more engaged. Fathers help out more when there are several children spaced close together, when the mother's attention is taken up with a newborn, and when the mother works outside the home—all conditions when mothers are otherwise occupied and a second parent is needed.

Fathers also provide more child care if there aren't other women around who could help the mother. For example, fathers are more active parents if the family lives apart from kin who might otherwise be available for child care. They help more in cultures where women have responsibilities outside the home, and they help more if the society isn't facing war on a regular basis. In short, fathering ebbs and flows with environmental conditions that make it more or less urgent. Fatherhood is a flexible system, indeed, and we have a big flexible brain to thank for it.

But fathering isn't identical to mothering either, even at its active best. Fathers are less likely than mothers to tend to basic care like feeding and changing; they focus instead on play. Fathers are more stimulating, vigorous, and disruptive with babies than mothers are, but since babies need stimulating, exciting times to mature properly (as well as the more soothing, less arousing times they get more often from mothers), this may be all to the good. Babies with involved, playful fathers are more social early in life and turn into more socially competent children than those whose fathers stay in the background.[17]

It is clear, then, that either parent can have a sensitive, responsive relationship with an infant. But fathers are more likely to take their cues from and respond to mothers' behavior and to the larger social context in which parenting occurs. From a biological standpoint, fatherhood may be a backup system, but if so, it is a very good backup system indeed.[18]

CLEARLY, HUMAN BEINGS are tenders. Both the biological evidence and the growing evidence concerning mothers' and fathers' behavior support this idea. How did we acquire this capacity for tending? In the next chapter, I suggest that it is wired into our brains as surely as the needs for food, sex, and safety.

CHAPTER 3

The Tending Brain

R udyard Kipling was a masterful storyteller who created fanciful explanations of mysterious phenomena in the animal kingdom, such as how the leopard got his spots or how the rhinoceros got his skin. In each "just so" story, Kipling singled out the feature that made the animal distinctive, crafting a tale around it that revealed the animal's inherent nature, whether peaceful, crafty, or curious.

Consider Kipling's tale of how the elephant got his trunk. One day, a baby elephant went down to the river to quench his thirst. As he leaned down to drink, a hungry crocodile grabbed him by his nose and tugged, trying to pull him into the water for a quick meal. With the help of a friendly python, the baby elephant pulled back, until the crocodile was forced to let go. As a result of the struggle, however, the little elephant was left with a very long nose. Initially, he lamented his predicament, but he soon discovered how handy it was for picking up grasses from the ground, for pulling fruit off trees, and for swatting flies, drinking water, and spanking his siblings. The crocodile, to his surprise, soon found his services to be in great demand, because once the other elephants saw how useful it was, they all wanted long noses.

To a child, a "just so" story is a delicious confection, a fantastic tale about the origins of the animal kingdom's most intriguing qualities. To a scientist, having one's work labeled as a "just so" story is a feared criticism, a shorthand way of saying that one has concocted an unsubstantiated, even wild tale of how something came to be. Yet in a basic sense, scientists are like Kipling, trying to understand how distinctive features came about and why they might have developed in one way as opposed to another. None of us was there 6 million years ago when the human species broke off from the chimpanzee line. We make educated guesses about our nature and why it developed as it did from the fossil record. We draw on evolutionary theory and the mechanisms it proposes for why things change and get passed on. But our theories are still stories, and it is sometimes hard to know if we are on firm ground. I say this by way of preface so that you will appreciate Rudyard Kipling's task a little more and respect the dilemma of scientists as well, as we try to reconstruct our origins when only traces remain.

Long noses serve elephants well, which is why they evolved as such. When you turn to humans, the most striking feature that differentiates us from other animals is our big brain. Bigger animals—elephants and hippos, for example—have much smaller brains relative to their size than we do, especially in the prefrontal cortex where crucial functions such as thinking, planning, and decision making take place. The products of this large brain are obvious: the invention of computers, the theory of relativity, and even our understanding of human evolution represent a modest sampling of what the large and complex human brain has been able to accomplish. But why does the human have such a big brain?

Theories about the origins of the big brain have abounded throughout scientific history. Perhaps we needed it to meet our complex nutritional needs? Or, alternatively, perhaps brain development was driven by our technological needs? After considering several possibilities and finding the evidence to be disappointingly lacking, scientists have largely settled on an answer. The big brain is fundamentally a social brain. We live by our ability to coordinate our needs with those of the people around us. Other animals have weapons, such as sharp teeth and claws, and good defenses against threat, such as colors that blend in with the landscape or quick speed for a rapid getaway. As Desmond Morris noted, humans are naked apes, hairless animals who can't outrun anyone, can't defend well against predators, and can't even stay warm without help. Our success as a species has come entirely from our gregarious nature. We live and work together, having found safety in numbers across the many thousands of years of our evolution.[1]

EXACTLY WHAT DROVE the evolution of the social brain, however, has been a matter of some debate. Male scientists have long been the proprietors of this story and as a result, in their interpretations, brain development revolved around men's activities. Men needed to coordinate their hunting activities with other men, and so big brains evolved (in men alone, by some accounts) because the big brain met the challenges of the hunt more successfully.

Natural selection would have favored the big brains of successful hunters for several reasons. More reliable sources of protein would lead to longer lives and opportunities to produce more offspring. As hunting improved and food sources became more reliable, bigger social groups would become more tenable. People could have more children spaced closer together because they could feed all of them, and the species would grow more numerous. According to the theory, sexual selection would have favored the successful hunter as well. Men with the ability to bring game home to their families would be attractive mating prospects, and be able to take their pick of one or more women, and, consequently, they would produce more offspring to whom they could pass on their genes for a big brain.

No less a figure than Charles Darwin, the father of evolutionary theory, first put forth this viewpoint in 1871, and his beliefs went largely unchallenged for decades. According to Darwin, men are subject to more selection pressures than women are, because they have so many important jobs to do—hunting, driving off rivals, using their charms to attract partners, and protecting their offspring and mates, just to name a few. Darwin concluded that these tasks require "the aid of the higher mental faculties, namely observation, reason, invention, or imagination. These various faculties will thus have been continually put to the test and selected during manhood."[2]

Darwin concluded that, as a result, man attains "a higher eminence, in whatever he takes up, than can woman—whether requiring deep thought, reason, or imagination, or merely the use of the senses and hands" with the result that "man has ultimately become superior to women." It's a good thing that children get their evolutionary heritage from both parents, Darwin concluded, because otherwise boys would just get smarter and smarter with each successive generation, whereas girls would fall further behind.[3]

The hunting theory is a good manly theory, and, indeed, it may well play a part in the story of the big social brain. It is probably, however, a much smaller part than its progenitors maintained. As Jared Diamond has argued in *Guns, Germs, and Steel*, the rapid increase in the size of the human social group came when a continuous food supply became available through the domestication of animals and the planting of crops, rather than with progress in hunting (or, for that matter, gathering) methods. This point suggests that hunting may not have been as pivotal an activity for human development as some scientists have made it out to be. Moreover, hunts are often unsuccessful, and so a continuous supply of animal protein through hunting is by no means guaranteed. The sexual selection argument, namely that successful hunters have more opportunities to mate and reproduce, has also been challenged in recent years. Big kills seem to have been distributed fairly evenly in hunting-and-gathering societies, and so the mates and offspring of successful hunters were not necessarily favored with extra food following a successful hunt.[4] These inconvenient points suggest a few cracks in the hunting account of the big social brain.

But let's persist, because this explanation does raise some intriguing questions about what drove brain development. The early theories of the social brain characterized man as aggressive and self-serving, manipulating the social environment for personal garnering of resources at the expense of others. Scientists have placed a lot of emphasis on the needs for tactical deception, misrepresentation, lying, and other techniques of social control as prominent among the skills that the big brain affords. In characterizing this account as masculine, I do not mean to imply that men have a corner on deception, lying, or other Machiavellian skills. Rather, the male tasks around which social brain explanations were crafted—hunting, forming coalitions to defend against enemies, and luring potential mates away from competitors—are well served by outsmarting and deceiving others, and so such tactical skills may, for these reasons, have loomed large in early scientific accounts of the social brain.

But while these skills may be important for survival, it is unlikely that the brain would have evolved primarily to furnish tactics of deception and manipulation. If so, we might well have tactically skewered one another right out of existence. By ignoring the kinder side of social life, we are left with, you might say, half a brain. When we consider what women were doing while men were out hunting, we can see quickly that the tasks they performed required a large social brain as well. Raising children, coordinating food gathering and child care, attracting and holding on to a mate, protecting one another, and often doing all these things simultaneously required substantial social skill.[5]

Happily, the science of the social brain now incorporates these warmer, more compassionate aspects of human nature. Scientists now consider the nurturant qualities of life—the parent-child bond, cooperation, and other benign social ties—to be critical attributes that drove brain development as well, accounting for our success as a species. Indeed, the ability to cooperate and to promote social harmony have clear survival advantages. You are more likely to survive to reproductive age if you avert war, for example, than if you win it.

So WHY DO we have this big social brain? I will argue that the social brain is devoted not just to hunting or to wary self-defense but to tending to others' needs and to ensuring that one's own needs are met by others as well. Support for this idea is found startlingly early in life. The infant begins life primed to be social. Within an hour after birth, a baby draws his head back to look into the eyes and face of the person who is holding him. Within the first few hours, he turns his head in the direction of his mother's voice. A social bond that was formed during pregnancy is already in place, and on it, other bonds will be built. After a few hours, the newborn can mimic an adult's expression, and, shortly thereafter, he or she can reciprocate another person's emotions. To demonstrate this amazing capacity, scientists show newborns close-ups of faces that are smiling, frowning, or expressing surprise. They film the babies looking at these pictures and then show the films to observers whose job it is to guess what picture the baby was looking at. Observers are often able to tell, because the baby spontaneously mimics the face in his or her own expression. Infants use this remarkably sophisticated innate system of emotional communication to signal their needs to their caretakers and evoke their tending,[6] and these interactions fuel the exuberant brain growth of infancy.

Nor is this communication one way. There is a biologically hardwired program by which mother and infant come to coordinate their emotions and expressions within a split second of each other. The synchrony with which they regulate each other's emotions and match their emotional states to each other is so striking as to suggest an intrinsic capacity for social relations with others. Indeed, evidence suggests that when the infant imitates the caregiver and reciprocates his or her emotions, corresponding brain regions of the caregivers are activated.[7]

This cooperative ability to share emotions with others, which is ready at birth, is the route by which interactions with caregivers regulate the child's brain development, on which more sophisticated social learning will depend. This learning relies on very primitive systems that we share with other species. For example, the mother-infant bond is virtually universal throughout the animal kingdom. Instinctive in lower animals, it is shaped both by these same old biological systems in humans, and also by social norms and by culture. A large brain is vital for learning these norms and cultural traditions. Like the mother-infant bond, mating, too, has old biological routes, but our mating patterns are also shaped by social and cultural forces that draw on the social brain. We tend to one another in other ways as well. We heal our sick rather than letting them die. We take care of our dependent elders. We are capable of great acts of altruism. All of these activities depend on a social brain.

Consider the manifold consequences of our cooperation with one another. The stores are open; the buses are running; people show up for work; children are dropped off at school, educated, and picked up again; most people are fed, clothed, and housed, and those who can't do these things for themselves often receive help. Toddlers, sick people, and the senile elderly are not left to roam the streets unattended; their relatives, friends, or institutions care for them. Cooperation is the norm, an art form so commonplace and so expected that we are no longer even aware of it. We institutionalize our tending in professions such as nursing, teaching, child care, and elder care. We institutionalize our aggressive and protective side as well, in military and civilian protective services, for example. But on the whole, daily life is largely devoted to the cooperative exchange of goods and services that help us to achieve a better life. The most marked characteristics of human daily life are caring and cooperation, not the unbridled selfishness that many describe as "human nature."

On the personal level, the social brain is engaged as well. Social life requires the ability to form friendships and alliances and to understand the meaning of social encounters. All of the challenges we faced in our prehistory benefited from coordinated activity—hunting, shared foraging, shared child care, and successful defense against predators or rival bands of humans. We have an extraordinary array of skills to help us do this. Social cues are highly varied and subtle, requiring a complexity of thought and interpretation that only a big social brain can provide. The sheer amount of social information we can comprehend in a second is staggering. We infer other people's intentions from what they say; we recognize the meaning of nonverbal signals, such as an averted gaze, a direct stare, or a smile. We hear a warning in a tone of voice. The knowledge that must be mastered about any social group is truly daunting—one must remember who everyone is, whether each person is friend or foe, who is friends or enemies with whom, who is whose relative or ally, with whom it's safe to leave your children, among other vital information.[8]

Is social life the reason we have a big brain? Let's put this idea to a test. The social brain theory argues that the size of the brain would have increased as the social system grew more complex. As bands of humans grew larger, they needed to accomplish more tasks together—coordinating food gathering, developing norms for choosing mates, and creating social groups for hunting, for example. All these tasks became exponentially more complex as the size of a social group increased. Accordingly, if the demands of social life have driven the evolution of brain size, we should see a relationship across the animal kingdom between the complexity of the social system and the size of the brain. This test succeeds. As brain size increases across primate species, one sees an ever more complex social system. Or, to put it the other way, as the social system becomes more complex, the brain, specifically the neocortex, becomes bigger.[9]

Each of us acquires this vital social understanding during our own lifetime. It is not present at birth, but instead requires active shaping. Where does all this knowledge come from? Human infants are dependent on their parents for many years after birth. This dependency is not to learn speed or stalking skills, which are some of the reasons for the relatively short periods of immaturity of other animals. Rather, it is so we can develop all the skills required for coordinating our needs with other people. At birth, the hardware of the human brain is essentially intact, but it contains little or no software. Imagine unpacking a computer, turning it on, and trying to get it to do something. Until you start loading the software and entering the data, it will be useless. The social brain works the same way.

Each of us has a big, flexible brain that is waiting to receive the specific information that will help us manage the unique environment into which we are born. Language is a big part of this coordination, and the cognitive skills we use to understand the world and make it work for us are also acquired during the long period of immaturity after birth. The breadth of social knowledge we acquire during these early years is impressive as well. We can come to understand the social norms of village life in New Guinea or skills for getting around New York City. We develop ways of getting along with kin and for making friends out of strangers. And we learn whom to fear.

Early social experiences provide the rudimentary software that starts to fill our big neocortex, the frontal part of the brain. What does the neocortex do? Most complex thought, planning, and reasoning occurs in this region. Consciousness itself, our awareness and intentional control of our thought processes, resides here. But perhaps most important for our story, the neocortex is also where social reasoning occurs. If this region is damaged, memory for people is not harmed, but social skills are grossly disrupted.[10]

Much of what we know about the social brain has come from studying people whose brains have been damaged in some way, either through an injury or because of incomplete development during pregnancy. This may be a crude way to learn about the brain, but it does provide us with important information. If you know where a lesion is in the brain, and you discover what process the individual can't perform, you may learn what activities that part of the brain would serve, were it intact.

Neuroscientist Antonio Damasio was one of the first researchers to recognize this important point in his groundbreaking work on the effects of brain damage on social behavior. The case of one man (we'll call him George) who lacked a left frontal lobe illustrates this well.

[George] was never able to hold a job. After some days of obedience he would lose interest in his activity, and even end up stealing or being disorderly. Any departure from routine would frustrate him easily and might cause a burst of bad temper, although in general he tended to be docile and polite. (He was described as having the courteous manner known as "English valet politeness.") His sexual interests were dim, and he never had an emotional involvement with any partner. His behavior was stereotyped, unimaginative, lacking in initiative, and he developed no professional skills or hobbies. Reward or punishment did not seem to influence his behavior. His memory was capricious; it failed in instances in which one would expect

learning to occur, and suddenly might succeed on some peripheral subject, such as a detailed knowledge of the makes of auto-
mobiles. [George] was neither happy nor sad, and his pleasure
and pain both seemed short-lived.[11]

George's dilemma suggests that the frontal cortex is vital, not for
mastering social information but for using it. He had a basic grasp of
social life—he learned people's names, knew what a job was for, and had
rudimentary social skills. George's problem lay in the fact that he could
not coordinate his needs with other people's, at least not for very long.
He lacked an understanding of both his own and others' reactions to
social situations, and his capacity for empathy was virtually nonexistent.
These particular failings, as will become evident, are quite critical to our
abilities to manage our social lives effectively. Another point in favor of
the social brain theory, then, is that research on people with damaged
brains demonstrates that the tools for social competence reside squarely
in the frontal cortex.

What other evidence can we muster? I've argued that the brain needs
software as well as hardware, and so we ought to be able to show that if
the software is missing, social understanding will be compromised, as it
is when the hardware is flawed. What is this software? In early social life,
the connections between the brain and social life are forged. Without
this experience, neither our social interactions nor the emotions that
accompany them work correctly. What should be a graceful, intimate
dance between the body and the mind is instead awkward, mistimed,
and out of step. Evidence for this assertion comes from a heartbreaking
source, namely a social "experiment" that failed miserably.

The end of communism in Romania in 1990 brought the grim discovery of hundreds of thousands of Romanian orphans housed together
in inadequate conditions without individual care. The economic poli-
cies of the Ceausescu government had made it difficult or impossible for
families to raise several children, and so children were often abandoned
by their parents at the doors of large orphanages called *leagane* (a word
that, ironically, means cradle). There were few workers to manage the
needs of these hundreds of children—on average, one worker for every

twenty or more children—and so most of the children received little more attention than food distribution permitted. Following the government collapse in 1990, the doors of the *leagane* were opened and the world was stunned by what was found. Shocked relief workers walked through room after room filled with children who rocked back and forth, hit their heads against the walls, and grimaced oddly, giving no sign they had registered that anyone new was present. Others simply stared at the strangers with big sad eyes.

The more normal of these children were adopted into welcoming families, and some of these adoptions have been successful. Many of the children have never been quite right, however, which becomes painfully evident by middle childhood. Their emotions are stunted. They take little pleasure or joy in their surroundings and are not really bothered by reprimands or criticisms. They just don't care. These children weren't, for the most part, beaten or starved. They weren't tortured or raped. They just weren't loved, held, hugged, or taught to feel emotions or how to recognize them in others. In many ways they appear as brain-damaged as George, and indeed they are. Yet George's problem is in the hardware—he has no left frontal lobe. The Romanian orphans' problem is in the software. They had no early nurturant experience to help them connect the hardware of the brain to what they encountered in the social world around them. Without both essential parts, a normal social life is out of reach.[12]

The first few years of life are critical for building these emotional responses to life. If a child fails to get warm, responsive contact with another person during those years, the disadvantages that result may never be fully overcome. This form of tending allows social bonds to develop, and babies who lack these bonds turn into adolescents and adults who have trouble with the basic tasks of life: finding a partner, making friends, and getting and keeping a job.

I'VE SAID THAT the experiences that link up the brain's software to its hardware are heavily emotional in nature. Why do we need this emotional information? One important reason is that it helps us manage threat. Starting early in life, we learn how to distinguish what is strange or threatening from what is familiar and comforting. Friend or foe? This is the first and most fundamental judgment we make about other people, and on it, all the rest of our understanding of social life builds.[13]

Do we truly decide whether someone is friend or foe so quickly and so decisively? We don't necessarily lump people into one of these two categories. For most of us, judgments about others are mildly positive most of the time. But the social brain makes other more subtle judgments about people who may be threatening (the pack of teens walking toward us), people who have power over us (a prospective employer), or people who have caused us harm (a callous old flame), among others toward whom we are cautious or wary.

If you need convincing, let me ask you to try out a test. Pick a friend, preferably someone who is not overly concerned with the niceties of social convention. Introduce your friend to someone new, and then later ask your friend for an assessment of this new person. If your friend is being candid, the first information you hear will be evaluative. "She seemed nice enough." "I thought he was a little cold." "She seemed to be trying to make a good impression." "Not my type." Social psychologists have conducted dozens of studies like this, and every time, the first and most important judgments that are made about another person are evaluative: good or bad, warm or cold, friendly or unfriendly. We pick up lots of other information, too, of course, but the primary judgment we make is positive or negative.[14]

Not that we're always right—how often have you formed a hasty impression of someone as perhaps a bit chilly or standoffish, only to discover that you really didn't have enough information to make that judgment? Evaluations are dominant over other facts and impressions we collect about people, and they are always being revised and updated as the social brain makes sense of the information it takes in.

Early tending by others helps us make these distinctions. We learn to discriminate what is comforting from what is not. These experiences are the building blocks of the big brain's social software. The prefrontal cortex can't do its job unless it can connect the neurocircuitry inside the body to emotional and social life outside the body. How are these connections made?

DEEP IN THE most primitive parts of our brains lies the amygdala. Long before there was even a glimmer of a prefrontal cortex, the amygdala monitored the environment, keeping an eye out for potential threats. The amygdala is activated anytime there is something new or unexpected in the environment, especially signs of danger. At these times, the amygdala (and its companions in the brain's limbic system) activates the body's stress-response systems.[15]

The rattlesnake has an amygdala that is not so different from ours. It goes on alert when there is danger, which sends a message to the motor centers of the brain to coil and strike. On the whole, these messages are fairly rare. For the most part, snakes just bask in the sun and don't do much unless they're provoked. A very silly dog I once had danced around a rattlesnake for nearly five minutes before I successfully collared him and dragged him away, and the snake did nothing but eventually crawl into the brush. Coiling takes energy, and striking uses up venom that may be needed for bigger threats. Old snakes know this. They wait to see if you're going to be stupid enough to step on them or try to pick them up. Even if they do strike you, they use only some of their venom, keeping a reserve in case a bigger threat comes along. Young snakes react more quickly; if they strike you, they use all their venom. If you should chance to stumble on a rattler during a hike, hope that it is an old one.

Human babies are not so different. Early on in life, the amygdala sends many messages of alarm. Any loud noise will set an infant off. A few months later, any stranger will provoke great distress. But mothers and fathers are comforting, and from them babies begin to learn about and adjust to the social world. Over time, they discover that "stranger" doesn't necessarily mean danger. Instead it can mean your parents' overbearing but well-intentioned friends, the aunt or uncle you are meeting for the first time, or your new baby-sitter. If a child isn't sure how to respond to a new situation, she can watch her parents' reactions; with time, she will learn to take her cues from their positive responses.[16]

Learning gets more sophisticated yet. By age six or so, we begin to infer others' intentions, and the shaping of the prefrontal cortex proceeds by leaps and bounds. We get upset at someone who meant to hurt us but not at someone who did so by accident. The rattlesnake never learns that you didn't mean to step on him—he will bite you regardless. This is where our social brain helps us. The prefrontal cortex gets intimately involved in the interpretation of social information. Eventually we can process very complex messages indeed. You know when a conversation with someone is going off in a wrong direction. You know when a friendship has moved to a new level of intimacy. You know very quickly into a first date whether you would welcome a second one.[17]

It must be evident that the amygdala has an important job. It helps shape the software of the brain by sending emotional messages about social experience. When the cues from the environment say "danger," the amygdala and the prefrontal cortex exchange messages and also activate arousal that puts us on alert. Through these experiences, the social brain grows increasingly sophisticated in ways that provide ever more finely tuned information about both the threatening and the comforting aspects of the social world.

The social brain, then, is fundamentally a system for managing threat. The bonds of attachment that begin early in life and that usually achieve full and intense expression in the first few years of life are a source of warmth and comfort. Through these relationships, we learn to form bonds with others; these bonds, in turn, become similarly comforting, and through them we learn to discriminate when to be wary and when to feel safe.

FRIEND OR FOE? This judgment affects much more than our impressions of other people. It also affects whether the body's systems of defense—our stress systems—are engaged. A sense of security, comfort, and familiarity disengages stress systems, whereas a sense of potential danger engages them.[18] We are one another's solace and one another's predators, and the developing brain grows increasingly adept at distinguishing between the two. In the absence of early nurturant learning, our default option is a judgment of danger that puts our stress systems on alert. When the amygdala tells you that a threat is imminent, and it's time to get moving, every system of the body listens and responds. The amygdala provides a fast lane to our stress responses.

Here is how it works: When a threat arises, the amygdala sends messages to the stress centers in the brain's hypothalamus, causing sympathetic arousal and the HPA stress responses to go up; when you escape the stress, sympathetic arousal and the HPA response go down. Both the original "up" part and the "down" at the end are necessary. If you don't react to stress at all, then your body isn't showing the normal protective mobilization that you need as an impetus for action. A more common problem is the body's failure to shut off sympathetic and HPA responses to stress. Once the threat has passed, if your body doesn't return to normal quickly enough, your overactive stress systems will take a biological toll on you.[19] Will tending from others in childhood protect you against this? The short answer is yes.

Our biological responses to stress are molded through social contact in early life. While it is certainly true that our stress systems are innate, the fine-tuning of these systems depends on social experience. Remember Michael Meaney's infant rats and how their mothers rushed over to soothe and nurse them when they were put back into the nest? Those babies got lifelong protection against stress as a result. To be very biologically specific for a moment, what happened was this: The little rats developed more receptors for the stress hormones of the HPA system (called glucocorticoids) in particular parts of the brain. Having more of these receptors means that the HPA response to stress became better regulated—quick to come up, quick to come down.[20]

There are important payoffs for behavior as well. Having a well-regulated stress response that comes from nurturant contact means that fewer things will cause you stress. During all those nurturing experiences when you learned to discriminate the familiar from the strange, more people and situations in your life got labeled "familiar and friendly." Fewer things in your life engaged your stress systems, giving you a freedom to explore new situations. And so it was with Meaney's baby rats. The rat pups who received so much care from their mothers were a bit more daring—more likely to explore a new territory, for example—than were rats that had not received this attention, and their stress responses to new situations were not as extreme. As they got older, their HPA systems looked "younger," not as sluggish as those of other aging rats, and they maintained their ability to solve problems—run through mazes, remember where the food was—better than the rats who lacked the attention in their early lives.

What about humans? Surely this doesn't mean that affection and attention in early life influence whether a person develops a stress-related disorder? Actually, it may well mean exactly that. Every bit of scientific evidence we have tells us that very much the same thing is true for humans. When babies experience stress, responsive loving attention is not only immediately soothing, but it has long-term payoffs in the form of better-developed regulatory systems that determine biological responses to stress.[21]

We've looked at how the social brain interprets danger and puts stress systems on alert. Now let's look at the other side of these early experiences, namely how we form a sense of what is comforting and familiar and how an initially frightening experience becomes a soothing one through the nurturant contact of social life.[22]

When I was about two years old, my parents, aunts, and uncles rented cottages for the summer on a lake in Maine. On the Fourth of July, we all went down to the shore to see the fireworks. I was the youngest, and they probably all told me how beautiful and exciting it would be. But I wasn't prepared for the loud noise, and when the first explosions came, I began to cry in fright. Everyone tried to comfort me but to no avail. With each burst, I grew more frightened. When it became clear that I was not going to calm down, my mother picked me up and carried me back to the porch of our cabin where we could see the fireworks from a safe distance. I still winced at each explosion, but when I did, I buried my face in my mother's clothes, taking in their familiar smell and listening to her soothing voice, and eventually the fireworks didn't seem scary anymore. Most of us have memories similar to this one.

You may be surprised to learn that psychologists study exactly this kind of mundane experience. They go into people's homes and quietly observe how parents manage the inevitable stresses of home life. If two siblings begin fighting, are they yelled at? Are they hit or slapped? Or is the moment used to teach them both something about how to get along with each other and resolve their differences more peacefully next time?

Researchers then bring these children into their laboratories and see how they react to new situations. The results are intriguing. Moments of stress are, indeed, pivotal learning points for developing social skills. Although most children are taught to be nice to people, what they're taught to do when their emotions are at fever pitch and their stress systems are throbbing matters a good deal more to their developing social skills and future behavior.[23]

Children who learn how to manage their stress actively, first of all, recognize other people's emotions better. They can look at a situation and figure out pretty quickly what the people in it are feeling—an important skill that foreshadows empathy. They can observe a potentially rancorous circumstance—such as a staged argument between two adults—and control their own emotional and biological reactions to it without getting too engaged or aroused.[24]

Offspring of the parents who yell and scream—the "hit him back" school of stress management—behave quite differently. Their understanding of emotions is impoverished. When researchers present them with stories involving emotional experiences—such as getting an injection at the doctor's office or having an argument with another person—they don't know what the people involved in the story are feeling. Because they are accustomed to conflict as a response to stress, they are sensitized to its potential occurrence in others. They become distressed, fearful, or angry at the slightest signs of rancor, and their stress systems are fully engaged. They are hypervigilant to threat, on the lookout for and overreacting to the smallest cues, as their amygdalas operate on overtime.[25] This is the foundation onto which their social life and health will build well into the future.

CHAPTER 4

Good and Bad Tending

I n a perfect world, everyone would be a good tender, and children would thrive as a result. In many families, this is exactly what happens. But the case for good tending is not self-evident. As a scientist, I cannot point to a well-tended child and say, "Look at those great gluco-corticoid receptors!" or "Check out that genetic expression," and expect you to be impressed. The well-tended child presents a picture of good functioning in large part because of what that child *doesn't* have, namely certain early signs of emotional distress or poorly regulated stress systems. I can, however, make this case by showing you the presence of these problems in children who are deprived of good tending in early life.[1]

I will start by telling you about a friend, Michael, whose early life was stressful, but not impossibly so. He came from what most of us would call a "good family"—well-to-do and successful, but it was also a family marred by an absence of good tending. Michael was always a mediocre student, and he used to get no end of criticism from his father night after night for his middling grades. Over dinner, his father made sarcastic remarks about Mike's abilities, berated him for his lack of effort, and otherwise made his life miserable. His three sisters for the most part escaped this daily abuse. Their father had low expectations for girls, and so he left them alone—no great pride or caring, but no insults either. Michael's father was not a bad man. His pride in his son led him to believe that Michael could do better, and so instead of expressing his love directly, it came out as criticism instead. That did not prevent its adverse effects on Michael, however.

Each night, as his father went after him, Michael kept his head low, shoveling food into his mouth, trying to pretend, perhaps, that nothing was happening or that it was normal for fathers to abuse their children over dinner. Michael's deepening color during each of these encounters betrayed his hurt and embarrassment but he otherwise kept his feelings to himself.

He had other ways of registering his unhappiness, though. He put insects that he collected into a box and tried to set them on fire using a magnifying glass that focused the sun's rays. He broke his sisters' favorite toys when they were out of the house and left the pieces lying on their beds so they'd be sure to see them when they got home. He picked on younger kids at school.

I've thought about Mike a lot over the years. He's only forty-eight, but I guessed that by now he would be starting to show the ill effects of his stressful early life. I saw him recently, and my intuition was well placed. He has severe hypertension. I learned a few other things about his life, too. He went to a good college after high school but was asked to leave after three semesters, not because he couldn't do the work but because he'd stopped going to classes and turning in assignments. He kicked around doing various jobs until finally, at age thirty-three, he got his degree by taking classes at night. He was married briefly, but his wife grew frustrated by his lack of ambition. And every now and then, he'd start screaming at her for no apparent reason, picking on everything from how she cooked to how she parked the car. These bouts not only angered her because they were unfair, but they scared her as well, and she decided not to wait around to see if he was going to turn physically violent.

Did Michael's early experiences of stress contribute to his current emotional and medical problems? I have no doubts. This sad account of Michael's life shows two important aspects of what I will call a "risky" family environment: its immediate fallout in the form of emotional distress and the trajectory it established for Michael's later life as well.

Most of us understand that physical abuse is toxic for children. We're all familiar to some degree with its legacy.[2] But recently it's become evident that more minor inadequacies in parenting produce long-term damage of a similar kind. In what I'm calling risky families, children don't get the warmth and nurturance that help them form the biological and emotional repertoire that early tending usually creates.[3] When children are left to fend for themselves, and when children just don't get a lot of physical affection and warmth, they are at risk for emotional disorders such as depression or anxiety, and for health problems as well. We have been quick to recognize the emotional consequences of these risky families, probably because it "makes sense" that cold or hostile parents might produce a depressed or angry child, and indeed the evidence for these adverse effects is very powerful.[4] But the fact that these families spawn chronic disease is a little more surprising.[5]

My interest in risky families began quite accidentally when I was asked to evaluate the evidence on how stressful environments "get under the skin," that is, turn into genuine health risks. Together with two colleagues, I sifted through the hundreds of relevant psychological and medical studies. We suspected, of course, that harsh or chaotic families would produce some damage in children, but we were completely unprepared for the sheer range of adverse outcomes these risky families seemed to foster.[6]

One of the most compelling studies was conducted by Vincent Felitti and his colleagues in a large Southern California health maintenance organization, the kind of health-care organization to which many of us belong. In the process of collecting information on family background, Felitti and his team asked the nearly 13,500 members of the HMO about certain aspects of their childhood to get at whether the family environment had been harsh, neglectful, or ridden with conflict. Some of the questions included how often they were insulted, sworn at, put down, or physically hit or kicked to the point of injury, whether they had been sexually abused, and whether they had grown up in a family with someone who was a problem drinker or a drug abuser, among other questions. More than half the people surveyed said they had experienced at least one of these conditions in childhood, making it clear just how common these risky families are. Felitti and his associates then looked at the medical records of their respondents to see what diseases or disorders they had, and the results were sobering indeed.

The people who had grown up in families marked by turmoil or neglect developed more health problems as adults. They were more likely to have had a bout of depression or to have tried suicide, and they had more problems with drugs, alcohol, and sexually transmitted diseases. Significantly, they also had a higher likelihood of heart disease, diabetes, stroke, chronic bronchitis, hepatitis, and cancer. The surprising aspect was that the effect of these risky families demonstrated what scientists call a dose-response relationship to the diseases studied: the riskier the family, the greater the likelihood that a person had each of these disorders. But even at low levels of riskiness, signs of problems were evident.[7]

Might it not simply be the case that people who are sick or distressed just remember their childhoods as more stressful? In some of the scientific evidence for risky families, this could be a concern. In many of the studies, though, researchers actually go into the home to see how parents and children interact with one another, and so there is independent evidence that the family environment is problematic. In other cases, researchers have confirmed the reports of a harsh background with detailed accounts of the events of early childhood.[8]

Nonetheless, like everyone, scientists are most convinced by evidence they see with their own eyes, and so my students and I decided to look at these processes firsthand. We recruited university students for a study of stress. First we screened out all those who had diagnosed psychological problems (such as depression) or health problems (such as hypertension). In short, we studied a fairly healthy group. We brought these young adults into our lab individually and first asked them to complete questionnaires, including some that inquired about their early family life. A few days later they came back for an interview, and we asked them more focused and detailed questions about their family background. Most of these students had only recently left home, and so their experiences were quite fresh in their minds. Many of them cheerily described their happy home lives, acknowledging the occasional arguments or pesky younger sibling with whom they had sometimes quarreled. Others, however, looked uncomfortable and clearly wanted to be elsewhere. These young adults seemed relieved to be away from home and not very enthusiastic about describing what they'd just left. With gentle probing, we extracted their stories of chronic conflict, chaotic disorganization, or neglect.

Next, we brought the students into our psychophysiology laboratory and put them through some stressful events and measured their heart rate, blood pressure, and cortisol responses to the stressors. (Cortisol level is an indicator of how the HPA stress system is working.) An example of the stressors we used required the students to count backward as rapidly as possible by 7s from 4,985 while being videotaped and being urged by an irritated lab assistant to "please go faster." (If you try this for a minute or two, you'll see that this is not easy to do, and if you imagine doing it in the presence of a person who is criticizing you, you'll quickly see how stressful it is.)

We then compared the responses of the students from the supportive families with those of the students from the "risky" families. On every indicator those from the riskier families looked worse. They were more anxious, depressed, and hostile, not at levels that would require therapeutic intervention, but at discernibly greater levels than was true of the students from the more supportive families. (We had excluded anyone in therapy from participating in the study on the grounds that the procedures might be too stressful for them to handle.) The physiological and neuroendocrine responses of the students from the risky families looked worse, too. Two of the young men already had borderline hypertension, and several of the students had cortisol responses to stress that are usually seen in people suffering from posttraumatic stress disorder. There was no question that the young adults from risky families were already showing poorly regulated stress responses, which with time might well lay the groundwork for more serious mental and physical health disorders.

Realize that these were normal, healthy college students. No one, to our knowledge, had been sexually or physically abused in childhood. We had no runaways or drug addicts. Their "risky" experiences were all in the range of normal family pathology—arguments, tension, lack of affection, chaos, and neglect.[9]

What should we make of evidence like this? I think it can be best characterized as a psychological and biological snapshot of young adulthood, a picture that tells us a little something about where these students came from and where they are headed. They are already showing the imprint of their early life and may well be laying down psychological and biological trajectories for the future—healthy ones, in the case of those young adults from supportive families, and less healthy ones, in the case of those from chaotic or conflict-ridden families.

As I write about the extraordinary impact that early tending has on children, I am mindful of the enormous controversy that this seemingly self-evident idea has generated over the past decade. In 1998, Judith Rich Harris gave popular voice to the assertions of behavioral geneticists who had concluded that parents have a relatively modest impact on their children's personal qualities.[10] How do I reconcile the behavioral geneticists' conclusions with my own evidence that even seemingly normal family strain produces some damage in their offspring? The behavioral geneticists do have valid points. If one asks whether good parents inevitably have good kids and bad parents inevitably have bad kids, the answer is no. The impact of early tending can assume more subtle forms, as we'll next see.[11]

O NE OF THE deepest mysteries raised by the research on risky families is why these families are linked to so many different adverse outcomes. As we confronted the evidence, we realized that risky families were fueling nearly every incipient problem a child could have. Mental health was affected, as was physical health. Risky families fostered depression, but they also fostered aggression. The children from these families had poorer health habits (they smoked and drank at early ages, for example); they coped badly with stress; they had fewer friends. By adulthood, they had more chronic diseases, and they developed them earlier. Usually, when we think of a disorder—depression, perhaps—we assume that it has a unique etiology that distinguishes it from other disorders a person might have—say, diabetes or heart disease—and so the evidence that risky families fuel such a broad array of vulnerabilities demands some mechanisms to explain it.

One answer to this surprising pattern is that poor tending in early life seems to interact with any preexisting vulnerability a child has, increasing its likelihood or worsening its course. If a child is at risk for problems with aggression (as, perhaps, from a genetic heritage), a risky family may bring those aggressive tendencies to the fore. If a child has an inherited risk for heart disease, a harsh family environment may increase that risk by constantly engaging the child's stress systems and the heart rate and blood pressure changes that go along with it. A child at risk for depression may become depressed if she has to deal unsuccessfully with the neglect and chaos of a risky family life. In essence, then, I'm arguing that the broad array of risks that have been linked to risky families may be plausibly understood as the interaction of poor tending with preexisting weaknesses.[12]

Some of the weaknesses that are exacerbated by risky families assume the form of gene-environment interactions.[13] By definition, the idea of a gene-environment interaction means that both the genetic risk and a family environment are needed for a person to express the genetic risk in a phenotype, which is what is actually observed. It also means that, in a nurturant, supportive family, the genetic risk may be expressed minimally or not at all. Think back to the little rats at genetic risk for hypertension who were cross-fostered to either a mother from the same hypertension-prone strain or to a mother who was not at risk for hypertension. In this latter case, few of the offspring showed elevated blood pressure responses to stress. So it is with risks in human families as well.

Increasingly, scientists are coming to appreciate that much psychological and physical pathology may assume the form of such gene-environment interactions. By making this point, I do not mean to trivialize the role of genetics in these processes. Not only does a genetic risk for, say, excessive aggression increase an offspring's likelihood of being overly aggressive, it also increases the likelihood that this child will grow up in an environment that fosters that risk, by virtue of the genetic heritage shared by the child and other family members.[14] So the potency of genes in these interactions can be great indeed. Yet the family environment is clearly crucial.

One risk that is affected by parenting is extreme shyness. Thought to have genetic origins, intensely shy children are difficult as babies and fearful as youngsters.[15] Yet parenting makes a great difference in how these kids turn out.

I met Emily when she was six years old, or rather I didn't meet her, because she was hiding behind her mother, Lynn, holding on to her skirt for dear life. She peeked out at me a few times during my chat with Lynn. To my amazement, Lynn seemed to find Emily's behavior neither unusual nor noteworthy. I left thinking that Emily was an odd child, and I wondered why her mother didn't do something about it.

It turns out that Lynn was doing quite a lot, and her efforts began with neither apologizing for her daughter's behavior nor by calling attention to it. Emily has what psychologists call a fearful, inhibited temperament, and children like her need more help managing their emotional and social life than other children do. Although many people are shy in social situations, the withdrawn fright that Emily showed often has a genetic basis. Like other children with this temperament, Emily has an overly active amygdala. Instead of reacting to new situations with initial wariness that quickly gives way to curiosity and interest, new things frighten Emily for longer. Consequently, Emily's stress systems are excessively activated in new situations as well. How should parents respond?

Although the likelihood of turning a child like Emily into a fun-loving extrovert is low, the prospects for turning her into a normal, happy adult with a partner, friends, and rewarding interests are excellent, if she has a parent invested in making sure these things happen. Emily is lucky, because Lynn is such a parent.

Berating a shy child, pushing her forward to meet strangers, and putting her in situations that badly tax her social skills are not ways out of this dilemma. What Lynn did successfully over the next ten years was to gradually build up Emily's emotional skills, to help her learn how to get through potentially stressful new situations without being immobilized with fear. She took her on outings with other mothers and children, ones in which the activity itself was so compelling—the zoo, for example—that Emily was able to enjoy the activity without being self-conscious. Lynn built on Emily's strengths—a natural athletic ability that led to good tennis strokes and a penchant for track. Through sports, Emily was able to focus on the activity rather than on her fear of social situations. In the relay, Emily bonded with her more extroverted teammates and began to get more comfortable with other people.

Lynn taught Emily the trick of asking questions, getting other people to talk and paying close enough attention to hear the answers. Ask other people enough questions about themselves, and they will usually chat away for some time before they notice your more modest contributions to the conversation, if indeed they ever do. At her mother's urging, Emily rehearsed a few things she might talk about when friends came to visit. On her first date, Emily went out armed with a list of questions in her handbag that she could use in case the conversation faltered, and she made a few well-timed trips to the restroom to refresh her memory.

Emily is always going to prefer reading to attending a party, and she will probably dread social occasions her entire life. But when I last saw her at sixteen, she greeted me warmly, introduced me to her friend, and then the two ran off happily, clearly enjoying each other's company.

The kind of parenting that Lynn practiced can ameliorate the genetically based temperament that Emily has. People who look at a mother-daughter relationship like this one from the outside may think, Why is that mother hovering? She's too involved. She needs to give that kid some room. She's making her shy. In fact, it's often the other way around. Mothers of children with a temperamental risk often sense that their child needs something extra, and so what looks like overly solicitous activity from the outside may instead be well-placed efforts to modulate this child's temperament, to make her less fearful, to help her gain skills that will get her through life.[16]

STORIES SUCH AS Emily's make up a key part of the argument for the importance of parenting. But, in truth, case histories are only that—single examples of an underlying process that may be compelling but that require proof. Obviously, we cannot take a child with a genetic risk, such as Emily has, and flip a coin to decide whether she gets a supportive or an unsupportive mother. We can, however, make such assignments in animal studies, and this is where the case for parenting is persuasively made, as it is in some intriguing studies of monkeys with high or low levels of serotonin.

Serotonin is a neurotransmitter, which means that it helps control the flow of chemical information throughout the body. It influences a person's behavior and emotions as well. For example, when serotonin levels are low, people often feel irritable or blue. Men with chronically low levels of serotonin also experience a tendency toward impulsive aggression, and so serotonin levels appear to be important for understanding human social behavior.

Several different genes control serotonin. Among them is the 5-HTT transporter gene, which affects how much serotonin is circulating at any given time. Many genes have alleles, that is, alternate forms of the gene, and the 5-HTT transporter gene has two, a long form, which usually leads to normal serotonin levels, and a short form, which is a concern because it is associated with lower circulating levels of serotonin. Studies conducted with rhesus monkeys at the primate center at Emory University in Atlanta by primatologists J. D. Higley, Steve Suomi, and their colleagues show just what this short allele can do.[17]

Roughhousing, chasing, and other playful forms of aggression are a normal part of a male rhesus monkey's early life. It provides young monkeys with opportunities to learn the boundaries of acceptable aggression, and so in this sense it is thought to be vital to early development. But monkeys with the 5-HTT short allele often get carried away. Instead of being playful, their roughhousing may escalate into physical damage, often to their own detriment. But whether the short allele of the 5-HTT gene leads to these outcomes depends heavily on how these little monkeys are raised.

Higley, Suomi, and their colleagues selected monkeys who had this genetic risk for impulsive aggression and who were raised either with their peers or by their own mothers. The peer-raised monkeys were separated from their mothers at birth, kept in a nursery for six months, and then housed with other monkeys of the same age. Although these monkeys formed strong relationships with one another, peers are not very good at raising one another, at least not as good as mothers are. What happened when the monkeys at biological risk for aggression (that is, with the short 5-HTT allele) grew up with their peers versus their mothers? The differences were dramatic.

The peer-raised monkeys with the short 5-HTT allele showed a variety of behavioral disturbances as they aged. They were involved in more aggressive acts of all kinds: more threats, more chases, and more bites. They showed little ability to de-escalate cycles of growing conflict—for example, they gave no signs of the submissiveness, lip smacking (an appeasement gesture), or fear grimaces that usually bring resolution to a fight. The peer-raised monkeys with the short allele often could be identified by sight, because they had more scars from bites and slashes. They did other risky things as well. Monkeys usually move carefully from tree to tree and avoid dangerous leaps, but these monkeys were prone to make unnecessarily dangerous leaps from tree to tree.

Their social lives were marred in other ways. Their little monkey friends eventually learned to avoid them. Grooming is the monkey's way of showing friendship, but no one groomed these low serotonin monkeys, and they didn't groom much in return. They spent a lot of time alone. They dropped to the bottom of the dominance hierarchy and stayed there.

By contrast, those monkeys sharing the same genetic risk who were raised by attentive mothers achieved normal levels of serotonin. Rather than succumbing to aggression and consequent rejection by their peers, they channeled their impulses into a constructive assertiveness that gained them acceptance throughout the monkey troop. They rose to the top of the dominance hierarchy and stayed there. In other words, the mother's nurturant tending reversed the effect of the gene. While it is unlikely to be the case that nurturance typically reverses the effects of a genetic risk factor on behavior, the case that tending moderates such risks is becoming ever more clear.

IN ADOLESCENCE, THE fallout from risky families starts to assume more menacing form. Children change abruptly into people who look like adults and sometimes behave like madmen. As teens assume control of their own social lives, they either begin to abuse tobacco, alcohol, and drugs, or not. They deal with their sexual maturity in either a restrained or promiscuous manner. They cope with stress either by engaging the environment or by withdrawing into sullen silence. They find or create peer groups of like-minded souls that may drive their parents to distraction. They use their freedom to experiment with new interests in a controlled manner or to crash their cars, drink themselves into oblivion, and otherwise test the border between life and death.

Children from risky families often turn into adolescents who are risk-prone.[18] They may smoke, do drugs, and have sex early; often they do all of these things. Indeed, what is notable about adolescents is how these behaviors cluster. No great surprise there, you may think—bad peers, bad behaviors. But the peers didn't come first. Who you spend time with in adolescence isn't some lottery akin to how you got your housing in college. You pick your friends, and they pick you. Offspring from risky families who reach adolescence with poor social and emotional skills and a moderate dose of peer rejection gravitate toward similar friends.[19]

But why *all* these problem behaviors? Take this question and turn it on its head. Instead of asking why some adolescents smoke, drink, sleep around, and do drugs, ask why so many adolescents don't. After all, each of these behaviors—drinking alcohol, smoking, doing drugs, and having sex—provides its share of pleasures.

Adolescents who grow up in warm, nurturant families and elude these temptations typically have three answers to this question. First, they are worried about the consequences of their behavior—the risk of disease from unprotected sex and the fear of arrest if they possess illegal drugs, for example, loom larger for the teens from nurturant families. They know they have a lot to lose from drugs, alcohol, smoking, and promiscuous sex, and they don't especially want to risk it.

Adolescents from nurturant families also say they don't want their parents to find out. Despite their increasing freedom, they know that their parents still have a pretty good idea of what they do, and they don't want the discomfort and awkwardness of disappointing them. Adolescents from risky families often have parents who don't monitor their activities as well to begin with, and so the likelihood of their getting caught is decreased. To some degree, these adolescents also care less about getting caught. Their parents' love, affection, and esteem are not things they have much of already, and so they lack the motivation to preserve them.[20] As Bob Dylan wrote, "When you got nothing, you got nothing to lose."

But unlike the adolescents from risky families, those from nurturant families also say they simply don't enjoy these activities that much, and this difference is important. Scientists who study substance abuse now think that abusing alcohol and drugs and even having promiscuous sex may not only be ways of compensating for poor social and emotional skills, but also constitute forms of self-medication that compensate for biological dysregulations that may have resulted in part from a risky family upbringing.

Why would this be the case? Offspring from risky families have stress systems that don't respond ideally to signals of danger. As a result, they also don't show the same patterns of arousal to stress that other adolescents show. In some cases, their arousal levels are just higher all the time. Others of these "risky" teens don't show the gradual arousal to oncoming stressful events that other people experience. Instead, they are hit full force with a stressor when it occurs. Even when they aren't under stress, these adolescents may not feel as good as other adolescents do. They aren't sick, but they feel vaguely uncomfortable, restless, and irritable much of the time.[21]

Early biological dysregulations that occur in risky families affect not only children's developing stress systems, but other systems as well, and among these are the neurotransmitters that are associated with mood. For example, children who grow up in harsh families may have disrupted patterns of serotonin activity, which can lead to irritable depression and other mood problems. Dopamine, a neurotransmitter associated with positive mood, may also be in shorter supply in offspring from risky families. Most of the evidence we currently have is from animal studies only, but it is certainly suggestive. Animals who are deprived of nurturant mothering early in life have permanent alterations in their dopamine and serotonin activity. Since using alcohol and drugs and even having sex can raise levels of these circulating neurotransmitters, at least temporarily, the adolescents who use them often find that their moods improve.[22]

When adolescents from supportive families say they don't do drugs, smoke cigarettes, or drink alcohol because these substances don't feel good to them, they mean it. These substances may affect them in different ways than is true for adolescents from risky families, and so they may not experience the same rewarding high that adolescents from risky families get from substance abuse. A "high" may just feel weird to them.

THE TRAJECTORIES THAT are laid down early in life by poor tending affect psychological health and biological stress responses, as we've seen. They also contribute to a layer of problems in adolescence, including propensities for behavioral problems or substance abuse, as just noted. How do these concatenating problems in childhood and adolescence lead to the increased risks for disease in adulthood that have now been so persuasively documented? These outcomes occur because of the long-term effects of grinding, chronic, unalleviated stress on the systems of the body. They come from the accelerated aging that poor tending fosters.[23] In essence, these biological systems just wear out.

In early human history, we needed a quick response to danger, as when a lurking predator threatened to attack. Occasionally we still need this quick response, as, for example, to jump out of the way of an approaching car or escape from a menacing dog. Most of the stressors we encounter in our current lives, though, don't call for the rapid physical mobilization required for fight or flight. At most, our flights are metaphorical—we unwind with a drink in front of the TV—and our fights involve intense verbal exchanges but not physical ones. Our bodies don't realize this, however, and instead prepare for a strenuous battle or a hasty exit.

These stress responses, though well suited to our early history and the kinds of threats we encountered then, don't serve us as well now. Startling at the sight of a real cobra cranks up our systems for good reason; startling at the sight of a cobra while watching *Indiana Jones* may give us a thrill, but from the body's standpoint, it's a wasted expenditure of resources. Of course, an *Indiana Jones* startle here and there has no long-term effects on the body, but the kinds of stressors we habitually get aroused by make a substantial difference.

Problems develop when, instead of being short-term reactions to an occasional emergency, stress responses instead become long-term reactions to more or less continuous stress.[24] Think of Michael dreading each evening dinner, for example. Repeated activation of these stress systems does no biological good. The fight-or-flight response is great for leaping out of the path of an oncoming car, but not for coping with an abusive father, quarreling parents, or a chaotic home life. In adulthood, the damage can worsen. Being pressured to complete a project, work through lunch, handle hostile clients, or put in overtime gets all those same hormones going but with no physical outlet, no massive burst of energy that the body has been cranked up to do and is, in a sense, anticipating. The stressors that most of us encounter are chronic and grinding, and the more we confront them, the worse it is for our bodies.

What happens? The fight-or-flight response leads to increases in heart rate and blood pressure, which is a perfectly normal short-term reaction to stress. But when this occurs repeatedly or continuously, there is wear and tear on the blood vessels, leading eventually to lesions in the walls of the arteries. Plaque builds up along these lesions, damaging the vessel walls further, and the heart has to work harder to pump blood through vessels that are narrowing and losing their elasticity, processes that lay the groundwork for hypertension and heart disease.[25] Psychologists have studied children from conflict-ridden families and found that, as early as eight years old, these children are showing risk factors for heart disease.[26]

Over the long term, repeated or chronic activation of the HPA stress system does damage as well. The glucocorticoids associated with a prolonged HPA response initially help us, but if they continually course through our bodies, the systems they activate can wear down. Continuous HPA activation can lead to immune deficiencies, cause or worsen depression, and disrupt memory and other thought processes as well.[27]

When glucocorticoids keep pounding against the brain, the neurons in a region called the hippocampus begin to atrophy and die, and the ongoing process of neural regeneration, that is, creating replacement neurons, gets inhibited. In the short term, these effects of stress interfere with attention, memory, and learning. This is one reason why children who are coping with a stressful home life often have trouble with schoolwork. With unremitting stress, the hippocampus shrinks, memory declines, and the ability to think clearly suffers permanently. The grandfather who inquires about how his grandson is doing in school three times in fifteen minutes may be showing this kind of damage.[28] People who lived their early lives in risky families or who were exposed to other chronically stressful conditions throughout life appear to develop these problems early.

Stress can lay the groundwork for diabetes as well. Glucocorticoids are released late in the body's responses to stress, and they increase the appetite for food and prompt activity designed to get it, in order to replenish energy after a period of physical exertion. This is a good adaptation left over from our early history, when we were fighting or fleeing from predators or hostile opponents. Once you've calmed down, you look for something to eat, to replenish the resources you just expended. But when your stressor is a deadline for a report, you may still reach for that bag of potato chips, even though you haven't expended the physical energy this response was designed to meet. If your glucocorticoids are always high because you're under stress, but you never actually do anything—run, flee, engage in combat—over time, the action of insulin to promote glucose uptake gets sluggish. Insulin levels increase, insulin and glucocorticoids together promote the deposit of fat in your abdomen (this is why your pants no longer fit), and you get plaque deposits in your coronary arteries. Enough years of this life will give you heart disease, hypertension, diabetes, or perhaps all three. All those chronic diseases that typically come with older age come earlier to people from risky families, the legacy of the early accumulation of poor tending, stress, and the accelerated aging they produce.[29]

The immune system works much the same way. In response to a short-term stress, the immune system gears up, ready to do battle. But with long-term, grinding stress, the immune system wears down. The cells that fight infection decrease in number and seem to grow weary of battle. The substances that heal wounds don't get to the wound as fast or heal it as quickly. The fatigued immune system leaves you susceptible to colds, flu, or even cancer.[30]

Why an increased risk of cancer? Part of the reason is that children from risky families often develop bad health habits in adolescence that contribute to this risk. Smoking is probably the clearest case, since it promotes lung cancer (as well as other lung disorders and heart disease), and abusing alcohol and drugs and eating a poor diet also contribute to the likelihood of certain cancers as well.

But risky families contribute to cancer in another insidious way. Because the stress systems of children from these families are engaged more often and for longer periods of time, the immune system eventually may get down regulated, which is to say it may work less efficiently than it should. This process may not cause a cancer, but it can weaken the surveillance function of the immune system so that a cancer may take root and begin to grow undetected. Not only are children from high stress backgrounds more vulnerable to cancer, they're more vulnerable to developing the disease earlier in life, and their cancers have a more rapid course.[31]

Across our lives, we nudge all of these disorders along. With age, our blood pressure goes up a little, our arteries get a little clogged, we get a little skin cancer, perhaps, our glucose response isn't what it once was, and our weight goes up. Most of us think of these changes not as diseases but as normal signs of aging. They are common, to be sure, but they are also the first signs that disease processes are in place. Many of us may never reach the point at which a physician diagnoses diabetes or hypertension. Your physician may look at your test results, assume a worried expression, and suggest that you temper your enthusiastic consumption of cheese, but you may not have to go on a diet for diabetes, or take drugs for controlling hypertension or lowering cholesterol. Most of us live with only the incipient signs of these diseases, until one of them—heart disease, cancer, or stroke most commonly—rears its ugly head in diagnosable form. On the other hand, some people will get these diseases, and they will get several of them at the same time. For people who have led poorly tended lives, these problems develop at a younger age.[32]

So which one will it be? Just as risky families are especially toxic for children with some psychological risk like shyness or aggression, they are most toxic for those with some biological vulnerability as well. That weakness can come from your genes—heart disease, hypertension, diabetes, and certain cancers all run in families. The weakness can come from a risk acquired in early life, a biological system that failed to develop normally because of premature birth, perhaps. Other times, the weakness comes from exposure to a carcinogen or toxic chemical. Sometimes you know the source of the vulnerability, but most of the time you don't.

In short, every biological process that stress sets into motion is helpful for meeting short-term challenges, yet with constant or repeated use, each system creates the vulnerabilities that lay the foundation for life-threatening diseases. The remarkable fight-or-flight response that helped us evade predators, flee from harm, take on challengers, and cope with natural disasters is poorly suited—even ill suited—for the chronic stresses of family conflict, grinding poverty, and the other ways we have of making one another's lives miserable. With good tending, stress responses to new situations are normal and short-term, if present at all. Without adequate tending, children accumulate this damage more rapidly. Early adversity, then, leads to what we might think of as accelerated aging.[33] All the diseases we're going to get if we live long enough—heart disease, hypertension, diabetes, cancer—start earlier and have a more rapid course when a person comes from a risky family.

Tending is a powerful force indeed. With supportive care, children develop the emotional and social skills they need to manage their daily lives and to confront new, potentially challenging situations. Without it, they grow up with overactive stress systems, poised to fight or flee at the first provocation. Wary hostility or nervous anxiety stalk their relationships with others, and any preexisting risk from genes or early life may become much worse. But the trajectories of mental and physical health are not written in stone at the end of the first few years.

CHAPTER 5

A Little Help from Friends and Strangers

The family lays the groundwork for physical and mental health, but what happens throughout the life span matters as well. We form friendships, find partners, console one another during stressful times, and raise children, barely aware of the deep-seated social nature that propels us into this social activity. We are not alone in this need. We undoubtedly come by our social nature in large part through a genetic heritage that we share with many of our primate relatives. For the most part, they draw heavily on kin for these protective bonds, although they form coalitions and friendships as well. Humans do much the same, drawing on kin when they can, but also on friends and even on total strangers, reaping much the same benefits. Our propensity for group living provides far more than the simple protection of numbers, however. Studies of many species, including humans, attest to the better health and longer life that we enjoy in one another's company. Social bonds are strong, and they provide benefits similar to those that early tending from parents so clearly confers.

These processes begin as early as the womb. At the moment of conception, the fetus develops a social life. For all practical purposes, the mother's social environment is the fetus's social environment. It is muffled and diluted to be sure, but the developing offspring is present and affected by everything the mother does and all that happens to her. When the mother goes to work, so does the fetus. When she listens to music, has a meal, or fights with her husband, the developing infant is there. But whether the mother and infant have support from others during this important time matters greatly to how the baby develops.

When a mother is under stress—from poverty, abuse, or fear of unemployment, for example—her HPA system is activated, releasing a hormone called CRF (corticotropin-releasing factor). CRF is necessary for the proper development of a baby, but at high levels, it can cause problems. It can act as a signal to the baby that it is time to be born. At the end of nine months, this is the job CRF should be doing, but when these levels are too high too early, a baby may be born prematurely or be low in birth weight.[1] Even among babies who make it through the full nine months, high levels of CRF can be a danger. If those hormones are constantly bombarding the vulnerable hippocampus of the developing infant, they can affect the baby in ways that will influence his concentration, ability to learn, and even his temperament.[2] Some startling evidence for this assertion comes from Israel's seven-day war.

In the spring of 1967, Israel came under siege by the armies of fourteen of its neighbors, and nearly all men of fighting age volunteered for duty. This situation left many young, pregnant women not only under intense wartime stress, but without the support of their husbands. What was the effect on their children? For the most part, their offspring were normal, but compared with boys born before the war, the boys born during wartime were more difficult and harder to console. They were also more withdrawn, irritable, and hyperactive. They walked and talked a little later and took longer to be toilet trained. As they grew older, some more subtle and disturbing difficulties emerged. Compared to their peers, the war boys were more aggressive and antisocial. The stress hormones, so evident in their mothers and unrelieved because of the absence of social support from their fathers, took a modest but permanent toll.[3]

Scientists have devoted much effort to identifying which mothers may be at risk for having babies with these kinds of problems. Psychologist Christine Dunkel-Schetter and her colleagues have been in the forefront of this issue, focusing especially on low-income women who face a barrage of stressors daily including overwork, insufficient help from others, and, in some cases, abandonment. The prospect for premature birth and its accompanying problems looms large for these women, in part because their CRF levels may be chronically high.[4]

Dunkel-Schetter's group finds that one factor reliably and consistently offers biological protection against these all-too-common adverse birth outcomes, and it is social support. Support from the baby's father or from the expectant mother's family and friends can keep her level of stress lower, decreasing the risk of prematurity and low birth weight. Support from an encouraging person during labor is important, too. It can influence how smoothly the birthing process goes and whether there are complications.[5] Beginning as early as the womb, then, the larger social environment affects us in important ways. When the environment provides resources and support, our tending is more successful.

We can think of human tending as like an onion in its structure: At the innermost layer is the mother and other constant caregivers, often the father. Immediately surrounding them are family and close friends who provide social support. Enveloping them is the neighborhood and the larger community that provides the resources on which good tending depends. Each layer protects those that lie closer to the core, first by providing a supportive environment that makes good tending possible, and also by providing additional tending resources when they are needed. To make this point, I will take as examples two boys who had a very similar and common problem, namely managing aggression. Yet these two boys turned out very differently because of the social context in which they were raised. Both are real case histories.

In a short and undistinguished career as a Cub Scout leader, I had responsibility for a high-spirited, unruly, rather mutinous little band of eight-year-old boys who rarely wanted to do what they were supposed to do, in quite the way it was supposed to be done. Our crafts projects usually ended with someone stuck to his chair, the "superglue" pranksters giggling in the background. Our nature walks were so boisterous that people came out of their homes to see if the neighborhood was under attack. But what really did us in was Allen.

Allen was unable to control his temper. An accidental bump or push by another boy led to quick retaliation—a violent shove or punch on the shoulder. And the unfortunate boy who responded to Allen's retaliation by striking back incurred an unbounded rage. Typically, it took two of us to physically pry him off his victim, as he continued to hit and punch and kick with no self-restraint. We took Allen out of the group, made him sit by himself, had him work on projects alone or with another well-controlled boy who knew to keep his distance, and yet no amount of threatening or cajoling or time-outs could change his behavior.

Aside from his uncontrolled bursts of violence, Allen had many good qualities—he was smart, outgoing, and funny—but the ease with which his behavior could turn to murderous rage frightened both the Cub Scout leaders and the other boys. After several draining meetings that were repeatedly interrupted by Allen's aggression, his mother was asked to attend to see if she could do anything. Each time he assaulted another boy, she drew him aside and talked to him calmly and rationally, explaining what he was doing wrong and why he needed to stop. It worked while she was there but not for long after she left.

Our scouting activities took place in an atmosphere of tense antici-pation. One of the coleaders took a tranquilizer before each meeting. Each week brought new discussions of what to do about Allen and how to ease him out of the troop. Unfortunately, Allen's interest in scouting showed no signs of abating, and so, with no mother willing to take on the leadership and a declining number of boys interested in participat-ing in the troop's activities alongside Allen, the troop was disbanded.

Will Allen go on to a career of violence? It seems doubtful. His father is a prominent attorney, and although he shows some of the same impul-sive aggression as Allen, he keeps it at the verbal level, intimidating other parents at school meetings and bullying small children from the sidelines of school soccer games. His aggression is irritating but offset by charm and success. Allen will probably be much the same. He has a high

IQ, his family is supportive, and these attributes will probably spare him the prison sentence his behavior might otherwise eventually draw.

When a child with this same penchant for aggression is raised in a hostile, punishing environment, however, the prospects are not as good. Consider Steve, who was profiled in *Science* as a disturbing example of what happens when inborn propensities and the environment feed on each other to foster aggression.

Signs that Steve was headed for big trouble were there from very early on if anyone had cared to read them. Born to an alcoholic teen mother who had raised him with an abusive alcoholic step-father, Steve was hyperactive, irritable, and disobedient as a toddler, according to his mother.

After dropping out of school at age 14, Steve spent his teen years fighting, stealing, taking drugs, and beating up girlfriends. His mother, according to the researcher who interviewed her, "did not seem to be aware of the son's behavioral problems." School counseling, a probation officer, and meetings with child protective services failed to forestall disaster: At 19, several weeks after his last interview with researchers, Steve visited a girlfriend who had recently dumped him, found her with another man, and shot him to death. The same day he tried to kill himself. Now he's serving a life sentence without parole.[6]

Steve is the worst-case scenario, a child with a risk for aggression similar to Allen's whose environment made things worse. The problems often begin in infancy, when a bewildered and inexperienced young mother finds that her image of a soft, cuddly, sleeping baby is dramatically contradicted by the inconsolable, irritable infant she got instead. The temptation to mistreat such a child—to shut him up or punish him—can be great. You don't have to be young or inexperienced to feel this strain. If you're poor, out of work, raising several kids on your own, or just under a lot of stress, a child like this makes things a lot worse.

But what happens to such a child when a combination of better parenting, community resources, and a good education has smoothed over the sharp edges of biological risk? When Allen's mother came to the

Cub Scout troop to help Allen get through the meeting without attacking anyone, she did exactly what the ideal mother in that unenviable situation should do. She got him to slow down, count to ten, and get a grip on his anger. She helped him see how he had been misinterpreting the situations that enraged him. A boy who bumps you, she explained, was probably bumped himself and didn't mean to jostle you. She carefully, patiently tutored him through each situation that made him angry, and over time, he learned how to control himself. Although Allen's mother was only partly successful during the existence of our Cub Scout troop, over the long term, she was actually successful. By age sixteen, Allen had become quite the model high school student. Yes, he interrupted other students in class, and yes, he still got involved in the occasional brawl in the school parking lot, but for the most part, he confined his aggression to the football field, where it served him well.

What makes Allen's mother look like the perfect picture of motherhood while Steve's mother looks so negligent? Here are a few things that Allen's mother has that Steve's mother did not have: a supportive husband who is committed to his son turning out well and being successful; a community with lots of organized sports; a strong religious and cultural tradition; neighbors who intervened when Allen got too boisterous; friends who understood the problem and could take him so his mother could recoup; a school that gave second, third, and fourth chances; no substance abuse problems in the family; no history of physical abuse in the family; relatives living in the same community; a counselor who talked with Allen about his feelings and how he could control them. The list goes on. The social environment either conspires to make genetic heritage a lifelong resource, as it may ultimately prove to be for Allen, or a life sentence, as it was for Steve.

Just as early family life can mute the effects of a genetic or acquired risk, community support—neighborhoods, schools—can do so as well. Even if a child like Allen doesn't grow up in a supportive family, the environmental advantage of living in a middle-class or upper-class community may offer that child some protection against an escalating cycle of problems. How does a community have these protective effects?

One way is through the peers a community provides. An at-risk child in a poor neighborhood can become susceptible to the influence of deviance-prone peers, whereas the high-risk child living in a middle-class neighborhood is surrounded by peers who are less likely to go that route and who may consequently deter that way of life. Neighborhoods also provide many eyes that can monitor the environment to be sure things remain safe and to see to it that would-be rule breakers are quickly discouraged or caught. Neighborhoods provide a wealth (or a dearth) of resources that give children constructive opportunities—good schools, youth groups, organized sports, and role models to help them pursue their goals. In ways you might never have imagined, our collective community-based tending has powerful effects in controlling how children turn out.[7]

THE SOCIAL WORLD is undeniably protective, a point that has been evident for decades. In the late 1800s, sociologist Emile Durkheim found that a key risk for suicide was a lack of social integration. With few ties to others, people self-destruct. Ties with family and close friends are protective of physical health as well: social isolation increases the risk for *all* causes of death, including heart disease, cancer, stroke, accidents, or suicide.[8]

One of the earliest studies to show this important point was conducted by epidemiologists Lisa Berkman and Leonard Syme, who followed nearly 7,000 California residents over a nine-year period to identify factors that contributed to their longevity or to early death. They looked at the obvious factors, such as whether or not people had good health habits and generally took care of themselves, but they also looked at whether people were married, had contacts with close friends and relatives, maintained memberships in formal groups such as churches or civic groups, or participated in informal groups, such as bridge or poker clubs, bowling leagues, and other leisure-time social activities.

They found that people who lacked social and community ties were much more likely to die of all causes during the nine-year follow-up period than those who cultivated or maintained their social relationships. Ties with family and close friends were particularly protective of health. When the researchers compared the importance of social ties with other factors known to affect health, such as consuming alcohol, getting enough sleep, eating a proper diet, and smoking, they found that social ties were at least as strong an influence on health. At first, these effects may seem quite magical, but as we'll see shortly, there is solid biology behind them. Our intimate and social relationships are potent resources, indeed. Over a hundred scientific studies have now shown that people who have ties to others—family, friends, and community—are happier, healthier, and live longer.[9]

Just how powerful social ties can be has been elegantly demonstrated by Carnegie Mellon psychologist Sheldon Cohen and his colleagues in their perverse experiments on cold viruses. Cohen and his colleagues recruited healthy community volunteers, paid them a lot of money, and then deliberately exposed them to cold or flu viruses by swabbing the inside of their nasal passages with virus-soaked cotton swabs. Then they watched to see who got sick and how sick they got. People experiencing a lot of stress were more likely to get ill than people under less stress, and the colds and flus they got were more serious as well. Those with more social ties, however, were less likely to get sick following exposure to the virus, and if they did, they were able to shake it off more quickly.[10]

OUR TENDENCY TO come together is especially great when we are under stress. This is perhaps the greatest evolutionary adaptation we have, for it is at these times when we need others most. This aspect of our social nature seems to be wired in as well. Among our primate relatives, threat also fosters tighter bonds. Consider our close relatives, the chimpanzees. Chimpanzees live in flexible groups, sometimes as large as a hundred or more in number. Although members of a group spend much of their leisure time in one another's company and return to the group at night, during the day, many chimps, especially the females, are solitary foragers. Each has her personal territory for food gathering, which helps keep competitive skirmishes over good food sources to a minimum. Solitary foraging is only possible in an environment largely free of predators, however, and if the environment should become more threatening, a more social style of life may become more likely. Indeed, in places where predators are a risk, female chimpanzees abandon their solitary style in favor of group foraging. For example, in the Tai forest of the Ivory Coast, where leopards are plentiful, a solitary forager can be easily picked off, and so the chimps have taken up group foraging instead. Moreover, they share food, defend one another's interests, and develop friendships, all of which are rare behaviors for female chimpanzees in the wild that attest to the bonds a common threat can encourage. Similarly, in the hills of Guinea, human beings have been encroaching on chimpanzee territory over the last few decades; and, as in the Tai forest, group foraging has become the norm.[11]

In times of tragedy, humans are much the same. A shared threat is a quick and reliable way to get people to band together. On January 23, 1994, Los Angeles was rocked by a major earthquake that injured many people, toppled buildings, disrupted transportation, and otherwise made life frightening and inconvenient. Moreover, it was followed by more than 1,100 aftershocks of strong enough magnitude to keep nerves raw. Coping with the aftermath of an earthquake is edgy business. The power goes out, you check your gas lines for leaks, each inspection of your house reveals some new possession broken or chipped. And just as you're starting to calm down, there's another aftershock. Nonetheless, life limps along.

A few days after the earthquake, I had to buy a gift, and so I ventured out to a nearby shopping center, expecting to find it sparsely and tensely populated. To my surprise, it was packed with cheerful people, only a few of whom seemed to be shopping. Most lolled around outside, basking in the warm sunlight and the companionable chatter of strangers. It was an impromptu party.

The cappuccino carts were clearly doing their best business of the year. People were nibbling on hot dogs, burritos, dim sum, pizza, and other food-court offerings. As I walked through this calm and pleasant crowd, my paced slowed, my errand seemed less insistent, and I'm sure my expression changed. I started acknowledging strangers who returned my greeting as if we were friends.

At one point, an aftershock rocked the shopping center. No one moved, as if we were all locked in a freeze frame. Within seconds, it ended and excited conversation resumed, more animated than before, marked by smiles, jokes, and visible signs of relief. I stayed perhaps an hour longer than I expected to and went away feeling quite soothed.

The comfort, help, and caregiving that people give to one another, often complete strangers, comes from the bonding that rapidly develops under conditions of collective threat.[12] My earthquake experience is a very modest example of this bonding. Discovering a common enemy—whether impersonal, as with a natural disaster, or personal, as in wartime—induces intense social bonds and is one of the fastest ways to get people to act on one another's behalf.

THE IDEA THAT perfect strangers can and do provide solace, affection, and support to one another went largely unexplored by scientists for decades. It has taken us a while to realize that we are all capable of providing this kind of "medicine." Indeed, we edged into this position only by seeing how this happens spontaneously, as in our coming together during times of intense stress.

People have been supporting one another for centuries, of course, but this role was usually filled by someone familiar, such as a family member, or someone empowered to do so, such as a minister or an elder. But it is not just the experts among us who have these abilities; those who share our experience do as well. We have elevated the concept of the ministering stranger to an art form.

The idea that expertise can come from someone whose only qualification is knowing what you're going through is a quite radical idea, and yet it works. Try as they might, psychologists have yet to come up with ways of helping problem drinkers that are noticeably more effective than Alcoholics Anonymous. Weight Watchers and similar organizations do nearly as well as many scientifically based interventions in helping people take off weight. Peer counselors help adolescents weather struggles that adults can hardly imagine.

Capitalizing on the expertise of the average person is also the idea behind support groups. In this novel approach to problem solving, a group of people who have gone through the same problem can give one another support and advice, even as each member extracts the same to meet his or her own needs. These processes draw on that same principle of bonding that characterizes our other tending relationships: shared adversity spawns ties with others. The ostensible purpose behind support groups is to provide emotional comfort, but they probably do their share of healing, too. It would be no great surprise if they did. We've known for decades that the solace provided by the tending of others disengages stress systems, an effect that benefits almost every biological system we have.

Stanford psychiatrist David Spiegel has been right in the thick of this issue. In 1989, he and his colleagues published a paper in the prominent British medical journal *The Lancet* that dramatically changed how the scientific community regarded support groups. Many physicians had thought of support groups as a way to make their patients feel better (and perhaps get them to take their time-consuming personal problems elsewhere), and so they recommended them to their patients, particularly the loquacious ones. But Spiegel's work told them that something far more important could happen in support groups.

Spiegel enrolled women with advanced breast cancer who were not expected to survive for long. This move was innovative in itself, because support groups have usually been considered as resources to help survivors return to full psychological health, not as ways of easing the transition to death. To see whether these groups could benefit terminally ill patients, Spiegel had some of the patients participate in small groups of about fifteen women each, whereas others constituted a comparison condition and did not participate in a group. All the women continued to receive medical care, of course.

The women attended the groups for about an hour and a half each week for over a year. The group discussions were guided by a psychiatrist or social worker and by a therapist who had also fought breast cancer, but for the most part, the women controlled the flow of the conversation. The topics they discussed ranged widely, from the effects the illness had had on their lives to the physical side effects of treatment and how to overcome them. The women shared their feelings of increasing isolation from other people, and they talked about how to be more assertive with doctors. They talked about the meaning their lives held, and how, paradoxically, the cancer had helped them recognize that meaning. They faced their losses together when a group member died.

After the year had ended, Spiegel and his colleagues followed these women to see what had become of them. Even Spiegel was surprised by the dramatic results. The women who had participated in the groups lived twice as long as those who had not—on average, nearly a year and a half longer.

How does simply talking things through with fellow patients lead to longer life? Part of the reason may have been that the women in the intervention became less anxious and depressed as they talked through the issues their cancers had raised. Having gotten advice from other group members, they also became more successful in controlling their pain. Anxiety, depression, and pain all activate stress systems, which adversely affect the functioning of the immune system. Women who were better able to manage these problems, as a result of their support group participation, may have had a slower course of illness because their immune systems waged a better battle than was true for the women whose depression, anxiety, and pain were less well controlled.[13]

Participating in just any group wouldn't confer these physical and mental benefits, of course. Those groups that reduce anxiety and depression, those that help their members control pain, and those that are truly supportive are most likely to extend life. But group members may benefit emotionally, regardless of whether or not the group is effective in other ways. When you've embarked on the roughest journey of all—dying—it's important to have some warm companionship along the way.

THE IDEA THAT social ties can maintain or improve health sometimes meets with skepticism, because it seems like magic rather than science. So let's put the science into it. Why is social support good medicine? Scientists are now quite confident that we understand some of its benefits. As many studies now attest, stress responses are lower when supportive people are around. The fight-or-flight response of sympathetic activation is lower and HPA activity is reduced. Consequently the immune system, which is influenced by both the sympathetic and HPA systems, functions better. Some psychologists and biologists think that social support may add something more, however, suggesting that social support not only reduces stress but may stimulate neuroendocrine benefits as well.[14]

One of those sources of neuroendocrine benefits is oxytocin, which appears to be both a cause and a consequence of social support. In the face of at least some threats, oxytocin is rapidly released. From what we know about its effects, oxytocin may be one of the biological factors that propels people and animals into one another's company in stressful situations: as an "affiliative" hormone, oxytocin leads people to seek contact with others. It is released in the company of others, so it may also be implicated in the emotional experiences of bonding that are seen in the aftermath of tragedy. Even a soothing touch can activate oxytocin's release, and so the stress-reducing benefits of hugging, massage, and other forms of affectionate physical contact can bring about a calmer response to stress.[15]

Growth hormone may be another neuroendocrine consequence of social support. Evidence for the role of growth hormone in combatting stress is indirect, much of it the product of studying abandoned infants, like the orphans in Romania. Very young babies who do not receive the affectionate attention of caregivers fail to thrive and may die. "Failure to thrive" is a complex disorder, characterized by an imbalance of catabolic hormones (such as stress hormones) to anabolic hormones (such as growth hormone and insulin). The overabundance of stress hormones so early in life can lead to the inhibition of growth hormone, as well as to problems in making use of the nutrients extracted from digested food, which further exacerbates growth problems. Infants who survive this kind of neglect nonetheless often have profound problems in physical and mental development, and their stress systems, most notably the HPA, show marked aberrations. By implication, higher levels of growth hormone may be associated with better neuroendocrine profiles. Indeed, in one study by psychologist Elissa Epel and her colleagues, women who showed resilience in the face of life traumas, such as illness, divorce, and death of a family member, had higher levels of growth hormone. From evidence like this, scientists have learned that growth hormone is affected by positive social experiences well into adulthood, and so its potential role in the benefits of social support is attracting well-deserved scrutiny.[16]

An increase in brain opioids (or endogenous opioid peptides) may be implicated in the benefits of social support as well. Just as there seems to be a two-way street between oxytocin and social contact, so, too, do EOPs and social contact influence each other. Low levels of EOPs lead animals to seek social contact, and positive social contact, in turn, leads to the release of EOPs. This process may provide a biological mechanism for wanting social contact with others. EOPs are certainly rewarding: when animals in research studies get a dose of EOPs in a particular place or in conjunction with a particular smell, they show a preference for that place or odor well after the effects of the EOPs have ended.

EOPs may even exert direct effects on stress hormones, reducing their strength. When animals are socially isolated, their levels of EOPs decline. When they rejoin their companions, EOP levels return to normal, accompanied by an emotional state that can only be described as euphoria. Neuroscientist Jaak Panksepp has suggested that EOPs may be the key to a mild form of social addiction, whereby the release of opioids in response to companionship sustains the need for that companionship. So far, only animal evidence for this idea has accumulated, so it is not yet known whether EOPs underlie the euphoria that human companionship can produce or the need to seek it out in the face of loneliness or isolation.[17]

Oxytocin, growth hormone, and EOPs almost certainly get some support from other hormones, including vasopressin, norepinephrine, prolactin, and serotonin. For example, in male prairie voles, vasopressin prompts pair bonding, and when the male prairie vole is under stress, he turns to his mate. Vasopressin and norepinephrine may play a role in social memory, that is, in the ability to remember who is friend and who is foe. High levels of serotonin are associated with social confidence and feelings of connectedness with others. Prolactin levels change in response to caregiving and grief in both humans and animals. Whether this list exhausts the hormones that help to regulate our social behavior, especially in times of stress, is not yet known. Do these hormones work together or back one another up to provide the health benefits of social support, or are the benefits all in the ability of social support to reduce stress hormones? These are the questions we will seek to answer about the neuroregulation of social behavior in the coming decades.[18]

I have brought you to the cutting edge of the science of social support. While some of the theories on the role of hormones are still speculative, one thing we do know is that people with social support have "younger" stress systems and consequently better protection against major chronic diseases.[19] In the last chapter, I described how the stress systems of offspring from risky families look "older" than those of children from supportive families. The reverse is true of people who feel supported by their friends and relatives. A study by Bert Uchino, John Cacioppo, and their colleagues makes this point well. As people age, reliable changes in the functioning of the cardiovascular system usually take place that can eventually lead to hypertension and heart disease, as we saw in the last chapter. Uchino and his colleagues reasoned that social support may guard against these age-related changes. To study this issue, they asked older men and women if they had at least one person with whom they could talk through their problems. Supporting their reasoning, the researchers found that the people in their study who said they did have such confidants had "younger" cardiovascular systems that, for the most part, did not show the adverse effects of aging.[20] There is a fountain of youth, it seems, although it is not to be found in an elusive spring but in the flow of support that runs from one person to another.

W HEN PSYCHOLOGISTS BEGAN studying social support, they emphasized the specific benefits that other people provide, such as advice and emotional sustenance. Friends and family bring food after a death in the family, or they drive you to the doctor if you're injured and can't get there on your own. You can talk through your fears—about starting school at age five or getting divorced at age forty—and other people help you understand what you're feeling. Friends and family provide information about issues large and small, such as where to get the best deal on a new appliance or how to break off a relationship gently.

But in truth, psychologists have probably overestimated the importance of these specific acts of social support and underestimated the importance of simple contact with others. When a person you care about is just there—reading the paper or puttering in the kitchen, for example—it's soothing, even when you aren't talking or doing anything helpful for each other. When you're ill and your family wants to close your bedroom door so you can get some sleep, you want the door left open so you can hear the comforting social sounds of the household. We regulate one another's biology without even realizing it.

Scientists have recently discovered exactly this: that "invisible" social support may actually be better for physical and mental health than real social support. People don't like putting their friends and relatives out, and so when they need to draw on others for help, they feel guilty and experience a sense of obligation to reciprocate that may detract from the benefits the support might otherwise give them. But just knowing others are there is stress-reducing, because even if you never have to use it, it is comforting to know it is available.[21]

To show this point, psychologists Sherry Broadwell and Kathleen Light brought married men into their laboratory and had them fill out a questionnaire about how much support they felt they had at home. Each man was then put through several stressful tasks, such as computing difficult arithmetic problems in his head. The men who said they had a lot of support from their families had lower blood pressure responses to the stressful tasks than the men who reported that they had less family support, suggesting that their families were providing support to them even when they weren't there! Just being in a happy family kept the men's stress responses low.[22]

Other people are a source of nurturant solace. They calm us down in times of stress. In early life, if we're fortunate, our parents are the source of this comfort, and throughout childhood and adulthood, we build on the early soothing relationships with parents to derive comfort from our social environment. For the most part, the others who provide this comfort are familiar to us, family and friends, but strangers can do so as well.

In the wake of a community trauma—a tornado, hurricane, or flood, for example—the survivors commonly remark on the intense bonds they developed with one another, how they never knew they had so many friends or that so many people cared for them. Our stress systems react less strongly when supportive people are about, and if our stress systems have already gotten engaged, they come back down faster with comforting people around.

WHO PROVIDES THE comforting resources of social support, the tending that brings stress systems down and keeps both mental and physical health on an even keel? As the next few chapters reveal, the answer, quite often, is women. Women are not only the tenders of children, but the tenders of men and one another as well. Women get much of their social support from their ties with other women, and are only somewhat benefited, both emotionally and in terms of health, from their ties with men. For example, the study by Sherry Broadwell and Kathleen Light, which I just described, included both married men and married women. Although men's stress responses were lower after they had described their supportive relationships at home, women's stress responses were not. Men, on the other hand, may get limited health and mental health benefits from their ties with men—indeed, as we'll see, ties with men seem to enhance many risks—but they do reap many emotional and health-related benefits from their ties with women.[23]

As a beginning peek into this revealing truth, consider the findings of a study on loneliness by University of Rochester psychologist Ladd Wheeler and his colleagues. They looked at students who remained behind at the university to complete exams while everyone else had gone home for the December holidays. The holiday season is a vulnerable time for depression and loneliness in any instance, and being away from family and under stress merely aggravates these problems. To see what kinds of experiences staved off these risks, Wheeler and his colleagues had the students keep records of how they spent their days, with whom they spent their time, and what emotions they experienced during that period.

The strongest determinant of how lonely the students were was how much contact they spent each day with women who had also remained behind during the holidays. The more time a student, man or woman, spent with women, the less lonely he or she was. The amount of time spent with men, for the most part, had no effect on either the male or the female students' mental health.[24] Nor is this finding distinctive to lonely college students. Across stressful and nonstressful times and across the life span, we all benefit from women's tending.

CHAPTER 6

Women Befriending

Shortly after she was married, my grandmother, Lizzie Ella, joined a quilting group of neighborhood women, which she participated in for most of her adult life. I have no firsthand knowledge of what it was like, of course, or why it was apparently so satisfying to its members that it lasted so long. But I imagine it to have been something like the one portrayed in the 1995 movie *How to Make an American Quilt*, filled with stories, confessions, and advice to the youngest member, though perhaps freer of the infidelities and dramatic skirmishes in the film. Or perhaps not.

A generation later, my mother and her friends formed a group called the Coterie, which met about once a month for nearly fifteen years, rotating among the six members' houses. On the nights the group met at our house, the food was especially good, since my mother was not about to look like a mediocre cook in front of her friends. After dinner, each woman pulled out the pile of knitting, mending, or darning that she had brought with her, and they talked and laughed for another couple hours until everyone left around 9:30 or 10:00.

By the time this multigenerational habit got to me, all pretense of constructive activity had vanished. No quilters, sewers, or darners we! We came together in Cambridge, Massachusetts, as a group of professional women who initially carpooled to distant greenhouses to buy plants, but soon we discovered that what we really enjoyed were the Saturday noons of food, wine, and laughter that preceded those trips. The plant part dropped out pretty quickly. Nonetheless, we called ourselves the Cambridge Ladies Garden Club, largely because the mother of one member had been nagging her to get involved in civic activities, and we felt that this very proper title would get her to back off.

When I moved to California, I found that I missed these nourishing afternoons of good food and good company, so I talked with some new acquaintances to see if they were interested in doing something similar. They were, and the six of us have now been getting together every three weeks for over twenty years. We have seen one another through relationships, marriages, divorces, and remarriages, the birth or adoption of eight children, and the deaths of six of our parents. We have made it through earthquakes, fires, and home construction. We have talked through career promotions, setbacks, and new directions. We have lived most of our adult lives together.

This is what women do, not necessarily in the formal and regular sense I've just described, but informally, getting together with other women to meet a common need. A neighbor of mine belongs to a group called the Coffee Klatsche, which originally formed because all the members had small children and no day care or any other way for their toddlers to meet other children. So they let the children play together while they shared their ideas about how to raise children and deal with problems like thumb sucking and bed-wetting, getting their husbands to help out more, and finding more time for themselves. The first day of kindergarten loomed sadly on the horizon, not because the women weren't ready to give up their little ones to school—they were more than ready—but because the Coffee Klatsche would cease to exist. And so they decided that it wouldn't, and they continued meeting as a group for years after.

Any woman with close friends knows this joy, this fun, this complete necessity of friendship. Women tell stories of awful blind dates, share suspicions about an errant husband, and compare notes on impossible adolescents. They celebrate successes together, seek comfort in setbacks, and plot to neutralize tormentors at work. They seek and usually get the validation that they need to manage their lives. Women's friendships are vital to mental health, and that is a large part of my story.

But women's preferences for one another's company may come not only from the rewarding companionship that other women provide, but also from an evolutionary heritage that has selected for female friendship. Women and children have literally stayed alive over the centuries because women form friendships. Our most insistent needs—for food and safety—and our most vital tasks—the care of children and the sustenance of the social group—have been met through these ties. This is a new and potentially controversial view of women's friendships, but one that, I think, is amply supported.

Women have formed bonds with other women for hundreds of thousands, perhaps millions, of years. We know very little about these early ties. What knowledge we have comes from how we think early people may have lived, and from the hunter-and-gatherer societies that have survived to the present time. We know that early women were foragers, who combed the land in search of roots, tubers, and other nutritious foods. We believe that they may have coordinated their foraging activity so that no isolate would be picked off by a predator and so that conflict over food sources could be kept low. From current-day foraging societies, we can infer that some food sharing among women also took place and that shared child-care arrangements, especially with kin, probably helped to free each woman to do her foraging.[1]

As humans began to cultivate the land, women farmed together, talking, singing, and laughing, as they still do in many countries, to let would-be predators know that they were there in numbers. From the Dogon women of Upper Volta who clean millet in village circles to the boisterous female relatives and friends who get Thanksgiving dinner on to the table, women prepare food together to nourish themselves and others. And they sew, knit, darn, and quilt while they talk through events of their lives and what they mean.

Would our prehistoric ancestors recognize the women's groups of the present? Certainly some of the forms they now assume would be unfamiliar. Women join book clubs to discuss a current bestseller, invest-ment clubs to manage their money, and theater groups when their part-ners eschew cultural activities. But other groups would be readily recognizable, especially the sewing and mending circles and the most common of women's groups, the Mommy and Me toddler get-togethers. Our ancestors would probably also understand the spirit of such groups, even without knowing one word of our language, for women's groups have a distinctive style.

Throughout life, women seek more close friends than men do. Begin-ning in early childhood, girls develop more intimate friendships than boys do and create larger social networks for themselves. Groups of women share more secrets, disclose more details about their lives, and express more empathy and affection for one another than do members of men's groups. They sit closer together and touch one another more than men in groups do. Women confide their problems to one another, seek-ing help and understanding. Men do so much more rarely.[2]

This inclination of women to bond together may be far older than we imagine, for the comfort that females enjoy in one another's company is not confined to humans; it is evident in animals as well. Psychologist Martha McClintock, who studies female reproductive hormones in ani-mals, noticed a curious phenomenon in her Norway rats. When too few individual cages necessitated housing the females together in groups of about five, the rats lived 40 percent longer than when they were housed alone. This surprising finding led McClintock to rethink how to house her animals, since the convention of one rat to a cage originally devel-oped to prevent male rats from attacking one another.[3]

Biologist Sue Carter, a pioneer in investigations of social affiliation in animals, noticed a similar curiosity. Carter studies prairie voles, the small rodent best known for its tendency to form strong, lifelong male-female pairs, as humans often do. When conditions become stressful for the voles, males seek contact with their mates. Under the same stressful conditions, however, female voles turn not to their mates, but to their female "friends"— that is, the other females with whom they have pre-viously been housed.[4]

Intrigued by observations like these, primatologist Sally Mendoza and her colleagues at the Regional Primate Center in Davis, California, conducted an experimental study in which they took female squirrel monkeys out of their familiar cages and placed them in an unfamiliar environment, a move that usually distresses monkeys and leaves them agitated. Half the females were put in the strange environment alone, and the other half were put there in the company of their female cage mates. Those who had the company of their cage mates showed less distress than those who were put there alone, suggesting that these familiar females protected them against the stress of the new environment.[5]

My interest in women's groups was initially piqued not by my own experiences but by these animal studies. For many years I have studied how people cope with stress; turning to the social group for safety and support, as I've noted, is one of the most common ways to do so. The fact that one can see a similar pattern in animals suggests that turning to others may have quite old biological origins. What particularly intrigued me, though, was how, in females, this desire for social contact seems to include a preference for female company. I began to look at women's groups with a new perspective and wondered whether they might represent more than the informal, pleasant social sororities they seem to be on the surface. Specifically, I began to think of them as possible buffers against stress.

I shared my interest with an anthropologist friend, a prominent investigator of social relationships. His immediate response was, "Women don't form groups." When I told him about the kinds of groups I was interested in—mother and toddler groups, fireside food preparation groups, and the like—his response was "Oh, those kinds of groups. Of course, women form those kinds of groups. They just don't form groups that matter."[6]

I contend that these groups matter a great deal, not only to the women who participate in them, but to the networks and communities in which they are embedded. Women's networks form an inner core of social life that may be barely visible in nonstressful times, but that leap to prominence when life becomes more difficult. These bonds may be based on kinship—with mothers, sisters, aunts, or nieces or on simple friendship, but regardless, the needs they meet are fundamental ones: raising children, getting food, protecting against violence, and coping with stress.

Turning to the social group in times of stress is beneficial to both men and women, of course.[7] Historically, however, the social group has probably been especially important to women because it provides safety for each woman and her children. For many centuries, women spent much of their adolescent and adult lives pregnant, nursing, or caring for their young. Unlike men, who could readily attack an invader or flee from a predator, women, as I've already noted, had to develop ways of managing stress that included protection for their young as well as themselves, and group life affords such protection.[8] But why would a specific preference for the company of other females develop? And what needs would that preference for female company meet?

OUR PRIMATE HERITAGE provides a good place to look for answers to these questions. Although bonds among females may be almost invisible in human societies some of the time, they are starkly evident in other primate groups, most notably the Old World monkeys—gorillas, orangutans, baboons, macaque monkeys, chimpanzees, and bonobos—who are our closest relatives.

First, a bit of background: Each primate society is organized somewhat differently, but most feature a hierarchical structure with dominant animals at the top, who commandeer resources for themselves, and subordinates further down, whose resources are few. How important the dominance hierarchy is varies a lot among the species. Macaque monkeys are very dominance-oriented, for example, whereas bonobos are quite egalitarian. Males, for the most part, are more dominance-oriented than females, aggressively attempting to ascend the hierarchy and defend their position against other males. Dominance in females is often based on kinship—a daughter's position in the hierarchy is determined by who her mother is—and female-dominance hierarchies are usually more stable and somewhat less rancorous than their male counterparts.[9]

In many primate societies, females stay in the troop in which they were born and males emigrate, which is one reason why kinship is the primary basis for female ties. But when females do emigrate, as is true among bonobos, friendships may actually be more important. Once settled in their new troops, female bonobos form intense, long-lasting bonds with other females. And even where bonds among females are based on kinship, unrelated females in several primate species form strong "friendships" as well.[10]

How are these bonds expressed? Grooming, the practice of picking through the coat of one's companion to remove parasites, is one important way. Primatologist Robin Dunbar calls it the primate equivalent of talking on the phone. Depending on who grooms whom for how long and under what circumstances, grooming can communicate very complex messages such as solace, solidarity, amends making, or, by its absence, rejection. Grooming keeps a friend's coat clean and attractive, and it is also a very soothing, comforting activity. Mothers groom daughters, and sisters and friends groom one another, an activity that can consume up to 10 to 20 percent of an animal's waking time. When you consider that as much as 70 percent of a female primate's waking time may go to foraging for food, this means that grooming fills much of what remains, making it a primary leisure-time activity. Grooming of males by other males, on the other hand, is less common in most primate species, and nearly unheard of in some.[11]

Female bonds among primates, then, are common, usually based on kin, sometimes based on "friendship," and maintained, in part, by grooming. What are the purposes of these alliances? Like mothers everywhere, female primates need to gather food and care for their young, and their female friends and relatives help them with these tasks. Indeed, primatologist Richard Wrangham believes that females' relationships with one another may have evolved primarily to manage food collection and distribution, with females sharing information about where the good food is, harvesting food collectively, and driving off rival groups of females from good food patches. Males need food, too, of course, but if they are providing primarily for their own needs, their food-gathering strategies don't have to take infants' needs into account to the same extent as mothers' strategies do. For females, getting enough food for everyone is vital.[12]

Just as coordinating food allocation is a major task for females, so is child care, and sharing this responsibility benefits mothers and offspring alike. Like human mothers, primate mothers often sit on the outskirts of a group of youngsters, seemingly interested primarily in communicating with (grooming) one another or resting, but usually keeping one eye on the group, ready to intervene if the boisterous play gets out of hand. Not surprisingly, when all the females are watching out for them, infants benefit. They are less likely to wander into harm's way and be killed or die from neglect.

Sometimes females trade off child care as well, with kin, with "friends," or with younger female "baby-sitters." The benefits of these exchanges are not confined to convenience. When care of infants is shared among females, they grow faster, whether because their mothers are more free to forage for food, or because their sitters help feed them, or both. It's a good arrangement all around, and it has a significant by-product as well: younger females who have not yet given birth learn how to be mothers, which is vital to how well they care for their own infants later on.[13]

All things considered, the female primate network can be an amazing little social system. Food gets distributed, babies are cared for, the mothers of the future get training, and everyone gets groomed and comforted in the process. This is the ideal situation, of course. Just as is true in groups of women, groups of female primates can go off in some unpleasant directions as well. Other females sometimes kill or eat babies rather than nurture them, and squabbles over food, friendships, or males can turn ugly. On the whole, though, if this system seems eerily familiar to many mothers, it is probably because, for the most part, it has been successful and has consequently made its way into our own genes and lives as well.

Bonds with other females also provide protection. If you know how often a female is groomed by others, and by whom, you can predict pretty well who will come to her aid if she is attacked by a female outside her group, the male in her own group, or an outside predator. Robin Dunbar describes such an encounter in Gelada baboons when the male head of a "harem" becomes too aggressive in his efforts to control the females[14]:

The male's attempts to ride herd on his females when they stray too far from him often backfire. The luckless victim's grooming partners invariably come to her aid. Standing shoulder-to-shoulder, they outface the male with outraged threats and furious barks of their own. The male will usually back off, and walk huffily away, endeavoring to maintain an air of ruffled dignity. However, occasionally, the male will persist, feeling, perhaps, unusually sensitive about his honor and security. This only leads to more of the group's females racing in to support their embattled sisters. The male invariably ends up being chased 'round the mountainside by his irate females in an impressive display of sisterly solidarity.[15]

When strong female bonds are absent, males are often aggressive, even abusive, toward females. For example, although chimpanzees and bonobos are very closely related, male chimps take out their frustrations on females much more often than male bonobos do to female bonobos. This is in large part because bonds among female chimps are not as strong as they are among bonobos. Even among chimpanzees, however, when the environment becomes especially stressful or threatening, female bonds may strengthen to meet the challenge.[16]

It is not unusual for females in a captive chimpanzee colony to band together to protect themselves against an abusive male. Given that such female coalitions can deliver quite a beating, the male is in an understandable hurry to get out of their way. He watches the other sex from a safe distance if he has been lucky enough to escape. Because none of the females matches him in strength and speed, their solidarity is crucial.[17]

Primatologist Sue Boinski found that female squirrel monkeys' ties to other females change in this fashion to cope with extreme stress. Like chimpanzees, female squirrel monkeys are typically lone foragers with relatively weak ties to other females. But during the period in which the females give birth, a plentiful supply of delicious little squirrel monkeys suddenly appears, attracting birds of prey. To reduce this threat, the previously solitary mothers begin traveling in close-knit groups. They often sit together, staring into the sky, swiveling their heads in search of the birds. Each time a falcon swoops down to pluck away a baby, it is mobbed by the vigilant females and driven off. Then, once the infants are mature enough to fend for themselves, the mothers return to their solitary foraging style. These intriguing animal studies suggest that female ties may be loose and variable in normal times but flexible enough to promote shared defense in stressful times.[18]

THIS IS THE picture of female bonds that we get from primates: Together, females provide food, groom one another, take care of off-spring, hold hostile males at bay, and come to one another's aid when threats appear. On the whole, this is a pretty fair characterization of women's bonds as well.

We'll start with food. Women seem to have a special relationship with food. It's not just that women are the ones who buy it, although they are, by a large margin, the food shoppers of the world. And it's not just that women prepare it, although this task, too, is more commonly a woman's province than a man's. Food seems to have a special meaning for women. When women want to celebrate a special occasion, they think of food. When they get together, eating is commonly the activity. "Having lunch" means something special to women that it doesn't nec-essarily mean to men. When women want to send a message of caring or affection to someone, they often cook for them. Men don't typically try new dishes out on one another or exchange recipes, as women do. And women's pathologies often revolve around food as well. Women are by no small margin the dieters, the anorexics, and the bulimics of the world. Women come by their interest—even obsession—with food quite honestly. Just as female primates did, early foraging women had the important job of ensuring that they and their offspring got fed. And the foraging mother faced a daunting task.

The human infant is vulnerable and matures slowly, requiring almost continuous care for the first few years of life, as every weary mother knows. Even after infancy, almost continual monitoring is needed to ensure the child's safety. Moreover, infants have an enormous need for food, estimated by one expert to be between 3 million and 10 million calories over the course of time it takes to bring an infant to maturity. Attempting to meet both her own and her offspring's nutritional needs by herself would have posed almost impossible demands on the foraging mother. She must have had help.[19]

In many cases, that help would have come from the baby's father or from the woman's partner—sometimes, but not always, the same person. For a variety of reasons, however, this would not have been a reliable source of help, so much as an occasional one. Relationships with partners do not always last, and so fathers may have abandoned their responsibilities to an old family as they assumed obligations to a new one. Paternity may have been uncertain, and a man may have been unwilling to provide food for a child he doubted was his. Hunts were not always successful, and even when they were, the food might not have found its way to the hunter's offspring. So to whom did women turn to get the food they needed to bring their offspring to maturity? They relied heavily on ties with other women.[20]

Sometimes they gave offspring to baby-sitters, typically girls who did not yet have children of their own, so they could forage more easily. Foraging is hard work. You have to move rocks and underbrush aside and then dig to get stubborn tubers out of the ground; trying to do so with an infant in tow makes the process even more difficult. Moreover, women foragers typically covered a lot of territory—an estimated 1,500 miles a year by some accounts—and to do so accompanied by an infant or child would have been difficult.[21]

But baby-sitters solve only the problem of freeing the mother to find food more efficiently. They don't address the problem of how the mother was able to provide the sheer amount of food required to satisfy the caloric needs of both herself and her offspring. What may have solved this caloric conundrum was food sharing with female kin and friends. Closest kin are most likely to have helped—a mother, sister, grandmother, or aunt—but other women with whom a mother had forged ties may also have provided food as well. Friends or relatives with infants of their own may have helped out by suckling the hungry baby of a mother who was off foraging. This kind of milk sharing is still found in some present-day foraging groups. Older women who had already had their children but who were able to obtain more food than they needed probably shared food with mothers of young offspring as well. Indeed, in present-day African foraging societies, such as the Hadza and the !Kung, where grandmothers contribute to the care and feeding of their grandchildren, those children who have a living grandmother are more likely to survive.[22]

Food gathering and child care were intimately tied to each other in early human existence. To some degree, that remains so today. Most women don't forage anymore, but they do other things to provide for their families—work, errands, chores—and the arrangements they make for child care with women friends and kin are similar, often startlingly so, to those that early women likely created for one another.

In particular, women continue to play the primary role in child care. I made this statement in a scientific paper recently, and a reviewer solemnly wagged a finger at me, pronouncing that with more egalitarian sex roles this is now much less true. I raced to the library to make sure I wasn't living on a different planet, and, yes, by a large margin, women continue to be the primary players in child care, both for their own children and for one another's. Women are more likely than men to stay home with children, and they do more child care than their husbands do, even when they work full-time. Baby-sitters are more commonly girls than boys, and child-care workers are more often women than men. The preferred form of child care continues to be care by a female relative.[23]

Just as early humans did, modern women also exchange child care. Your kids come to our house where I watch them, and my kids go to your house where you watch them. It isn't that men can't or shouldn't care for kids. Men just don't do so to the degree that women do. So, as was true for our early ancestors, women get food and care for children with the help of the women around them.

For women to form and maintain these vital bonds with one another, some sort of social "glue" needs to exist to hold the relationships together. In primates, the glue that cements social bonds is grooming. What do women do? Robin Dunbar has suggested that the human equivalent of grooming is conversation.[24] While for primates most of the communication of bonding happens through touch, women get closer to one another through talk—endlessly sharing information about what is going on in the social world. Indeed, about two-thirds of conversational time goes to social matters: relationships, social events, likes and dislikes, and what other people are up to. No other topic—politics, work, or even sports—comes close. But is it fair to see conversation as a specifically female kind of social glue? Talking is certainly not unique to women, but it may play an especially important role in building and maintaining women's relationships. Women's verbal abilities are a bit better than men's to begin with. Conversation is a more vital part of women's relationships with one another than is true in men's relationships. Psychologists point out that men friends often do things together—playing sports or working on projects—but the primary activity that women enjoy together is talking.

If you've ever sat in a restaurant next to a table of women, you know that the noise can be overwhelming. Usually everybody is talking very fast and all at the same time. This is hardly useless gossip, however. A great deal of social information gets exchanged quite quickly, and everyone leaves the table very well informed. This is how you might find a book to help you understand your son's attention deficit disorder; a treatment program for your daughter's bulimia; the best divorce lawyer in town; an inexpensive, well-run nursing home for your mother; a recommendation of a surgeon in St. Louis that your sister can see for her breast cancer; the name of an agent for the book of short stories you are writing; a restaurant recommendation that your parents will enjoy and not find too expensive when they visit; a caterer for your son's bar mitzvah; a Web site that discusses golden retrievers' bladder problems; and on and on. For almost any difficulty you may have, however great or small, a group of women can probably point you toward a solution.

As I will argue later, women are heavily involved in stitching up all the little rips and tears in the social fabric. They take care of parents, spouses, children, friends, relatives, and even the family pets. No one tells a woman how to do this, however, and each little crisis is maddeningly unique. This is where women friends come in. They know who had a similar problem, so you have someone to get advice from or commiserate with. If the burden of life's small problems (and many of its larger ones as well) falls on your shoulders, this is often the best way to solve them. But beyond the help that provides a solution to a particular problem is the emotional support that comes from talking. The simple process of conversation makes relationships among women meaningful and holds them together as well.

D‍O TIES AMONG women also provide protection, as they do in primates? Usually that role has been accorded to bonds with men. In our early history, mothers attempting to protect both themselves and their children from predators would have needed help from others, and a protective male is likely to have provided some of that assistance. The fact that men and women pair up may be, in part, an evolutionary adaptation that protected females and offspring against predators.

Men and women in foraging societies spent much of their lives apart, however, with men involved in hunting with other males, and women involved in foraging activities, alone or in groups. Thus, men would not have been a constant source of protection. Ties between men and women can be unstable as well, so that protection at one time may not have been there at another time.

Moreover, as concerns about leopards, tigers, and other animal predators have abated, men themselves have come to be women's primary predators. Women have much to fear from men in the form of rape, assault, abuse, murder, and the mistreatment of their children. In some societies, any woman alone is at risk. Even being in the wrong place at the wrong time can be considered an open invitation to sexual assault. This is when the mere company of other women can be protective. Anthropologists Yolanda and Robert Murphy describe this situation in the Mundurucu of Brazil:

> Any woman who sets out on her own is a mark for the men, and the women guarantee each other's propriety by constantly being in the company of other females. Every morning and evening when the women go to fetch water and bathe, they leave the village in a group. And when they work in their gardens it is always in the company of at least one other woman, and preferably

more. The woman who leaves the village by herself is always considered to be heading for a tryst and, even if she is not, any male has the right to accost her and demand that she have intercourse. These events sometimes approximate rape.[25]

Many women have good reason to fear their own male partners as well. Surveys estimate that between 20 and 50 percent of women in North America have been assaulted at some time by their partner, and crime data reveal that women are most likely to be killed by their own partners. With other women nearby who could provide protection a would-be perpetrator, whether husband or stranger, may think twice.[26]

The evidence that women can protect one another from aggression by a partner is quite plentiful. Let's look at Papua New Guinea to see what factors influence whether a woman is abused by her husband. You may wonder why I focus on Papua New Guinea when there is plenty of domestic violence to look at in other societies, including the United States. In Papua New Guinea, unlike many countries, domestic abuse was, until recently, an accepted part of the culture, and so it was not only common but fairly openly acknowledged.[27] As such, it offers a rare documented example of what happens in societies with overt domestic abuse.

A 1987 study of domestic violence in Papua New Guinea found astonishingly high levels of wife beating, as high as 97 percent in some provinces. In two communities, however, the Wape and the Nagovisi, domestic abuse is very low. One reason why Wape women may escape the abuse that dominates the lives of their sisters in neighboring provinces is that they have real social power. This power comes from at least two sources: Women provide most of the food, first of all, and so husbands are economically dependent on their wives. Wape women also participate in choosing their husbands and may thereby gain a certain leverage in their marriages.[28]

Perhaps the most important reason why Wape women enjoy a life relatively free of abuse may be because of the bonds they form with other women, both their own kin and friends in the village. Anthropologist William Mitchell recounts the following story:

The women of a hamlet, or at least the one in which I lived, develop strong solidarity bonds. In the unlikely event that a couple becomes so angry during a quarrel that they begin to shout at each other, women of the hamlet, a few sometimes armed with large sticks, descend upon the house and stand around it until the woman joins them outside.[29]

By not permitting verbal aggression to escalate, Wape women keep physical violence at a minimum. Among the Nagovisi, where domestic violence is also relatively rare, villages are formed around a group of women related through maternal lines, and men marry into these family units, moving from their own families to live with their wives' families. These close ties among female kin help deter domestic violence.[30] In fact, generally speaking, when women live near their kin, domestic violence is low.

When women leave their own families to move near their husbands' families, they are at much greater risk for being abused, a risk that increases with the distance the woman has moved.[31] Under these circumstances, men wield most of the family power, and it can be difficult for women to form bonds with one another. Isolation from kin makes alliances with one's mother or sisters difficult to maintain, and friendships may be hard to form as well. A husband's female kin—his mother and sisters—may also be abusive and harassing.

Anthropologist Margery Wolf studied young Chinese brides and the isolation and risk of physical abuse they experienced when they moved to live near their husband's family.

It is considered bad form for [the new wife] to visit her natal family often, and even her mother discourages frequent trips home. If she is seriously maltreated by her husband or his family, her father and brothers might intervene, but occasional slaps and frequent harsh words are too unexceptional to rate more than commiseration by her mother. Her closest and most important source of protection from her husband's family and solace in her most unbearable hours of loneliness is the group of women who live nearby but are not related to her husband's family.[32]

Women who are isolated from other women can be in danger. The kinship and companionship of other women is protective, both implicitly, by providing a watchful group, and explicitly, by coming to a woman's aid. When women friends or kin are absent, a woman's vulnerability is that much greater.

I'VE ARGUED THAT, as is true of social groups more generally, women especially activate their bonds with one another under stressful conditions. Indeed, in more than thirty scientific studies of stress and how people cope with it, women turned to the social group more than men did. This was true for every stressor studied, ranging from job stress to a cancer diagnosis to the threat of fatal violence.[33] Consider the following study.

In August 1990, the University of Florida, Gainesville, was rocked by a string of random and quite gruesome serial murders. More than 700 students withdrew from the university, and others armed themselves, anxiously awaiting the next event. In the meantime, the students coped as best they could with the mounting sense of panic that pervaded the campus. Psychologists Monica Biernat and Michael Herkov looked at what these students were doing to control their anxiety and found that how the students coped varied a lot by gender. Whereas men more commonly continued to go it alone, most of the women made arrangements to walk with one another when they had to go out. They called their friends on the phone or got together with them to talk about what they were doing and feeling much more than men did. Perhaps because they shared so much information, the women also took more basic safety precautions than men did, including checking their doors and window locks, carrying mace, leaving their lights on when they went out, and installing alarms in their apartments. In short, the women drew on their social contacts with other women for support and advice.[34]

No doubt, they asked male friends to walk them home from time to time, but on the whole they sought the company of women like themselves who were scared and trying to cope. Other scientists looking at the evidence might argue that women are simply more social than men and that this difference comes out both in stressful times and in day-to-day life. Women, many scientists say, are collectively oriented and have a keen sense of their connections to other people, whereas men are more individualistic.[35]

There is certainly some truth to this generalization. Women do give more social support to others than men do. They readily get involved when a friend or relative needs help, whether because of a death in the family, a divorce, a layoff, or another family tragedy. They notice the stressful events that occur in their social networks, for instance, whose child is sick or whose mother broke her hip. University of Michigan psychologist Joseph Veroff and his colleagues found that women were 30 percent more likely than men to have provided some type of social support in response to stress among their relatives and friends, including work-related difficulties, arguments, death, and illness. Nor are these patterns confined to Western societies. In the more than eighteen cultures in which anthropologists have looked at this issue, all eighteen found similar patterns: women and girls give more help than men do to both the men and the women in their networks.[36]

But from whom do women seek support when they need it? Are they as selectively oriented toward other women as the Florida study implies? The following research helps to answer this question. In the 1950s, a social psychologist named Stanley Schachter explored whether people have a need to affiliate with others. Schachter's interest stemmed from his observation that groups seem to promote feelings of security and reduce the anxiety people experience in uncertain situations. He set up a rather diabolical experiment to test his ideas. He brought college students into his laboratory individually, told them he was studying pain tolerance, and mentioned that he would be giving them a series of strong electric shocks shortly. The shocks would do no permanent damage, he assured them, but they would be painful. He then explained that some additional preparations for the study had to be completed and asked the now quite fearful student whether he or she would prefer to wait alone or with a few other people (always of the same sex as the student) who were also going to participate in the experiment. (The students never actually received any electric shocks. Schachter's interest was only in learning whether people prefer the company of others or to be alone when they are anticipating a threatening event.)

Fortunately for Schachter, the first students who participated in his study were women. When they were given a choice of waiting alone or with other women, they preferred to wait with the other women. However, when Schachter included men in the study, he found a quite different pattern. The men preferred to wait alone. After tinkering with the mechanics of the study a few times and finding no conditions that would lead men to choose to wait with other men, Schachter shrugged and spent the next several years studying only women.[37] The convention stuck, and for the next forty years, psychologists studying the desire to be with other people when awaiting stressful events typically included only women in their studies. Curiously, no one thought to attach any significance to this pattern.

Forty years later psychologists Brian Lewis and Darwin Linder at the University of Arizona decided to see if women really do prefer to be with other women when they are under stress or if any old companion will do. In one of their studies, they gave women awaiting electric shock a choice to be alone or to wait with a man—not someone they knew, but someone who would also be participating in the study. Given that choice, women chose to wait alone.[38]

Why would women choose to be with other women in response to stressful conditions? The answer seems to be that other women reduce women's neuroendocrine responses to stress, calming them down, at least more than men do. Psychologists discovered this intriguing benefit of the company of women by doing stress studies in the laboratory. They invite women individually into their labs to do stressful tasks like mental arithmetic and public speaking and provide the company of a supportive woman or man during the stress tasks. Women's stress responses are typically greater, not lower, in response to a supportive male companion (even if he is the woman's own boyfriend!), but when the supportive companion is another woman, stress responses usually go down.[39]

In times of stress, then, women often choose to be with women. Adolescent girls say they turn to their girlfriends for support, more than boys say they turn to their male friends. Women college students say that they have more same-sex friends who can help them, and they receive more help from those friends, than college men do. Adult women, too, draw on social support in times of stress more than men—again mostly from female relatives and friends—and they rely less heavily than men on their spouses for social support. All across the life span, women turn to other women for help.

In 1932, during the darkest period of the Great Depression, *The Ladies Home Journal* put out an inspirational editorial to its readership, exhorting women to knuckle down and use their resourcefulness to hold their families together and make every penny count. It read in part:

> When money is plenty, this is a man's world. When money is scarce, it is a woman's world. When all else seems to have failed, the woman's instinct comes in. She does the job. That is a reason why, in spite of all that happens, we continue to have a world.

When we look at communities under intense stress, the vital role that networks of women play in holding families and communities together becomes especially clear. From Afghanistan to the inner city, when jobs are scarce, the political system is in upheaval, and buildings are bombed out or empty, babies continue to be born, people need to eat, sick people need care, laundry needs to get done, and children need to be kept out of harm's way. These activities, mundane as they may seem, provide a semblance of social order when the formal order has broken down, and they are usually performed by women. Nor is this a small accomplishment. In times such as these, it takes cooperation and ingenuity to accomplish these fundamental tasks of living. This is when networks of women become especially important.

This point is made especially well in studies of families trying to cope with the threat of poverty and the risks—crime, illness, unemployment—that inevitably accompany it.[40] One such study was recently conducted by Harvard anthropologist Katherine Newman, who interviewed

Harlem residents employed in the fast-food business making minimum wage or just above it. She found that women's ties with other women were often the mainstay of these poor families. Nearly a third of the people she talked with lived in female-headed households, and many more lived with other female relatives. Women—often older women who had already had their children—provided a home, food, and other necessities of life. Shaquena, one of Newman's respondents, comments:

> My aunt . . . lives right across the street from us. Like last night, my grandmother ran out of sugar. My grandmother called my aunt and my aunt brought her the sugar. The guy down the hall, he real cool with us, he give us stuff, and my grandmother's cool with a lot of elderly on our floor. She will ask her daughter, my aunt, for things before she asks a friend, but she's got friends [to ask]. If I need something, I go right upstairs, because my best friend lives right upstairs. Her grandmother and my grandmother are friends and they keep a kitchen full of food.[41]

Food is one basic need that is met by these female-headed networks; safety is another. The possibility of violence is always lurking, and gunfire threatens the safety of the children who play in the streets. Temptations to accept the drugs offered on a front stoop, or to participate in the crimes that mark any poor community, beckon a youngster ready to cut school in favor of something seemingly more interesting. And so women monitor the streets.

> Mothers on welfare often shoulder the burden for working mothers who simply cannot be around enough to exercise vigilance. They provide an adult presence in the parks and on the sidewalks where it is most needed. Without these stay-at-home moms in the neighborhood, many a working-poor parent would have no choice but to force the kids to stay home alone all day during the summer vacation, where they would at least be safe.[42]

These networks meet other needs as well, such as finding work. Tamara provides an example:

People in my family find jobs mostly through my grandmother. My grandmother is like the one source . . . "Grandma, we need a job," we say. She goes to this place, she knows that person, she knows about this job, that thing. I think she knows so many people because of her job. She's been there for maybe seventeen, nineteen years. She works at the Simmons Day Care Center. She knows, it seems she knows everybody in the world.[43]

Sometimes these networks become so intense that they collapse under their own weight. Newman describes one instance in which the female head of such a network had to take the drastic action of selling her house and moving to a small apartment to control the demands made on her by her relatives and friends.

These nearly invisible women's networks—or the groups that don't matter, as my anthropologist friend put it—provide the lifeblood of communities under stress. At their core are older women who cook, nurse sick children and adults, take people in who are temporarily homeless, and care for others' children when they are out seeking employment or working. Studies of low-income families of all ethnic backgrounds attest to the help and emotional support shared among female kin, friends, and neighbors.[44]

To show you how women's ties become especially important in stressful times, I have emphasized their importance in conditions of intense poverty or social turmoil. In a sense, though, these examples may be misleading. Women's networks provide support whenever stress and uncertainty abound, but poverty is, by no means, the only such condition.

I told you earlier about the Cambridge Ladies Garden Club and how much fun it was. What I didn't tell you was how badly we needed one another. Most of us were connected in some way with Harvard University, and in those days, Harvard had almost no women faculty and few women graduate students. Each of us felt intensely isolated. What a relief it was to meet other women who were experiencing so many of the same problems and asking the same questions: Why am I doing more than the men are? Why wasn't I given secretarial help like they were? Isn't that professor's suggestive behavior inappropriate? (The term "sexual harassment" was not yet in use.) Is this unfair, or am I overreacting?

By sharing our questions and, more important, by offering some preliminary answers, we were able to give one another help that was as vital to our bewildering lives as the more fundamental needs for food and child care that women's ties so often provide.

IN THE DELIGHTFUL romp through women's friendship entitled *I Know Just What You Mean*, Ellen Goodman remarks of her friendship with coauthor Patricia O'Brien, "We were becoming part of each other's DNA." She meant the comment metaphorically, but before the scientific study of women's friendships is finished, I think the DNA may very well turn out to be the right place to look.

Earlier I pointed out that nature does not leave critical tasks like caring for children to chance, and consequently it provides hormones that help females bond with their newborns. These hormones, which include oxytocin and EOPs, promote a sense of relaxation, warmth, and closeness with others, among other psychological and physical changes. There is now reason to believe that these same hormones—this same affiliative circuitry, as neuroscientists put it—may be implicated in women's friendships as well. Neuroendocrinologist Eric Keverne and colleagues have suggested that female bonding may have piggybacked, in the evolutionary sense, onto the mother-infant bonding process, and the hormones implicated in mother-infant bonding may also be implicated in the ties that women form with one another.[45]

What is the evidence for this idea? Some of it comes from studies of primates. Let's return to grooming, that slow, soothing process of cleaning the coat that is so comforting to our primate relatives. Some biologists suspect that grooming releases hormones that produce these calming, stress-reducing benefits. As noted earlier, oxytocin is released in response to massage, hugging, and other forms of affectionate touching, and it is known to have soothing, stress-reducing properties. Naturally produced opioids likewise produce a state of calm relaxation, and positive affectionate social contact seems to prompt opioid release as well. Scientists have learned that animals prefer to spend time with other animals with whom they have experienced high levels of brain oxytocin and opioids in the past, suggesting that these experiences have been reinforcing to them in ways that maintain the social relationship.[46] Are these chemicals one reason why friendships are maintained across time?

One way to find out would be to block these chemicals with a neurochemical agent to see if signs of friendship decline. In theory, if animals (or people) aren't getting their usual hits of oxytocin and opioids from their contacts with others, then they should reduce their social contacts because those contacts are no longer rewarding. In a study that did exactly this, female rhesus macaque monkeys were given a neurochemical agent that blocked the release of opioids. In response, the females substantially cut back their grooming of one another, the macaque way of expressing friendship. (The study did not include males because males don't groom one another reliably or form friendships in the ways that female macaques do.)[47]

There is some evidence that similar biological processes may underlie women's social behavior. In a study with college students, psychologist Larry Jamner and his colleagues injected men and women with a long-lasting opioid-blocking agent that markedly reduced their levels of circulating opioids. Although men's social behavior was unaffected by this chemical, women's social behavior changed quite a lot. They spent less time with their friends, called them less on the phone, spent more time alone, and said that when they did spend time with others, the occasions were less pleasant than usual. In short, just as with animals, blocking opioids inhibited the rewards that women got from socializing with their friends, and so they cut back on their social contacts.[48]

At present, the idea that women's bonds with one another are maintained, in part, by the affiliative neurocircuitry is a hypothesis rather than a well-established truth. But these intriguing bits of evidence do tell scientists where to look to understand the neurological bases of women's friendships more completely. For the moment, we have to be content with these hints.

Wʜᴀᴛ sʜᴏᴜʟᴅ ᴡᴇ take away from the study of women's bonds with one another? A first insight stems from the realization that these bonds are old and deep. They may have been "selected for," in the evolutionary sense, because they provided nourishment and safety for women and children. Women who bonded with other women were able to fend off more threats than those who did not, thereby ensuring their own survival and enhancing the likelihood that their children would survive as well. Second, these bonds are emotionally close, characterized by a sense of comfort and even physical closeness. Women seem to be less rattled by the stressful experiences they encounter when there are familiar women close by. As noted, there may be a biological basis for this sense of comfort. Third, these bonds meet important needs, which include providing food and child care, teaching younger females how to be mothers, and providing protection.

By focusing so heavily on the useful aspects of women's ties, though, we run the risk of ignoring some of their most important benefits. Women provide one another with solace, affection, laughter, and comfort. If we have learned anything about the value of social ties, it is that tangible help is only a small part of their benefits. Emotional ties are at least as important and perhaps more so. Certainly safety and survival were important benefits of women's ties in prehistoric times, yet it is hard to imagine that emotional needs would have been an insignificant part of these relationships. Friendship, caring, and love are not recent inventions. As women's ties were in early history, so they are likely to be today, nudged by biological pressures from our evolutionary heritage but sustained by the sheer joy of companionship.

CHAPTER 7

Tending in Marriage

My father-in-law is ninety-six years old and none too pleased about it. He has been ready to die for several years. Every few weeks, he goes for a haircut, and as he's leaving, he tells the barber, "Last haircut!" and the barber says, "We'll miss you, Theo," but a few weeks later, he's back. "Last Christmas!" he tells his assembled grown children each December, and they all smile and say, "We'll miss you, Daddy." His black suit is hanging in the closet and his good shoes are polished, but to his surprise and mild irritation, death keeps knocking on other doors.

Theo's "problem" is Mina, his wife of fifty-eight years, who has been meeting his every need since she was twenty-two years old. She's cooked his favorite meals, run his errands, done most of the child care, maintained his wardrobe, and entertained his relatives and friends. Theo has little reason to die. Although he's faced many threats in his life, some of them quite severe, he's done so with the stable and loving companionship of Mina close by.

A long companionable relationship filled with love, laughter, and children is what most of us imagine when we marry. The implicit promise that someone will be there in tough times sustains us during those inevitable moments when the marriage seems rocky. And although it takes many of us more than once to get it right, our faith in marriage is not, for the most part, misplaced. For decades, psychological studies have found that marriage—not money, not children, not a host of other things that could make you happy—is the primary determinant of emotional well-being.[1]

Marriage is in many ways a microcosm of the social forces that affect our health and happiness. In its intensity, it illustrates, as few other relationships can, both the potency of tending and the potency of the absence of tending. Marriage entails risks, to be sure, but the risks of not pairing up are greater still. As a tending system, marriage protects the health and happiness of men, and the happiness of women as well. Marriage is some of the best medicine we have.[2]

But there is no question that men reap more benefits from marriage than women do. Indeed, one of the great paradoxes of social life is why women so often want to marry, whereas men want to remain uncommitted. Viewed objectively from the outside, marriage is a great opportunity for men. Just as children get physiological and neuroendocrine protection from their mothers, so do men get much of the same protection from their girlfriends and wives. If you are a man and you want to live a long and healthy life, the very best thing that you can do for your health is to get married and stay married. It increases the chances of living past age sixty-five from 65 percent to over 90 percent.[3] If you're a woman, you may enjoy happiness in marriage, but your life expectancy will not be affected.

I'm going to look at marriage as a tending system, and argue that one reason why men fare so well in marriage and women fare a little less well is that women typically tend to men's needs in ways that directly affect their health and happiness. Men tend to women's needs as well—traditionally as providers, more recently as partners—but the evidence suggests that their tending is different and not as protective of health as women's is.

The ways in which women tend to men (and not the reverse) are ubiquitous and often mundane. Married men typically get many perks that single men and married women do not usually enjoy. For example, depending on the marriage, husbands may be fed, clothed, and picked up after, at least more so than is true for single men or for women. Someone else very often shops, cooks, cleans the house, does the laundry, and may even buy their clothes and do their errands. Men's lives may, as a result, be freer of interruptions, competing obligations, and minor hassles than women's lives are.

Marriage also protects men from the adverse company of other men, at least from a health standpoint, by acting as a brake on health-threatening personal habits. Compared with single men, married men eat more nutritious meals, have a more reliable pattern of sleep, and are less likely to smoke cigarettes, drink heavily, or abuse illegal drugs.[4]

Men work fewer hours than women do, especially when women combine work outside the home with housework. One study found that working women in the United States averaged three hours a day of housework, while their husbands averaged seventeen minutes. As for time spent exclusively with children, women averaged fifty minutes a day; men, twelve minutes. On the other hand, men spent more time sleeping, watching TV, and pursuing leisure-time interests such as sports than their wives did. These different patterns of work translate directly into physiological benefits for men.[5]

During the course of a workday, when a person encounters social conflict, time pressures, and other stressful events, the catecholamines epinephrine and norepinephrine are secreted, leading to predictable feelings of agitation and arousal—the fight-or-flight response that is all too recognizable. Most of us experience these feelings a number of times each day; by the end of a workday, our levels of catecholamines are often fairly high. When men come home after a day at work, the secretion of these chemicals begins to fall off, as if men's bodies are telling them, Relax. You are in a safe place.

Married women do not share this experience. Long into the evening, their catecholamines remain elevated, as if their bodies are telling them, Heads up! You're still working. The first scientist to recognize this pattern was the pioneer stress researcher Marianne Frankenhaeuser. The Swedish workingwomen she studied typically came home to prepare dinner and get the housework done before they were able to go to bed and truly relax. Frankenhaeuser credited their prolonged daily stress response to this dual set of expectations of work both outside and inside the home.[6]

The fact that married women work more hours than married men do, with the resulting hormonal effects, may be one reason why marriage protects the health of men but not of women. Chronically elevated stress hormones erode health, and so whatever benefits women get from the emotional and physical closeness of marriage may be offset by the stress of living more of each day in a state of agitation or arousal.

WOMEN ARE SOOTHING to men in ways that men very often are not soothing to women. To see this difference, one need only look at the divergent ways in which men and women communicate with one another. Linguist Deborah Tannen's 1990 book *You Just Don't Understand* provided stark evidence of just how different the communication styles of men and women can be. The book was snapped up by millions of readers, men and women alike, who felt it summed up exactly the problems in their marriages.

According to Tannen, wives see their job as supporting their husbands, and so when a husband tells his wife about a stressful event in his day, she will often respond with sympathy, expressing concern, love, and affection, sharing his indignation and anger, making him feel that she is on his side. Men, on the other hand, may see their job as providing perspective and wisdom. And so, if a wife tells her husband about a stressful event in her day, he is less likely to respond with emotional support; instead, he either suggests that the problem isn't as great as she thinks it is, or gives advice about what she might do to solve it. Often, this advice falls on deaf ears and leaves the woman feeling unhappy and criticized, rather than supported.[7]

Whose style is better, men's or women's? From a health standpoint, the answer is women's. For while men's responses to women may well contain some good advice, they have little of the calming effects that their wives' responses typically have.[8] (Consequently, women often turn to their women friends for comfort after one of these unsatisfying exchanges.)

Women may be more invested in their marriages than men are, which may also leave them more vulnerable to marital stresses. Certainly, they have a better idea of what is going on in their marriages than men do. In the classic film *Gigi*, Maurice Chevalier and Hermione Gingold share a humorous duet, "Yes, I Remember It Well," which embodies the difference between men and women and their recollections of their relationships. It goes, in part:

He: That carriage ride . . .
She: You walked me home.
He: You lost a glove.
She: I lost a comb.
He: Ah yes, I remember it well.

Psychologists Michael Ross and Diane Holmberg at the University of Waterloo, Canada, conducted a Maurice Chevalier study to see who really *does* remember the history of relationships. You can try a version of it out on your own partner. Ask him or her how you met, where you were, and who else was present. Where and when was your first date and what did you do? Ross and Holmberg asked their couples questions like these and found that men were quite poor at remembering these basic details. The wives' memories on these points were excellent—women, clearly, are the historians of relationships.[9]

Women's greater awareness of the details of their relationships extends into current events as well. Wives are better reporters of stressors that have taken place in the family than their husbands. Harvard sociologist Ronald Kessler tells the following account that characterizes the differences he sees between the men and women he interviews. In the process of interviewing couples about their relationships, Kessler asked one husband whether there had been any stressful events in his extended family during the past year. The husband thought for a moment, and said no. His wife looked surprised, touched him gently on the arm, and whispered, "Dear, your mother died."

Women's keener awareness of events in the marriage may develop, in part, because they are more likely than their husbands to be pulled into the ongoing events of their extended family networks, in both their own families and their husbands'. Women make 10 to 20 percent more long-distance phone calls to family and friends than men do, they write two to three times more letters than men, and they buy and send three times as many greeting cards and gifts. They remember birthdays and anniversaries and coordinate family attendance at weddings, funerals, and other family events. For women, marriage often carries with it daughterly ties to two families, whereas men are more likely to opt out of maintaining ties even to their own families after they marry. While marriage increases the number of greeting cards that women send, it cuts in half the number of cards that men send.[10]

Much of this is just the "work" of maintaining family ties, which falls disproportionately on women's shoulders. But women also get pulled into family crises more than men do and feel their effects more acutely. When men list the stressors they have encountered over the past year, they tend to describe work-related or impersonal problems, whereas women mention events in their social networks—family and friends—as their most common stressful times. A woman knows which family member is on the outs with whom and which daughter-in-law Mother doesn't really like very much. She remembers the wounding comment a careless uncle made about her oldest son during Christmas dinner and how the cousins' games seem so often to exclude her daughter.[11]

Another reason, then, why marriage protects men's health but not women's may be that women manage the inevitable family conflicts and crises, whereas marriage enables men to enjoy the benefits of supportive family relationships while evading some of the more stressful aspects of family life. Comedian George Burns summed up this benefit by observing that "happiness is having a large, loving, caring, close-knit family in another city." Metaphorically speaking, many men may be in another city.

Economists have recently found a way to put a dollar figure on the tending men receive in marriage. When you compare the earnings of married men to single men of the same background and education, married men earn, on average, 12.4 percent more an hour than single men. The gap is even greater for men whose wives are full-time tenders. Married men with stay-at-home wives earn 31 percent more per hour than do men who have never been married, but this advantage shrinks to a mere 3.4 percent for a man whose wife works full-time outside the home. (Of course, this latter man is able to enjoy the fruits of his wife's full-time salary, and so any sympathy one might feel for his loss in earnings should be tempered by this fact.) The marriage premium may come from a combination of pressures on men to be diligent providers and from the extra time, care, and good health they get from the special attentions of women. Clearly, tending pays off for men; they are the recipients of psychological and physiological benefits *and* economic benefits.[12]

Men's protection in marriage goes further still, protecting them even from the stress of marital conflict. Consider a representative couple, call them Dan and Laura, married, in their mid-thirties, who have volunteered to participate in a typical psychological study of marriage. For $150, they sit face-to-face, each attached to a machine that measures heart rate and blood pressure, and discuss the topics the researcher picks for them. "Let's talk about some areas of conflict," he says. "I'd like you to pick an aspect of your marriage that causes some problems for you, that leads you to argue fairly regularly, one that you both think is an unresolved issue." "Money," Laura and Dan say simultaneously, and then laugh at how readily they have agreed on the topic. "Let's talk about money, then," says the researcher. "What about money causes you to argue?"

"She spends too much," says Dan, looking to the researcher for validation. "I don't. I stay in the budget almost every month," responds Laura defensively. "You buy all those clothes that you hardly ever wear. Some of them still have their tags on," says Dan. "What about the eight-hundred-dollar chair you bought for your back?" responds Laura. "That was a medical necessity," snaps Dan. And they're off, continuing in this vein for the next twenty minutes.

If we were to take a peek at the machine that measures their physiological processes, what would we see? Laura's heart rate has gone up. Her blood pressure, too, is beginning to rise. What about Dan? His responses are nearly flat, his heart rate and blood pressure up only slightly. Dan and Laura are quite typical of the married couples who pass through laboratories like these. The wives show strong heart rate and blood pressure changes during marital conflict, and the husbands react much less, if at all. Based on their biological responses, it is hard to believe that the husbands are even aware of the argument.[13]

With only this information to go on, we might assume that women simply react more strongly to stress in general than men do, but the reality is more complicated. Let's do a thought experiment and pluck Dan out of the argument with his wife and put him face-to-face with another man, again hooked up to a machine that measures heart rate and blood pressure. As in the first experiment, the researcher assigns them a stressful topic to discuss: "Imagine that both of you need to take a particular airline flight, but there is only one seat left. The one who makes the better case to the ticket agent will get the seat." Dan and his partner begin their competition. The seat is imaginary, of course, unlike the money problems that Dan and Laura so often experience. But what happens to Dan's physiological responses? Five minutes into the discussion, his heart rate is up and his blood pressure has soared. He really wants to get that seat!

This thought experiment, too, reflects most man-to-man encounters that psychologists have studied in the laboratory. In competitive situations with other men, a man typically rises to the challenge quite literally, as his blood pressure and heart rate go up.[14] But in response to a conflict with his wife, these stress responses are far less likely.

Psychologist Janice Kiecolt-Glaser, virologist Ron Glaser, and their colleagues are among the scientists who have explored these important and robust differences in men's and women's responses to marital conflict. In some of their studies, they bring newlyweds into their lab and ask them to discuss areas of conflict. Typically, they find that these discussions lead to increases in the stress hormones epinephrine and norepinephrine, especially in women, as was true for Laura. The more distressed the marriage, the more adversely the wives react.[15]

Overall, the evidence that women show more adverse physiological changes to marital conflict is very compelling. There is a certain irony in the evidence concerning men: typically, men respond to stressful events with greater physiological changes, particularly in blood pressure, than women do. It is only in this one particular arena, marriage, that they enjoy this striking physiological protection.

Is THERE A biological basis for this difference in how husbands and wives approach their marriages? Are women the tenders in marriage for reasons far deeper than the conventions of social roles? The ancient neurocircuitry for nurturance that is so critical to maternal care may also underlie women's attraction to men. Specifically, the limbic areas of the woman's brain that influence maternal nurturance are closely inter-meshed with those that control sexuality. Oxytocin affects social and sexual behavior in females just as it affects maternal behavior.

For example, female prairie voles—those little rodents with the devoted male partners—require extensive contact with a would-be mate before they become sexually receptive. University of Maryland biolo-gists Bruce Cushing and Sue Carter reasoned that oxytocin, as an affilia-tive hormone, might be released during these repeated social contacts and play a role in the eventual receptivity the females show. To test their idea, they decided to speed up the process with an intervention. For each of several days before giving them contact with a male, the females were injected with either a small dose of oxytocin or a placebo. The results confirmed their suspicions. Those females who had been pre-treated with the oxytocin were far more likely to mate with the male upon first meeting than were those who had received the sham injec-tions. Presumably the oxytocin injections had "tricked" the females into believing that the partner was a familiar companion, worthy of a sexual response.[16]

Although the specific hormones and receptors underlying social and sexual receptivity in females vary from species to species, these findings suggest the possibility that females' attraction to males may piggy-back onto the neurocircuitry for affiliation more generally.[17] The same hormones—oxytocin and endogenous opioids—that seem to influence maternal behavior and affectionate contact may also provide the impetus for women to bond with men, both initially and over the long term as well. Is this why women take care of men—because their nurturance circuits are engaged along with their sexual interest and desire for companionship?

I am not the first to have noticed the proximity of these systems, nor the first to impute possible significance to it. Jaak Panksepp, an eminent neuroscientist, argues that the evolution of maternal circuits in the brain probably emerged from more primitive brain systems that initially governed sexual urges and encouraged mating behavior in females.[18] In other words, he suggests that sexuality came first and maternal behavior may have piggybacked onto it. However, there are some reasons for believing that the opposite may be true.

The male-female pair bond assumes many different forms in primates, ranging from the only occasional interest of gibbons to the "harem" organizations of gorillas and baboons to outright promiscuity among bonobos. In contrast, the maternal-child bond is more uniform across mammalian species. Indeed, it is one of the few cross-species consistencies that is seen in social behavior. This consistency suggests that the maternal circuitry may be deep and old, whereas the more variable sexual circuitry may be a more recent evolutionary development. Weak, variable, and "recent" behaviors typically piggyback onto older systems, not vice versa.

Moreover, maternal bonding is far more critical to infant care than pair bonding is to sexuality. For females to mate with males does not require either sexual attraction or pair bonding. In fact, it does not even require passing interest, since rape can impregnate a female nearly as well as an affectionate sexual encounter can. Nor need this bond last more than the minute or two that is required for a successful copulation to occur. Certainly, a female's chances of successfully bringing her offspring to maturity are greatly improved if the male stays around, but it is not essential. In contrast, maternal care is absolutely critical to the lives of offspring. An abandoned infant dies. For the offspring's survival to be assured until maturity, the bond must be maintained continually. Typically, this means years of attentiveness, far longer than the moments required for copulation.

The maternal-infant bond, then, may be the primary relationship onto which women's sexual attraction to men and their caring for them piggybacked, rather than the reverse. I am in good company with anthropologist Sarah Hrdy, who observes:

Maternal sensations have clear evolutionary priority in the pleasure sphere. Long before any woman found sexual foreplay or intercourse pleasurable, her ancestors were selected to respond positively to similar sensations produced by birth and suckling, because finding these activities pleasurable would help condition her in ways that kept her infant alive. It would be more nearly correct, then, to refer to the "afterglow" from climax as an ancient "maternal" rather than sexual response.[19]

What about men's sexual attraction? Is their interest in females bound up in neurocircuitry related to nurturance? No. In fact, in males the neurocircuitry for sexuality is in close proximity to the neurocircuitry for aggression, and the hormones that promote male sexuality also promote certain types of aggression. Among early primates, a male's sexual access to females often required him to do battle with rivals; over time, this liaison necessitated continual vigilance to defend against the competition. Thus, the hormonal link between sexuality and aggression may have been essential to ensure a male's reproductive success. Scientists' work on male prairie voles and vasopressin illuminates this fascinating connection.

In male prairie voles, as we've seen, vasopressin is associated with guarding and protecting females. Testosterone stimulates the production of vasopressin, which may be significant for the bonds that males form with females. Vasopressin plays a role in male sexual courtship, in the marking of territory, and in male-male aggression. When vasopressin is injected into the preoptic area of the brain, which is involved in successful male copulation, these rodents become more territorial: they actively patrol and mark their territories, and they aggress against invaders. Vasopressin may also be implicated in jealousy in males; after sexual activity, males are more likely to attack an intruder, but this does not happen if a vasopressin-blocking agent has been administered. Vasopressin is also implicated in male sexual behavior, and during sexual activity, vasopressin is released from the pituitary gland.[20]

What do these differences mean with respect to the caregiving that men receive in marriage? It means that men are very lucky. They may be the inadvertent but very fortunate recipients of a system that developed initially as a caregiving system for infants and children, but that has come to spill over into their lives as well. Or perhaps it isn't luck but an evolutionary adaptation instead.

Recall that one of the constant dilemmas faced by women in early societies was finding enough food to nourish both themselves and their children. Women who were able to attract and hold on to a male part-ner were perhaps somewhat better at solving this problem than those without partners, because male partners could bring in food through hunting. In addition, women drew on their mates for protection for themselves and their children, and so activities that could attract and hold a partner would help to ensure that this protection was available when needed. To keep a male partner invested in both his partner and his offspring continuously enough to ensure protection and a constant supply of food was a tricky task, which, I argued in Chapter 6, is one rea-son why women historically also enlisted the cooperation of kin and female friends.

What would keep a man invested in his partner and his offspring? Presumably a relationship in which many needs, not just sexual ones, were satisfied: freedom from arduous chores, care during illness or injury, access to plentiful food supplies from his partner's successful gathering, and nurturance and succor. Exclusive and solicitous caregiving lets a man know that his mate is truly his and may also provide some (re)assur-ance that his offspring are his as well, cementing his commitment to their welfare. Solicitous caregiving is also a striking social cue. In her actions, the woman sends a signal both to the man and to the social group that this is her mate, which may inhibit solicitations from other women and discourage her mate from initiating sexual activity outside of the relationship.

Women who tended to their husbands' needs may have enjoyed a double advantage: an increased likelihood of attracting a partner to pro-duce offspring and a greater chance that their offspring would survive because of the male's willingness to continuously provide resources. "Just so" story, or natural and sexual selection? It's hard to say, but it's

almost certainly the case that women did more to secure long-term com-
mitments from their male partners than simply satisfy their sexual needs.

I've made some claims for the protective role that women play in
men's lives and argued that women's tending promotes both happiness
and good health. The evidence is certainly suggestive. What happens
when men are cut off from the tending networks of women? A partial
answer to this question is provided by the following dramatic and compelling historical example.

On November 10, 1989, people around the world awoke to discover
that the Berlin Wall, long a symbol of communist oppression, had been
toppled. Television cameras captured images of jubilant East and West
Berliners disassembling the wall piece by piece, clasping and hugging
one another in joyous disbelief. Over the next two years, the world
watched in astonishment as the entire communist bloc crumbled, country by country, in an almost synchronous dismantling of an entire political way of life.

Many onlookers no doubt felt that, once the Soviet Union and the
countries of Eastern Europe were out from under the communist yoke,
life would improve. Only it did not work out that way. Instead, the
people of these "liberated" nations experienced an abrupt decline in the
marriage rate; a staggering increase in divorce; a precipitous decline in
the birth rate; dramatic increases in heart disease, fatal accidents, and
alcohol-related deaths; and a plummeting life expectancy.[21] They were
in the grip of a profound trauma.

Bewildered scientists flocked to Eastern Europe to try to understand
why people who were supposed to be living into their seventies were
dying in their forties and fifties instead. With each effort to comprehend
the problem, the mystery deepened. Divorce rates in some of the
affected countries were higher than marriage rates, and in many places,
the birth rate was insufficient to replace the population. As scientists
watched in disbelief, the social devastation and death rates worsened.[22]

Who died and what did they die of? The threats to life expectancy in
Eastern Europe hit one group especially hard: young and middle-aged
men. In 1989, a Russian man could expect to live to age sixty-four; by

1994, his life expectancy was fifty-seven. Men in the former East Germany experienced a 40 percent increase in their death rate. In 1990, an East German man of age thirty-seven was 70 percent more likely to die of heart disease, 156 percent more likely to die of injuries, and 200 percent more likely to die of cirrhosis than his West German counterpart.[23]

Although women's lives shortened somewhat as well, on the whole, men fared much worse. In Russia, for example, women live an average of twelve years longer than men. Estonia and Hungary have similar gender gaps. Compare this with figures from France, where men live to roughly age seventy-four and women to eighty-two, a gap of only eight years, or the United States where men live to seventy-three and women to eighty, a gap of only seven years.[24]

Moreover, exactly who was dying was informative. The excess mortality among middle-aged men in Eastern Europe was heavily (and in some countries, almost entirely) among unmarried—not married—men. For example, in Poland, following the end of communist rule, the death rate for married men in their early sixties increased by threefold, but unmarried or divorced men in this age group experienced a startling sixfold increase. In Hungary, the entire increase in death rate among middle-aged men following the end of communist rule was among unmarried men. Unmarried men who stayed alive had worse health than married men as well, although marriage did not affect health for women.[25] What was killing off the men?

Many Eastern European men had hoped to raise their standard of living when they joined the West, and so in the wake of the profound changes in government, they had developed great expectations for the future. However, East European workers were less skilled than the West Europeans, and with a low demand for manual labor, they were less competitive in the market. Instead of the boom they anticipated, they found their former meager standard of living slipping away. Middle-aged men in manual labor occupations who lived in urban areas were especially hard hit. As these now angry, depressed, belligerent men struggled to find good work in a disappointing economic climate, they stopped getting married or left the families they could no longer support. When they hooked up with other men, drinking, smoking, accidents of all kinds, homicide, and suicide all went up. And so these men died of heart disease, accidents, alcohol poisoning, and, to a lesser extent, cancer.[26]

The alcohol story is particularly significant in accounting for the galloping death rate of Russian men. On a daily basis, Russian men do not appear to drink so much more than men in other European countries. When they do drink, however, they often binge. In the company of other men, they consume large amounts of vodka very rapidly, with very little food, often long into an evening. One survey of Siberian men, for example, found that 80 percent engaged in binge drinking (at least 80 g of alcohol in a single occasion) at least once a month, and 20 percent consumed more than 120 g of alcohol in a single occasion at least once a week. I worked this out in my kitchen with a shot glass and water, and I'm guessing that heavy binge drinkers consume roughly ten to fifteen shots of pure vodka on an almost empty stomach over approximately three to four hours. That's a lot of vodka, and, to be honest, it's probably an underestimate.

A British scientist who had gone to Russia to study the changing death rates found himself in such a group one evening. He described the scene as a lengthy series of toasts, each followed by roughly a shot of vodka. " To life!" (everyone drinks). "To Russia!" (everyone drinks). "To women!" (everyone drinks). "To the British!" (everyone drinks). "To life!" And so on, until the men began to pass out. The British scientist, who had stopped drinking rather early in the evening, nonetheless spent the next day in bed, nursing a serious hangover. After contemplating the effects of multiple evenings of this sort, he came away from his experience somewhat less surprised that Russian men are dying in droves.

For while alcohol in moderation seems to have protective effects on health, binge drinking is disastrous. At the levels consumed by Russian men, alcohol greatly increases the likelihood of death from heart attack or stroke, because it alters cholesterol levels, affects how the blood coagulates, and increases the likelihood of disturbances in the heart's rhythms. Excess consumption of alcohol is also the leading cause of cirrhosis of the liver. More immediately, binge drinking can cause alcohol poisoning and accidental death, especially from automobile accidents. The binging parties may sound quite jolly, but alcohol fosters aggression, and so these parties can turn nasty in a heartbeat: researchers estimate that alcohol was implicated in more than half of the murders and suicides that occurred in the postcommunist era.

Why were men so much more affected by these problems than women? One explanation offered by scientists is that men are on the front lines of the economic and social fallout of stressful conditions, seeking to support themselves and their families and encountering few opportunities. As such, they are the "canaries" who fly into the mines of social change, breathe in the toxic air, and die.[27]

While the metaphor has considerable appeal, the argument is less than completely persuasive. Why should a man of age thirty seeking employment be any more on the front lines than a woman of thirty with perhaps a child or two to care for, seeking work for herself or hoping that her husband finds work, and praying that she is not abandoned? When economic conditions deteriorate, abandonment is a real risk, and women and children are often left to fend for themselves. Women's problems in times of poverty are at least as substantial as men's, and probably more so, because they often have others for whom to care.

A variant of the "males on the front lines" explanation puts the blame on gender roles. According to this argument, to be a man one must be gainfully employed and supporting a family. Consequently, men feel the effects of a deteriorating economy more keenly than women, and their feelings of inadequacy or uselessness lead them into deteriorating health and self-destructive behavior.[28] This is a plausible hypothesis, but there is some inconvenient evidence that calls it into question. Such gender role pressures might be expected to fall most heavily on married men, because they are the ones on whose employment the family depends and for whom the traditional male role may exert the most psychological and economic pressure. But as noted, this was not the case. Unmarried men suffered the worse consequences.

What may shock the minds and bodies of these men is a sense that their lives may be meaningless and may stay that way. But what men *do* in response to these realizations may be even more lethal. They turn to the perilous company of other similarly afflicted men, and engage in risky, drunken camaraderie, which allows them to forget temporarily that their lives have little meaning. Instead of putting themselves into situations in which their masculinity might be challenged and their self-esteem undermined, such as unsuccessfully seeking work, these men join with others like themselves, creating an alternative norm of drinking and carousing, largely unfettered by the influences of a wife, responsibilities to a family, and, in many cases, steady employment.[29]

Women fared better than men because they had informal ties in place that helped them negotiate the new social and economic order.[30] Before the fall of communism, women had been responsible for obtaining food and household goods, often by trading and sharing information with other women. By using these well-honed networking skills in the new social order, they were able to acquire food and other goods to maintain their now-reduced standard of living. But men's informal social networks, far from providing them with access to the basics of life, instead put them at risk. Cut off from the healthier networks of women and children by choice or circumstance, they turned instead to groups of men and the blinding alcoholic binges that poisoned or killed so many. Older men, who were divorced or widowed and who already risked heart disease after years of smoking and eating a poor diet, abruptly died without the support of the women on whom they had previously depended. Women and children died, too, but in far fewer numbers, sustained through the transition by the social bonds they had created and nurtured.

The Eastern Europe situation is not a long-term scenario. Already, it is evident that marriage and birth rates are climbing again.[31] But it is a dramatic example of a profoundly important point: When a society's tending system breaks down, illness and death can follow, sometimes in astonishingly short order. Men, in particular, are vulnerable. Because they rely so heavily on women for their emotional sustenance, and receive so much less support from groups of men, they show the effects of these intense stressors more keenly. Yet, there are some surprising ways in which men tend to one another's needs, as we next see.

CHAPTER 8

Men's Groups

A ny parent of boys knows the good-natured chaos that sweeps through the house when boys are at play—the simulated gunfire, bodies dropping in pretend agony, a figure leaping out from behind curtains or furniture, embarrassed to discover that it is you and not the juvenile enemy he expected.

One day, you notice that the voices are much lower and sound eerily like those of soldiers on maneuvers. You think, They are becoming men, no longer boys. Then on the Fourth of July, they spray-paint the dog red, white, and blue, and the illusion of manhood vanishes.

To understand groups of boys or men, we need to make sense of this energetic playfulness, this rowdy camaraderie. We need to understand the symbolic predation, hunting, and aggression these groups often spawn as well. For groups of men and boys are filled with a dynamic spirit that is usually lively and good-natured, but which can unexpectedly turn serious, even violent.

From early childhood, boys have their groups and girls have theirs, and as the saying goes, never the twain shall meet. Both genders resist playing with the other. Groups of boys are strikingly different than groups of girls—rowdier, more active, more aggressive.[1] Whereas girls' groups exist primarily for their own sake, groups of boys are more frequently organized around specific tasks, such as sports, games, or projects. Boys *do* things together. And quite quickly into the task, a dominance hierarchy is formed, first through play and aggression, and then through mutual, if reluctant, agreement. Norms about who's at the top and who's further down are established early.[2]

The sheer energy of boys' groups differentiates them from girls' groups as well. In their classic work *The Psychology of Sex Differences*, psychologists Eleanor Maccoby and Carol Jacklin described how one boy acts as an "evocative stimulus" for another, a gentle characterization that belies what actually happens. One boy studies, reads, plays his music too loud, kicks a ball around his room, but is otherwise not so unlike one girl. Two or three boys together create bedlam.[3]

This energy and its accompanying capacity for aggression have formed the core of many accounts of men in groups, most notably Lionel Tiger's book of that title, Karl Lorenz's work *On Aggression*, and Robert Ardrey's *African Genesis*. These authors argue that, despite a potential dark side, raw male aggression underlies much that is distinctive, even laudable, about humans, including the ability to shoot to the top of a hierarchy, pursue goals single-mindedly, even engage in warfare.

I will argue that this focus has distracted us from understanding some important purposes of men's groups. The struggle for dominance and the use of aggression to get it are certainly present, but ultimately, as I will explain, rather than fostering aggression, these hierarchies often control, contain, and marginalize it. Contrary to stereotype, the most aggressive men are not the ones who typically make it to the top of male hierarchies; instead, those with social skills, with the ability to work with others, to form coalitions and relationships, to lure, appease, and cajole, and to get rid of those who can't play by the rules are the ones who make it to the top. This realization yields a radically different portrait of men in groups than has been painted by past writings, but one that, I think, is defensible. Although they are different in form and style, like women's groups, men's groups are tending systems.[4]

Our template for men's groups has come from studying our primate relatives. Scientists have noticed and emphasized these commonalities, particularly hierarchy, coalition formation, and aggression, and, indeed, the parallels are instructive. Our male primate relatives typically live in groups with clear dominance hierarchies, with an alpha male at the top, his lieutenants directly under him, and the rest of the males further down. This hierarchy heavily determines how well any individual fares. High-status males gain access to females, enabling them to mate and pass on their genes. They also have the pick of the food. They are more likely to be groomed by females than lower-status males are, and in some species they are groomed by other males as well. When they are in the company of others, they are deferred to; on those occasions when they must defend their position, they can often call upon their lieutenants and other allies to fend off an adversary, sometimes with fatal consequences for the challenger.[5]

But because of the almost constant threat that other males can pose, male-male encounters proceed cautiously in an environment charged with tension. It's a delicate balance—forging cooperative bonds with other males, while remaining ever watchful of the risk of conflict and aggression. Primatologist Frans de Waal describes this trade-off from the standpoint of the male chimpanzee:

> He absolutely needs to get along with his male group mates: united they can stand against (and commit) brutal acts of territorial aggression. At the same time, he vies with these very same males for dominance. He must constantly keep track of his allies and rivals, as he may owe his rank to the first and run risks in the presence of the second.[6]

The dominance hierarchy periodically becomes unstable. Those lower down try to work their way up; tough juveniles come into maturity and want a shot at the top; a leader grows old and other males look to replace him; a male refugee from another troop tries to find a place in the new troop: many things may conspire to upset the dominance hierarchy. When this happens, the stress systems of the males operate at full throttle, especially those of dominant animals, because now their privileged situation is threatened. Testosterone gets engaged in this process, too, with levels rising and falling with each success and failure. Dominance struggles produce a rich soup of chemicals.[7]

M EN ARE NOT so different from other primates in their zest for dominance. Some need in men seems to seek, even relish hierarchy. As soon as a group forms, the men often set about establishing a pecking order, and within hours, sometimes minutes, there's a leader, his allies, a few more men further down, and a few outliers who are marginalized. Men establish a hierarchy in even their most informal groups, and much struggle can ensue over one's position in it.[8] Stress hormones are dramatically engaged, just as is true in nonhuman primate groups. Indeed, one of the reasons why men get heart disease earlier than women do may stem from their lifelong concern with issues of dominance.[9] If you're constantly involved in power struggles with other men at work, for example, your catecholamines are regularly rising and falling as competitive situations come up.

Why do men form these groups? According to anthropologists, from the very beginning of human existence, groups of men have taken on specific tasks for the social group—hunting, defense, and war, most commonly. Currently, among other tasks, they protect the community; fight fires, floods, and other natural disasters; defend the country against invaders; and protect families from harm. When a group is organized around a particular task, a hierarchy is beneficial because it provides a chain of command and a structure for coordinated action.[10]

Men's groups also often have an opponent—another team, an enemy army, for example, something that must be overcome. In the absence of a natural enemy, they may create one that will do for the occasion. For example, men peel off into opposing sports teams, and friends temporarily become adversaries. A group of men getting together on a Saturday to finish a project and then breaking up into a three-on-three touch football game does not seem incongruous. It is rare to find a group of women doing the same thing.

The enemy seems to give a focus to the group and fuel its actions. Our neighborhood men's soccer group is never so cohesive as when the park ranger is trying to oust them from their field. Most of the time, they squabble and bicker about who is playing poorly or causing injury to whom, whether the teams are evenly matched, or who isn't trying as hard as he should be. Each Saturday at least one indignant player stomps off the field, vowing never to return. He does return, of course, the next Saturday, and the grousing continues. But when the park ranger comes to complain about the damage their cleats do to the grass and the distress their colorful language has caused for nearby picnicking families, they are as one, shoulder to shoulder, ready to take on the entire Department of the Interior.

The case for status and aggression would seem to be clear: The toughest, most aggressive men get to the top. Yet a closer look suggests that rather than rewarding aggression, men's groups control and channel it instead. How does this happen? Some surprising clues come from elephants.

THE YEARS FROM 1992 to 1997 were trying ones for the gamekeepers of South Africa's Pilanesberg region. They had a major elephant problem on their hands. To expand their population, young orphaned male elephants had been introduced to the park, but instead of quietly joining the existing herds, they had hooked up with one another, often going on rampages. Among their acts of destruction was the killing of more than forty white rhinos. Elephants and rhinos do not mix well in the best of times, but this killing spree was unprecedented in the park's experience.

The situation was aggravated by "musth," a state in which a male elephant experiences dramatic surges in testosterone, contributing to high levels of sexual and aggressive behavior. Male elephants normally start to have short periods of musth of a few days' or a couple weeks' duration when they reach about age twenty-five. As they get bigger and have experience winning aggressive encounters with other males, periods of musth lengthen to a couple months. These lengthening periods are thought to help them adjust to their rising levels of testosterone. But in the orphaned young teenagers of Pilanesberg, musth began early and was lasting as long as five months.

Rob Slotow and his colleagues from the Environmental Sciences Department at the University of Natal were called in to see if they could help. They studied the elephants' movements and could see that they were breeding successfully, but they were doing so in groups that lacked adult males. A previous study of elephants in Amboseli, Kenya, had found that young male elephants were much less likely to be in musth if a larger older male in musth was present. And so to see if they could control these aggressive juveniles, Slotow and his colleagues brought in six older males to join the eighty-five elephants of Pilanesberg. When the experiment began, six of the seventeen young males were in musth. Within hours of encountering the new older males, the juveniles began to exhibit fewer signs of musth. Within two weeks, only a few young males were in musth and for a much shorter time. The killing of the white rhinos ceased.

When confronted with an older, higher-ranking male, these young males backed off, both physically and biologically. The older, more experienced males would have succeeded in any aggressive encounter, and so dropping out of musth was protective for the younger elephants. Natural selection favors males who can assess the qualities of potential rivals and adjust their behavior accordingly, and, almost immediately, the juvenile males of Pilanesberg showed this self-protective response because they stood little chance of winning a fight with the more experienced males. Soon their periods of musth shortened until they were able to manage their bursts of testosterone with the maturity that comes with age and experience. The dominant older elephants, then, controlled the aggression of those further down in the hierarchy, in part by suppressing their testosterone levels.[11]

Scientists have taken a fresh look at male groups and arrived at a conclusion not unlike that reached by the gamekeepers of Pilanesberg: Rather than encouraging lawless aggression, the hierarchies of all-male groups, particularly the presence of experienced males at the top, often manage and control it. The hierarchies that are so ubiquitous in male groups may be an evolutionary adaptation to control conflict, reduce the frequency of aggression, and limit the likelihood of escalating violence.

Now that we know what to look for, scientists have realized that primate studies reveal much the same pattern. True, aggression is high when a troop's dominance structure is unstable, but once the hierarchy is established, it is more rare and plays only a modest role in maintaining the social structure. Dominance hierarchies implicitly solve problems of aggression because they establish who is where in the hierarchy. Once this hierarchy is in place, spontaneous submission averts much conflict, and grooming and alliances keep it stable. Active interventions by the high-status males smooth over much of the incipient conflict that may remain.

High-ranking male primates are not necessarily the strongest or the most aggressive; they are those with good social skills. They form alliances with a few other group members to defeat challengers. They have methods of reconciliation, reassurance, and appeasement for restoring social relationships following aggressive encounters. Dominant males know how to tell the difference between minor provocations and major struggles. They don't overreact to a subordinate male who happens to be napping too close or who bumps into them by accident. A sideways glance or tensing of the body may be enough to deter a potential challenge. Dominant males who can't make these distinctions tend not to remain dominant for long. Dominant males who remain dominant have social intelligence.[12]

Among the well-studied chimpanzees of Gombe, for example, the alpha male maintains social control through savvy skill and gentle bullying. He stops fights that break out, sometimes by rushing into the middle of them and knocking the opponents to the ground. He may sit between quarreling parties to keep them from renewing their conflict. Eventually, he may induce them to come together to make up, through a combination of social pressure and subterfuge.[13]

Support for this new view of male groups comes from studies with humans as well. These processes begin by growing up with a father, an older male who, much like all high-status primates, keeps his juveniles in hand. The mere presence of a father seems to help boys manage their aggression, by teaching them how to substitute social skills instead. The range of adverse outcomes for boys whose fathers are absent is plentiful. Despite the often Herculean efforts of mothers, boys without fathers have a greater risk of delinquency, drug use, and poor academic achievement, as well as a risk for hostility, anxiety, and depression.[14] Psychologist Mark Flinn and his colleagues studied the endocrine profiles of boys whose fathers were present or absent while they were growing up. Among the father-absent boys, testosterone was higher in adolescence than was true of father-present boys. In adulthood, however, the men who had been raised without fathers had lower testosterone levels and higher cortisol levels, a profile suggesting they were anxious subordinates in their adult male peer group. Indeed, they were perceived by others to be lacking some basic social skills.[15]

Experience with male peers also plays an important role in shaping social skills, especially rough-and-tumble play. Common among young males of many species, this energetic, physical activity may have some specific functions. Once thought of as practice in aggression, it may instead teach males how to control it. In one study that led to these conclusions, Jaap Koolhaas and his colleagues raised young male rats without any contact with male peers. They then compared their behavior in adulthood with that of male rats who had grown up with the normal rough-and-tumble play of the male peer group. The rats without the rough-and-tumble play experience were less able to deal with both friendly and aggressive encounters from other males as adults, whereas those who had this experience managed both types of encounters more successfully.[16] Why does this occur? Rough-and-tumble play not only helps you practice your moves, it gives you opportunities to size up opponents' strengths and weaknesses, helping you learn whom and what to avoid. It helps you distinguish playful roughhousing from real threats. And it helps you learn to calm down and reconcile following a strenuous bout of aggressive play as well.

Boys on the playground learn much the same skills. They quarrel, have a brief fistfight, and then make up on the spot by shaking hands or by getting back to a sports game or other joint activity, as if nothing had happened. The idea that this pattern of aggressive bouts, followed by reconciliation, is fundamental to men's groups gets some credibility from the fact that groups of girls and women have very different patterns of quarreling and reconciliation. Although quarrels and aggression are less common in female groups, when an incident does occur, the females are less likely to reconcile and the activity that sparked the controversy is more likely to come to an end.[17]

Men who are socially skilled, capable, and mature rise to the top of a hierarchy and marginalize the more aggressive, often younger men, harnessing their energy in service of the group without letting their potential for aggression get out of control. Why has it taken scientists so long to recognize this important truth? One answer is that scientists interpret what they see: in men's groups aggression is, if not omnipresent, then certainly common. No one sees aggression that doesn't happen, and so the forces in male groups that reduce its frequency have gone largely unappreciated until recently.

What role does testosterone play in these processes? In the elephants of Pilanesberg, much of the control exerted by the older males was chemical. Humans are not elephants, of course, and men do not go into periods of musth as they mature biologically. They do, however, experience great surges in testosterone that can fuel aggressive behavior. Lots of other things like genes and sexual activity control testosterone, too, of course, but contacts with other males are unquestionably a potent influence. Testosterone increases naturally when men compete, as they do in their struggles for dominance. Just before an athletic contest, for example, men's testosterone levels rise, and the winner's testosterone level continues to stay up, while the loser's testosterone level drops.[18]

The popular literature has alternately blamed and lauded testosterone, viewing risk taking, aggression, and even violence as the darker side of a hormone that is responsible for great benefits, including competition, achievement, sex, and ultimately life itself. Testosterone *is* linked to aggression, but not to impulsive, destructive aggression. The aggression of the man with high testosterone is often managed in more restrained, socially acceptable ways.[19]

These are the guys who are in the friendly touch football game to win. They're the first ones to the door to challenge uninvited arrivals to a party, making it clear that the party is private. They like to win arguments and may press a point a little too long, but once they win, a friendly clap on the shoulder of the opponent largely returns them to good-natured affability. Provoked or threatened, these men may respond with greater aggression than men with low testosterone, but impulse does not typically rule their nature. Moreover, testosterone is associated with many positive qualities such as toughness, social assertiveness, dominance, competitiveness, and physical vigor. As is true for elephants and monkeys, our society typically rewards men with these qualities.

Perhaps the best way to test this new view of men in groups would be if we could show that unmanaged aggression sends you to the bottom of a male hierarchy and good social skills get you to the top. In an earlier chapter, I showed you some indirect evidence for this assertion. Monkeys with a risk for impulsive aggression who possessed the short allele of the 5-HTT serotonin transporter gene dropped to the bottom of the hierarchy when they had been raised by peers and lacked monkey social skills for grooming, peacemaking, and other forms of affiliation; those who had the same genetic risk but who instead were raised by nurturant mothers rose to the top of the dominance hierarchy.[20]

Let's look at what may be even more direct evidence for the tending role of male groups. Researcher Michael Raleigh and his colleagues have long studied the biological underpinnings of affiliation, rank, and dominance, focusing especially on the potential role of serotonin in these processes. Among other findings, they have observed that, when monkeys are given a dose of the serotonin precursor tryptophan or other drug treatments that increase levels of circulating serotonin, the monkeys become more social, grooming one another and showing other signs of affiliation. Conversely, drugs that diminish brain serotonergic functioning reduce affiliative behavior and increase aggression instead.

Raleigh wanted to see what would happen if he systematically manipulated levels of serotonin in male monkeys who were striving for dominance. Would the aggressive monkeys win out or would the leaders be those who approached their peers with friendly, affiliative gestures and grooming instead?

Raleigh and his colleagues created small groups of vervet monkeys, each with three adult males and at least three adult females and their offspring. They waited until a dominance hierarchy was in place among the males and then removed the dominant male from the group. They then selected one of the two remaining subordinate males and gave him either a drug that enhanced serotonergic activity or a drug that diminished it. In every case, the monkey who was treated with a serotonergic enhancer—and therefore grew more affiliative—became the dominant monkey. And when the monkey received the drug that reduced his serotonin levels—making him irritably aggressive—his male cage mate became dominant. In short, it was social skills, not aggression, that propelled these monkeys into leadership positions.

The reasons why social skills moved a monkey into a dominant position are revealing. It wasn't simply that he won out over the more aggressive, mean-spirited subordinate. With social skills, he "convinced" the females that he should be the dominant one, and so, to a degree, he ruled at their discretion. More generally, in nonhuman, primate-dominance hierarchies, the males jockey for top positions, but the females watch what is going on very carefully. If by chance an aggressive leader, who is abusive to the females or who harms the infants or juveniles, should rise to the dominant position, the females may throw their support to another leader or to a coalition that will oust the leader, sometimes with fatal force, and replace him with a socially skilled leader who enjoys the broader support of the females.[21]

THE VIEW OF men's groups as regulators of aggression through dominance struggles and corresponding fluctuation in testosterone levels tells only part of the story. As with our other social ties—the parent-child relationship, women's connections with one another, group responses to stress—there is a force that keeps men committed to one another, even as they join forces in competitive or aggressive action against others.

What is this glue that holds men's groups together? In nurturant early family life, the bonds of attachment tie child to parent and parent to child. In times of threat, bonding brings the social group together, with strangers commonly tending to one another's needs. In women's groups, there is substantial evidence of bonding cemented through conversation. Much writing about men's groups has taken a more dispassionate focus, however, seeking to show how coalition formation among small alliances of men may ensure that common needs are met, with coalitions breaking down if resources are unsuccessfully defended against outsiders.[22]

But as threats to men's groups increase, so does evidence of emotional bonding that looks much the same as that found in other circumstances of stress. Lionel Tiger was, perhaps, the first to describe the phenomenon. He characterized bonding in men's groups as a commitment to other men that inhibits aggression to help men cooperate. Tiger describes it vaguely, in almost sexualized terms, but he credits it with an energy that ties men to one another, and you can sense it when you are around groups of boys or men.[23]

The armed forces have developed this intuition to an art form. The dilemma that war poses is how to ensure that a group of unrelated men will work together and bond sufficiently with one another so that, when they are attacked, each man will watch out for his comrades and not merely for himself. Traditionally, these bonds have been instilled in several ways. Drawing on that segment of the population that is fearless, risk taking, and prone to aggression, namely young men, is a good beginning. It provides the raw material for the aggressive action of war. Something to fight for—an enemy, a noble cause, an entitlement, or retribution, for example—gives focus to what might otherwise threaten to be a meaningless contest. And last, but certainly not least, is bonding. Basic training reduces the salience of ties to family and friends, replacing them with ties, formed in adversity, to fellow soldiers. Through boot camp and other hazings, the bonds of shared misery develop so that when sacrifice and heroism are needed in wartime, the basis for heroism will be there.

In their investigations of wartime comradeship, sociologists Glen Elder and Elizabeth Clipp explored the psychology of bonding among men who had served together in World War II and Korea. Bonding through adversity is a persistent theme in these wartime accounts.[24] An injured Marine who decided to rejoin his unit after being wounded, rather then accept an early discharge, explained:

Those men on the line were my family, my home. They were closer to me than I can say, closer than any friends had been or ever would be. They had never let me down, and I couldn't do it to them. I had to be with them rather than let them die and me live with the knowledge that I might have saved them.[25]

As a bomber pilot put it:

We did it because it was given to us to do, or perhaps we did it because we could not bear the shame of being less than the man beside us. We fought because he fought.[26]

The veterans commonly said that they supported each other because they didn't want to let the other men down. As one Marine who had been in Okinawa during World War II put it, "All I could think of was how I could get him to the hospital . . . not that I was in danger of being killed. It never occurred to me that way. We were a mutual survival society."[27]

Whereas bonding might enhance the likelihood that men would act on one another's behalf in war, we might expect that it would put them at risk psychologically, making it hard to cope with the death or injury of fellow soldiers. Elder and Clipp explain this paradox by distinguishing between friendship and comradeship. Friendship is a personal bond of liking between two people, whereas comradeship is less a commitment to an individual man than to the group. The wartime bonds depended on the latter: if you got too close to another man, you were emotionally vulnerable because he could die at any moment. Comradeship enabled each man to take heroic action and make sacrifices for others without being immobilized by fear for his own survival or that of friends.

Indeed, adversity actually strengthens bonding. Elder and Clipp found that evidence of bonding increased the more a unit had been under attack and the more casualties it had sustained. A World War II veteran remarked, "Any one of these men would have given up his life for me, and some of them did," referring to the members of his unit who had died.[28]

These men met one another's needs in a second way as well. When they returned from the war, the bonds they had forged with one another helped them recover from the psychological trauma of combat experience. You might imagine that men who had stayed aloof during the action would be better protected against the trauma of losing comrades in battle. Yet the opposite was the case. The men who did not forge bonds with their mates or who had remained socially isolated from the other men fared less well, both in wartime and in the aftermath of psychological recovery. The bonds of wartime, then, made it possible for these men to fight and die on one another's behalf, but they also provided them with the sustenance to cope with the horrors they had witnessed, once the war had ended.[29]

STILL, THERE IS a chilling underside to men's groups. Many aggressive men do not learn how to manage their aggression through exposure to the regulating effects of other men. What happens to intensely aggressive males who disrupt the otherwise smooth pace of social life? One answer is that they, too, bond with one another, but in ways that may ultimately foreshadow their destruction.

Consider the case of Gelada baboons. These primates typically live in small bands, each led by a male with several, often related females and their offspring. Males who are low in status and who therefore do not have their own "harems" typically merge into an all-male group and act as a buffer between the females and an attacking predator. They are essentially on the front lines. Anthropologist Lionel Tiger, who was one of the first scientists to draw intriguing parallels between the Geladas and human aggression, describes these groups of low-status unattached males in somewhat romanticized terms as quite stable and loyal, the primate equivalent of Robin Hood's band of merry men. In fact, life is far more harsh. The stability Tiger referred to rarely lasts longer than a few months or weeks because these unattached males are vulnerable, and after a time they are never seen again, seemingly swallowed up by the land they inhabit.[30]

At a recent animal conference, primatologist Jeanne Altman presented her field work on baboons in the wild and talked about these luckless males, noting that after several unsuccessful efforts to mate with females or to move up in the dominance hierarchy, they simply disappear. Disappear? The audience was startled. "We assume they die," Altman added. "Of what?" asked one audience member. Precisely because these males disappear, we do not know exactly what happens to them, but we can make a few educated guesses.

These unattached males typically form a roaming band that lives on the fringes of a troop. The males in these bands are young and aggressive and often inflict injuries on one another that can fester with fatal consequences. Because they are marginal to the main troop, they are easily picked off by predators. Without female companionship, they are rarely groomed, and so parasites may live undisturbed until they form a life-threatening infection. In short, these unattached, sexually mature males create for themselves a fatal lifestyle.

Across all primate species, the group most likely both to cause harm and to get in harm's way is juvenile and young adult males. They are in the vanguard of nearly every risky behavior primates can undertake. When one macaque monkey spies a snake, he sends out an alert cry, and the entire troop heads for the trees. But within minutes, the juvenile males are back on the ground, poking and prodding the snake until it gets one of them or slithers away. Groups of young men are not so different. Young men commit more crimes, get into more automobile accidents, commit suicide more often, and kill one another more than any other group in the population.

At any given time in the world, there are bands of teenage and young adult males roaming the countryside or the cities, leaving a trail of destruction, rape, and murder in their wake. Sometimes these groups have an ostensible political purpose; other times they emerge from poor economic conditions. Whatever their apparent cause, they seem to be an inevitable fact of the human social landscape. Often we ignore them or interpret them as local responses to specific conditions, such as the outgrowth of politics in Burma, tribal warfare in Rwanda, religious fanaticism in the Mideast, soccer hooliganism in Britain, or gang rivalries in Los Angeles. Whatever the cause, their form is much the same, and so are their dynamics. They cause chaos and spread fear, and ultimately their members often die young in the midst of their destructive activity. They are the harsh casualties of the status struggles among men.

THE NEW VIEW of men's groups, then, argues that through experiences with other males, socially skilled men rise to the top and help to control the aggression of those below them, often marginalizing, even ostracizing those who fail to use these skills. Rather than the ubiquitous aggression emphasized by such writers as Karl Lorenz, we have come to see these groups as flexible systems that respond to the need to manage the twin demands of competition and cooperation. Certainly these groups can be harsh and lethal, punitively ostracizing the most aggressive in their numbers; but they are marked by the same bonding and capacity for sacrifice that distinguish all our tending systems.

| CHAPTER 9 |

Where Altruism May Reside

On January 13, 1982, Air Florida flight 90 crashed into Washington, D.C.'s 14th Street Bridge shortly after takeoff. Lenny Skutnik, a U.S. Parks policeman, watched in horror as the diving plane hit three cars and plunged into the icy waters of the Potomac River. Soon cries for help could be heard. Without thinking, Skutnik dove into the water and pulled one of the survivors to safety, a woman who would certainly have succumbed to the Potomac's freezing temperature had Skutnik not followed his impulses.

There was another hero that day. Arland Williams was one of the passengers in the water. As a rescue helicopter hovered overhead, Williams passed the lifeline repeatedly to others, and four of his fellow travelers were saved by his efforts. But when it was Williams's turn, he was gone. In all, only five people survived the Air Florida crash, and all five had been saved by heroes.[1]

If we needed any additional proof that tending to others is an intrinsic part of our human nature, it comes from heroism, both the dramatic acts of helping and the more quiet acts of caregiving that are a part of everyday life. Who behaves heroically? What are we to make of the brave and selfless acts so many people undertake?

Tending reaches its most dramatic and celebrated form when people deliberately risk their own health and safety for others' welfare. These remarkable acts of altruism, while common, have been difficult to understand from the conventional vantage point of evolutionary biology. Put in its most simple form, the paradox is, How do we pass on our altruistic genes to future generations if those very genes put us at increased risk for early death, thereby reducing the probability that we will pass on our genes at all?

In Chapter 1, I argued that nature does not leave vital tasks to chance, but rather backstops important functions through redundant hormones, organs, and neurocircuitries to ensure that vital functions will be performed one way or another. Altruism may be one of these vital functions—so fundamental, so essential to the survival of human beings that it has taken root in neurocircuitries designed for other purposes, finding its expression in numerous unexpected, but largely successful ways. I will suggest that, far from being paradoxical, altruism emerges quite naturally from the neurocircuitries for aggression, caregiving, and dominance and from our capacity for bonding. In other words, altruism builds quite readily on tending systems that are already in place.

We think of altruism as motivated by compassion, and if it isn't, then it's not altruism but something else—duty, perhaps. In fact, a lot of altruism doesn't fit this mold. It's wired in, impulsive in some cases, more like aggression or duty than kindness. It's not that compassion and empathy are absent from our many acts of heroism, but that our helping of others, like other forms of tending, is nudged by several different neurochemistries, by cultural norms and roles, and only sometimes by the emotions we credit with giving rise to it. Some of these origins are sex-specific, which is why men's and women's heroism so often assumes different forms. In men, heroism is often a spontaneous, automatic act of aggression against an enemy, whether human or nonhuman. In women, heroism seems more commonly to have piggybacked onto the caregiving that initially evolved for the protection of children. Is this a fair contrast? A look at heroism and caregiving is revealing.

In Los Angeles, as in many cities, people who have performed heroic acts such as taking a bullet for a friend, saving a drowning child, or pulling others from burning buildings are regularly honored by the mayor. These ceremonies are nice to watch because they are so uplifting. There is one recurrent emotion in the honorees, however—not universal, but common enough to be noteworthy. Embarrassment. What do the heroes say when invited to comment after their citations are read? "Anyone would have done the same thing." "I was just doing my job." "I didn't think about it, I just did it." The embarrassment comes, I think, from the feeling that heroism should be on purpose, prompted by empathy in the spirit of self-sacrifice. One should see a victim, feel compassion, recognize the potential danger to oneself but decide to take action despite the risks. It often doesn't happen that way. Our reluctant heroes are quite right. In many instances, almost anyone would have done the same thing.

In 1966, the state of California passed a good samaritan law to provide compensation to people who were injured as a result of helping others in life-threatening circumstances. Psychologist Ted Huston and his associates used the opportunity to study the question, Who is a hero? The original goal was to see what kind of person willingly puts his or her life in danger in order to help others. What are the roots of the compassion on which society so clearly depends? Huston and his colleagues were very surprised by what they found.[2]

From police records, they identified thirty-two people who had intervened in assaults, holdups, and other serious crimes and been injured in the process. They contacted these people and asked them to complete questionnaires and interviews, so they could understand the motives behind their brave actions a little better.

Significantly, the heroes were not distinguished by any psychological attributes—contrary to expectation, there was no altruistic hero type. Instead, they seemed to have had quite minimum qualifications for the actions they performed, namely large size and a little experience. They were taller and heavier than average, and most of them had received some kind of emergency training such as first aid, life saving, or police work. As this profile implies, almost all of the heroes were men. (The lone heroine was an elderly woman who went to check on her neighbor when she heard a commotion and was stabbed by her neighbor's attacker as he fled.)

Most of the heroes were on familiar terms with crime as well, having witnessed crimes personally or been a victim of one. They regarded themselves as aggressive. As Huston and his colleagues gradually began to realize, most of their "heroes" were all too ready for violence. They were believers in law and order. Many lived in high-crime areas, and most regarded crime as one of the highest priority issues facing the public. Over 80 percent were gun owners. When each was asked to describe how he would respond to several hypothetical provocative situations—such as his car not starting, someone butting into an argument, or hitting his thumb with a hammer—the heroes proved to be easily and extremely provoked. These Angry Samaritans, as Huston came to call them, were less angels of mercy than risk takers with a history of over-reacting to stress.

Compassion for the victim had not typically prompted their actions. Indeed, several of the heroes wondered aloud how the people they had saved had been so stupid as to get themselves in their predicaments. Rather than regarding themselves as heroes, several of the men saw themselves as in a contest with the criminal. In one well-publicized incident, a motorist saw a truck strike a pedestrian and then drive away. The motorist gave chase in his car—in part, as he later confessed, because his car was new and he wanted to see if he could catch the truck. He did, and he forced the hit-and-run driver to the side of the road. He then took out a shotgun from the trunk of his car and held the truck driver at gunpoint until the police arrived. Meanwhile, the woman who had been hit by the truck was left lying in the road; she died an hour later at the hospital.

While the men that Huston and his colleagues studied may not be typical of those heroes who sacrifice their personal safety for others, they do illustrate an important point about heroism. Much of what we think of as heroic behavior springs, not from some impetus for altruism, but from the hardware for aggression instead. Society makes use of this raw, aggressive energy, channeling it into the services that protect and defend.

We selectively recruit young, physically fit men ready for risk and adventure to serve these needs. In essence, heroism may be cut from the same cloth as the bravery of police, firefighters, and soldiers. It is a somewhat impulsive aggression, spontaneous, not thought through, but commonly benefiting total strangers.

WHEN WE THINK of heroism, we usually envision a young, fit man putting himself at risk to save others. So potent is this image that it shapes our very definition of heroism, restricting and constraining it to dramatic events such as these. While it is true that women less often hurl themselves in harm's way to protect people other than their own children, their heroism is as legitimate, if not as celebrated, as men's. It is a quieter kind, but in important ways just as risky as men's, involving sacrifice and risks to health and well-being.

A friend, Linda, has been taking care of her mother for four years. Her father died in his fifties, and her mother lived alone until age seventy-eight, when she could no longer manage on her own. Arthritis made it hard for her to get around, and she was growing forgetful, so Linda moved her mother into their home, where she cares for her alongside her two adolescent children.

Linda's mother is a lot of work. In the last two years, she's had several small strokes, and she now suffers from multi-infarct dementia, a condition not too different from Alzheimer's, which is marked by forgetfulness and faulty reasoning. Linda hired a woman to come in during the day to help, but she calls from work several times a day to make sure everything is all right. In the evening, Linda takes over from the caregiver, feeding her mother and helping her change and bathe, checking on her when she wakes up several times a night crying because she can't remember where she is.

Linda's friends tell her she is a saint, and it always annoys her when they do. What is she supposed to do? Abandon her mother? She is a reluctant hero who doesn't see her actions as particularly exceptional. Moreover, Linda's unwillingness to accept her friends' accolades of sainthood stems from something else she'd rather not talk about. She really does not like this caregiving at all. She's mentally and physically exhausted all the time. Occasionally her mother seems appreciative, but much of the time she's complaining and critical. Linda is trying to hold on to the memory of the strong, cheerful woman who raised her, but it is giving way to the image of the frail, petulant old woman who now sucks up every second of Linda's leisure time.

Just as men are the world's heroes, women are the world's caregivers, and by a large margin. Looking at caregiving overall, about 79 percent of it is provided by mothers, daughters, and wives. Daughters care for their aging parents (sons are only one-fourth as likely to give care to their parents), mothers care for their disabled children, and, most commonly, women care for their husbands. In the United States, the typical caregiver is a sixty-year-old low-income woman with a disabled or ill spouse.[3]

Another group of quiet caregivers is grandmothers. At the present time, about 1.7 million children in the United States are living with grandparents, usually cared for by their grandmother. The reasons are not altogether unexpected. Many of these children have parents with drug or alcohol problems or HIV infection. In other cases, their parents are divorced, dead, or imprisoned. In the last decade alone, the number of grandparent-headed households has increased by 53 percent, and as the reasons suggest, most of these families are poor.[4]

But these are contemporary patterns of caregiving. Can we truly argue that they result from evolutionary processes that selected for giving care? Certainly a case can be made. Early people must have had caregiving systems in place that extended beyond the obvious need to protect children. While we have no proof that this was so, evidence from prehistoric human skeletons shows clearly that people were injured, often more than once, yet survived their injuries. They could not have done so without a caregiving system—at least one person who saw to their needs for food, water, and protection until their wounds or broken bones had mended.

Who cared for the sick and injured? Who saw them through the inevitable convalescences that ensured return to a full life? I believe it was women. Women in early societies took care of young children and foraged, a way of life potentially flexible enough to absorb such responsibilities.

Moreover, caregiving involved tasks quite similar to those women were already doing with respect to children, and so it would have required a minimal extension of skills and activities already in place. (By minimal, I mean with respect to complexity and not effort.) Men whose hunting demanded coordinated, interdependent action and often required several-day excursions from home would have had lives less suited to the continuous responsibilities of long-term care. In search of evidence for these conjectures, I have cornered many an anthropologist, thus far to no avail.[5] I am on somewhat safer footing with respect to grandmothers.

Care by grandmothers is as old as humanity itself. Indeed, one account of why women live so much longer than men maintains that long-lived grandmothers were selected for through evolutionary processes. Older women who no longer had children to support nonetheless had very well developed foraging skills that would have enabled them to gather more food than they needed. By sharing it with their children and grandchildren, they increased the likelihood that these kin would survive. These kin, in turn, would have passed on the genes for female longevity. Evolution gave women long lives and, with them, the dubious opportunities to care for others throughout their lives.[6]

The costs of caregiving can be great. It is a tough, grinding, chronic stressor. Over half of contemporary caregivers work outside the home, and many more need to quit their jobs or reduce their hours to accommodate the time caregiving requires, on average more than ten hours a day. It interferes with all the other necessary activities of life, including working, raising children, running a household, or just attending to personal needs. For older people, it can be a fatal undertaking. Caregivers, as a result, are at risk for physical and mental health problems. Nearly 60 percent show signs of clinical depression. They're unhappier and lonelier than their age mates who aren't caregivers, and when another stressor hits them on top of their caregiving responsibilities, their stress systems are that much more strained. The cardiovascular systems of elderly caregivers typically show the precursors of heart disease. Their immune systems aren't very efficient. When flu season hits in November, caregivers are at double risk; they are more vulnerable to the flu because their immune systems are compromised, and they show a poorer response to the influenza vaccine for the same reason. Caregivers shake off infectious diseases very slowly, and they are also at heightened risk for death. University of Pittsburgh psychologists Richard Schulz and Scott Beach found that the chances of dying in a given four-year period for an elderly person involved in stressful caregiving were 63 percent higher than for elderly people without these arduous and draining responsibilities. Caregiving may be quieter, but it is no less dangerous than heroism.[7]

ALTRUISM OF THE sort that ultimately can lead to self-sacrifice has, as noted, been one of the thorniest evolutionary issues to resolve. Prior to the 1960s, evolutionary theory credited a cooperative nature as one of the factors that favored the survival of *Homo sapiens* as a species. The group survived because our individual acts of altruism, fueled by an intrinsically cooperative nature, benefited all. Group survival is an idea that deserves to be true. Yet the evidence that we pass on qualities that favor group survival has been meager.[8] Increasingly, evolutionary biologists have taken a gene's eye view instead, emphasizing how qualities are passed on by maximizing an individual's likelihood of surviving and leaving viable offspring. But cooperation, altruism, and selfless heroism have remained in our nature, and as such, they are difficult issues for evolutionary theory.

Consider, as an example, the warning cry of the sentinel, common to some rodent species. On the lookout for danger, the sentinel sees a predator—a hawk, perhaps—and lets out a loud and distinctive cry that sends his companions scampering for safety. In so doing, however, he calls attention to himself, increasing the likelihood that he will be the hawk's dinner. If altruism is rewarded by death, how does it survive in the genes?

William Hamilton, a British biologist, was one of the earliest scientists to take on the dilemma of altruism from an evolutionary vantage point. He argued that heroism can be understood from a gene's eye view if one adopts a principle of kin selection. He showed that in the animal kingdom, heroism often has the effect of saving relatives who share one's genes and who will live on in greater numbers than if your heroic act hadn't occurred and you merely quietly saved yourself. So long as your efforts are most likely to benefit those closely related to you, who will pass on your genes in your stead, altruistic genes can thrive.[9]

Caregiving is good evidence for Hamilton's point. Caring for children quite obviously increases the likelihood that those children will survive. Caregiving to men may be similarly explained. When a woman cares for her mate, she increases her chances of having additional children and increases the likelihood that her partner will survive and help provide for existing offspring. Caring for grandchildren allows one's genes to be passed on and, as noted, provides a possible basis for why women have long lives. Yet, oddly enough, caregiving is rarely discussed in the literature on altruism. Many of the evolutionary scientists who have written about altruism have explicitly excluded caregiving from their discussions. Maternal behavior, they sniff, is nepotism, not altruism.

But to exclude maternal behavior (and other forms of caregiving) from analyses of altruism is to miss the point entirely. Nature is a thrifty designer, and neurocircuitries designed for one purpose—maternal behavior, for example—may provide the underpinnings of other behavior patterns—caregiving, more generally. From one efficient set of genes, we may get a host of related behaviors—care of children, care of mate, nursing of the sick or injured, and care by grandmothers.

So it may be with our rough-and-ready heroes whose neurocircuitries for aggression are, metaphorically speaking, just itching to be turned to the good as well. As we saw in Chapter 8, men's aggression spontaneously seeks an enemy, and when an attacker, a criminal, or even an impersonal event like a flood slips into that slot, aggression in the altruistic service of others may be the result, whether compassion is at the heart of the behavior or not.[10]

Moreover, a lot of heroic behavior may not need much neurocircuitry behind it, because the learning on which it depends is in place. The play that occupies so much of children's time and that accompanies the enormous brain development of the first few years of life is heavily organized around sex-typed tasks. Boys get lots of practice in potential self-sacrifice, even when it is only on the sports field. They put their heads in front of someone's foot; throw themselves in front of a goal; intentionally make violent, full-body contact with an opponent. Military training further hones this willingness to forgo personal safety. And so, when another person's life is threatened, those whose fears for their own safety have been carefully trained out or whose aggressive impulses to overcome threat are well honed may have not a second's hesitation before intervening, albeit at potential cost to self. Huston's descriptions of his Angry Samaritans make this case well—big, aggressive men trained in emergency preparedness were the typical heroes. Those of us with lesser training in aggressive self-sacrifice may nervously eye the same situation, confident we would neither save anyone nor come out of the situation alive.

Learning may similarly benefit the type of heroism distinctive to women. If we look across cultures, we see that girls typically receive training in tending from an early age, beginning with playing with dolls and caring for younger siblings, extending to baby-sitting for others' children, and finally to caring for their own children. It is a modest extension of this same learning to care for an infirm husband or elderly parent.

Am I able to prove my argument, namely that much of what we call altruistic behavior derives from neurocircuitries and correspondent learning that serves other survival-related purposes? Can I demonstrate that the same patterns of activation and hormones that foster aggression or caregiving for the young underlie impulsive self-sacrifice or arduous tending to others? I cannot do so at this point. The science of altruism is currently conducted far away from this perspective, studied in lower species and even in computer models, and rarely is focused on the neurobiology of human behavior.[11] Were I a scientist who studied altruism, this is where I would look, but for the present I can show you only these intriguing parallels.

JUST AS AGGRESSION and caregiving may lie at the root of much heroic behavior, so other acts of altruism may arise from the quest for dominance. That is, once we abandon the scenario of dominance as the triumph of aggression and recognize that dominance is instead founded heavily on social skills, altruism is easier to understand. Although the short-term risks of altruism may be quite real, involving potential self-sacrifice for others, in the long term the effects may be quite self-serving and, thus, perfectly compatible with our selfish genes. Among most primates, as we've seen, males and, to a lesser extent, females form dominance hierarchies. Altruism can be an effective way of achieving and cementing a strong position in such a hierarchy.

Some years back, when my husband and I were visiting friends in India, a large male rhesus monkey appeared on the balcony outside the dining room. Since rhesus males can be quite confrontational, we watched him from the safety of the kitchen. Once in the dining room, he looked around for food; spying a long loaf of sliced bread, he seized it, ran to the balcony, and climbed up into the trees and across the street to a field where his fellow monkeys were waiting. As we watched, they all sat down, our thief patiently unwrapped the bread, and one by one, he handed a slice to each member of the waiting group. As the alpha male, it was no doubt his role to undertake such risky activities, but in doing so, he helped to ensure his continued role as leader through his beneficence.

In hunter-and-gatherer societies, a similar pattern has been documented among the successful hunters of the group. Rather than hoarding their kills for their own families, successful hunters commonly share the meat with the entire group. The behavior is well documented by anthropologists, although the interpretation of it varies depending on the point the writer is trying to make—some have used this behavior as an example of human beings' intrinsically egalitarian nature; others have written more cynically about the self-aggrandizing behavior of these successful men. Whichever version you choose to believe, the effect is the same. High status is cemented through generosity.

Status and altruism go hand in hand in our current lives as well. The wealthy put their names on the sides of hospitals or clinics to provide care for others. Universities sell auditoriums, even classrooms, to the highest bidders in exchange for a commemorative plaque. My children's school has a fund-raising campaign each year, and, like most schools, they publish a list of who gave what in categories designed to obscure the exact size of the gift: $500–$999 is one category, $1,000–$2,499 is another, and so on. Let's take the $1,000–$2,499 category. How many of the seventy or so families in that category would you guess gave exactly $1,000? Most of them, would be my guess. And how many gave, say, $2,300? None, would be my guess. For a mere $200 more, you could get your name into the next category. I don't mean to malign the motives of those who give, because they *did* give, after all, often lots of money, and it's money they no longer have. Moreover, one could have chosen not to give at all without being noticed, at least not immediately. The altruism of status-related giving may have its rewards in the admiration and deference of others, but it is altruism nonetheless.

Why would altruism thrive in the neurocircuitry for dominance? As just noted, we now know that dominance hierarchies are formed and maintained through social skills and savvy, not through raw aggression and domineering behavior. It's not too hard to see why genes related to dominance might harbor altruistic tendencies. Virtually by definition, altruism goes in one direction: from those who have to those who need. Dominant animals (or people) are often those with the resources to be altruistic. They get many benefits from being dominant, of course, including good health, long life, and partners for grooming and sex; as such, altruism may represent one of the "costs" of power. Those who rule over others, whether a band of rhesus monkeys or a business organization, are expected to give something back. Why else would followers continue to agree to subordination? The social skills of dominance include signs of warmth and affection, the willingness to demonstrate compassion and empathy, the ability to sense another's need and act on it. Even small acts of kindness and solace get noticed by others and contribute to the perception that you are someone to be trusted, or even favored. Altruism can help one secure a strong position in a dominance hierarchy. As anyone who has called in a favor knows, the goodwill and stockpile of obligations that modest but repeated acts of altruism can build will benefit you and your kin.[12]

THERE ARE MANY origins of altruism, and another of these is the human capacity to form strong bonds with others quickly, especially when times are stressful. As we saw in Chapter 5, human beings are distinctive in the bonds they easily and rapidly form with strangers, bonds that may be based on some of the same hormonal underpinnings as attachment or kinship. Much altruism depends on these emotional ties—the capacities for empathy and caring that evolve from the emotional and social knowledge that develops in early life. We act in the service of others in part because we feel for them.

Scientists still know little about the deep structure of altruism in humans, especially altruism toward strangers. But it is likely that the capacity for bonding may be a genetic proxy for kinship, and that this fuels much of our willingness to care for strangers. Adversity is the stimulus that gives rise to altruism, but a bond—quickly, easily, and intensely formed—is what propels the altruistic action for another.[13]

These bonds draw on the storehouse of emotional knowledge laid down in early life—the capacity for empathy, the ability to be distressed by another's need. To be sure, some altruism, especially of the heroic kind, does not seem to require bonding, building instead on arousal, aggression, and a penchant for risk. But the ability to bond with others that comes from our emotional neurocircuitry is yet another force that propels us into heroic action.

As we look at the various forms of tending throughout society—the parent-child bond, group responses to threat, and groups of men or women responding to stressful situations—all are marked by the experience of bonding. Although the research evidence is limited, there may be some commonalities in the neurochemistry that maps onto these subjective, yet widely shared experiences: oxytocin and EOPs are two of the possibilities. This program for bonding that lies deep within our nature underlies our commitment to offspring, other kin, and friends. The insistent neurochemistry that influences human bonding allows us to tend to strangers as well. When a shared stress occurs, this bonding is ready to be engaged. The emotions we came to understand in early life, the capacity for empathy that emotional understanding affords, our wired-in sensitivity to distress signals from others, all conspire to make heroic altruistic behavior on behalf of others the most normal yet enobling aspect of our nature.

Do we now have an understanding of our altruism, the heroics and caregiving that are so ubiquitous in our lives? I would say not yet. It's impossible to read the evolutionary accounts of altruism without developing a sense that we haven't quite got all the pieces. Far from being resolved, altruism is currently an academic battleground throughout the social and biological sciences, with "selfish gene" explanations increasingly coming under fire in fields as diverse as economics, anthropology, and political science as well as in biology. Whether the next few years will bring resolution remains to be seen.

Many of these skirmishes have focused on a narrow paradox concerning altruism, namely the warning cry of the sentinel, largely ignoring the breadth of altruistic behavior. Yet the forms of altruistic behavior in which humans engage are manifold, tenacious, and widespread. Altruism seems to have crept into a number of our neurocircuitries initially "designed" for other tasks. Moreover, much of what we might call altruism is cultural in origin. Our willingness to donate time and money to causes we care about comes from our socialization.

We are a caring species, capable of extraordinary acts of heroism and caregiving, often at great personal risk. No simple explanation can cover the range of this altruistic behavior, and while it may build on neurocircuitries for other functions—dominance, aggression, maternal caregiving—it is also engaged by bonding that we seem to slip into remarkably easily, especially when we share adverse experiences with others. Drawing on the emotional and social knowledge that is acquired in the first few years of life, our capacities to bond with others, to empathize with their experience, and to feel emotions vicariously have enabled our species to minister to total strangers as well as to kin.

CHAPTER 10

The Social Context of Tending

In response to threat, we care for our children, give one another social support, and otherwise band together to drive off a common enemy. But when stress is a chronic, grinding, unrelenting source of strain, it has exactly the opposite effect. On the biological level, it drains us of disease-fighting resources. The immune system goes limp. Much the same thing happens to relationships as well. That chronic stress can provoke harsh relationships is a robust and unhappy fact of life. When too much is going on, money is tight, and life is unpredictable, relationships can start to look frazzled and erratic. Nowhere is this story more clearly told than in the relationship of social class to health.

My FAMILY CAME to America during the first wave of Irish immigration in the late 1600s and early 1700s. We were Presbyterian Scots-Irish traders who had made a good living shipping between Belfast and Glasgow, and, by any standard, we were affluent. The economic plan for our transition to the colonies apparently involved trading between Maine and the islands off the coast of Massachusetts, and so Nantucket is where we landed. But as anyone who has ever spent time in Nantucket knows, there is nothing to ship but tourists, and in the 1700s, there weren't any tourists yet. So we relocated to Maine, hoping to find more promising cargo. Unfortunately, this plan proved to be as ill conceived as the first. Our third effort really sent our fortunes tumbling. In a state known at the time for its prosperous fishing industry, my family hit on the idea of farming the harsh stone-filled land of central Maine instead, and so rather than heading up the promising coastline, we made an abrupt, ill-chosen left turn inward. By the early 1800s, we were really poor.

Lack of good fortune did not prevent the peculiarly American fascination with genealogy from taking hold in my family, however, and toward the end of her life, my mother became passionately dedicated to constructing our family tree. The Internet had not yet been invented, and so the task required endless phone calls and letters to town halls and church parishes throughout the British Isles to track down exactly when and where specific Taylors had been born and died. This is an exceptionally tricky business with a common last name like ours; among the few clues that allow one to distinguish one line from another is the appearance of distinctive first names across generations. Between "Druisilla" and "Diantha," my mother managed to trace one line back to the Battle of Hastings before it disappeared into a great tangle of Saxons, Angles, and Normans. On my twenty-first birthday, I was presented with a giant circular document that contained the names, birth dates, and death dates of most of my ancestors, going back quite reliably to the 1600s.

When you peruse this document, a pattern leaps out immediately. The affluent relatives of the 1600s and 1700s were routinely living into their seventies and eighties at a time when people rarely lived beyond age fifty-five. This was quite an achievement, and it no doubt reflects the comfortable lifestyle that the trading business afforded. Equally striking is the fact that, as our family fortunes waned in the 1800s, our lives grew much shorter, rarely past age sixty and often only to age forty or forty-five.

Family stories from this era suggest that many of these early deaths were what scientists call "preventable deaths." A wheel came off a poorly maintained wagon, tossing one ancestor into a culvert and snapping his neck. Another fell asleep in a drunken stupor, unaware that the embers from his pipe were burning the house down around him. Others succumbed to heart attacks in their mid-forties. Most of the women died in childbirth, a result of inadequate medical care in less than sanitary conditions. And then, as our fortunes improved in the 1900s, so did our life expectancy.

Nowhere is this pattern more clear than with the offspring of my grandfather, Charles. Charles was married to Ida, and together they had three children, Alice, Elizabeth, and Charles Jr. (my father). Shortly after Charles Jr. was born, Ida died of ptomaine poisoning, and after a brief period of mourning, Charles proposed marriage to a much younger, lively woman named Evelyn. Evelyn was ready to marry, but she was not ready to care for three children, and so, in deference to her wishes, Charles gave his three children away. Elizabeth went to Ida's sister, a wealthy woman with no children of her own who doted on Elizabeth and made every opportunity available to her, including a college education—a rarity for young women in Maine in the 1920s. Alice and Charles Jr. went to their father's two unmarried sisters who ran a small farm and lived in considerably less affluent circumstances. Nonetheless, enough money was eventually scraped together to send Charles Jr. to college, where scholarships and part-time jobs made up the difference. Alice remained on the farm.

As adults, Alice married a neighboring farmer and lived out much the same life as that in which she had been raised. Charles Jr. married my mother and made a good living as a high school teacher. Elizabeth married up and was wealthy throughout her adult life. And so three children of the same parents with roughly the same genetic heritage lived their lives in three different social classes. What was the effect on their health?

Alice died of a stroke at age seventy-six, the result of obesity and its inevitable companion, hypertension. Charles Jr. lived to age eighty-three, eventually succumbing to heart damage caused by two childhood bouts with rheumatic fever. Elizabeth is in her nineties and still plays a wicked game of bridge.

$\sim$

M<small>Y FAMILY'S FORTUNES</small> and misfortunes are mirrored in every country in the world. More affluent, better educated people live longer and healthier lives. This is true for nearly every cause of death and under every system of medical care that has so far been invented. It is true in Sweden, where people have socialized medicine and live into their eighties, and in Bangladesh, where medical practice is catch as catch can, and people often die in their forties or earlier. People higher in the social hierarchy enjoy better health than those below them.[1]

Some of the most dramatic evidence for the effects of hierarchy on health have come from the Whitehall studies directed by physician-researcher Sir Michael Marmot—studies named for the street on which much of the British Civil Service is housed. If you want to know a British civil servant's risk of dying of a heart attack, knowing his level in the civil service will give you some idea. It will also tell you something about how vulnerable he is to cancer, diabetes, infectious disease, and respiratory illness. It will give you some idea of how likely he is to be depressed, an alcoholic, or a smoker. If he's already sick, his civil service grade will give you a rough idea of how likely he is to get worse.[2]

When people first hear about social class differences in health, most are not surprised. Yes, they nod sadly, poor people die younger than rich people. We expect poor people to die of illness, poor nutrition, drug abuse, and unsanitary living conditions. But that is not what I mean. All along the social class gradient, at each of its levels, richer and more socially or professionally prominent people live longer than poorer and less advantaged people. The Whitehall civil servants, for instance, are a pretty privileged bunch, on the whole. Far from being poverty stricken, these bureaucrats all make decent incomes, enjoy a hazard-free work environment, and have job tenure. But even in this advantaged group, those higher up in the hierarchy are healthier than those lower down. All causes of death are affected, from the chances of developing heart disease to the simple likelihood of slipping on the front steps.

Thus, a person making $20,000 dollars a year is likely to die earlier than someone making $70,000; a person making $80,000 may well die earlier than someone making $130,000; a person making $250,000 may die earlier than someone making $300,000. Why does a higher social class give you extra life all along the social class gradient? Clearly, if extra income is buying you longer life, regardless of where you fall on the class gradient, the relation of social class to health is not explained by poverty.[3]

ONCE WE ELIMINATE poverty as an explanation for the effects of social class on health, most people look toward health care. If the quality of health care you receive—preventative care, checkups, quality of doctors—varies with education and income, wouldn't that explain effects on health? It could, but it doesn't. If top-flight health care were available to all, a laudatory goal in its own right, it would make only a dent in the gradient. Countries that provide health care for everyone, such as the Scandinavian countries, show the same social class gradient in health as those countries that lack universal health insurance, such as the United States.

In fact, the gradient is nearly as evident within the upper classes, where health care is uniformly available, as it is in the lower classes, where access to health care is irregular. Indeed, the gradient is roughly the same for health problems that are unresponsive to medical care (for example, incurable cancers) as it is for disorders that are responsive to health care (for example, treatable cancers, like breast cancer). Differential access to quality health care doesn't explain the effects of social class on health.[4]

What about health habits? If better educated and affluent people are less likely to smoke, drink to excess, and abuse drugs, and are more likely to exercise and eat a healthful diet, wouldn't this explain the effects of social class on health? Not only do health habits affect your chances of getting a lot of illnesses, many of them also vary with social class. For example, smoking shows a rough class gradient, with poorer people more likely to smoke than wealthier people. Better educated people are more likely to exercise and to consume a healthful diet than less educated people. And wealthier people typically drink in moderation, whereas the less well-to-do are more likely either to abstain from alcohol altogether or abuse it. Since moderate drinking is the healthy pattern, the well-to-do look better on this front, too.[5]

All the arguments would seem to be in place for a compelling explanation of the relation of social class to health. But when you take health habits into account, they explain only about one-quarter of the effect of social class on health. So with the most obvious explanations—poverty, health care, and health habits—explaining only part of the social class and health gradient, what's left?

Some scholars have concluded that it may be social position itself, one's status and position in the hierarchy, that explains the effect. With vague references to our chest-beating primate ancestors (what I will call the great apes theory of social class and health), some have simply thrown up their hands and concluded that the health effects of social class may somehow be intrinsic to the social order. In recent years, a number of popular magazines have run stories on inequalities in health and reached the same judgment, namely that such inequalities may be the inevitable consequence of any ranked society. One article in *Forbes* concluded:

If rank alone explains why the rich outlive the poor, the problem would seem to be as intractable as human nature. Can medicine, or education, or even radical socialism pretend to offer a cure?[6]

Such an account gives little hope or impetus for change. Moreover, it undermines efforts to understand the situation or improve it. Still, since the basis for this dismal conclusion relies heavily on intuitions about our primate heritage, let's turn again to this rich source of information on hierarchies and health and see what insights it provides.

ALMOST ALL PRIMATE troops have some form of dominance hierarchy, and, as we've already seen, where you fall in it makes a big difference to the quality of your life. If you are high in the dominance hierarchy, you get better food, more reliable protection when a predator is nearby, access to sex whenever you feel like it (if you are male), and someone to groom you whenever you want. From a primate's vantage point, it's a wonderful life.

Correspondingly, if you are low in the dominance hierarchy, you get the food that's left over, and even if you are lucky enough to find a great food source or make a great kill, someone higher in the dominance hierarchy may well come along and take it away. When a predator threatens the troop, you're out there on the front lines risking life and limb to protect everyone else. If you are male, you rarely get to have sex; if you do, often your sexual encounters must be surreptitious, since you may get beaten if you're caught. If you are female, you may be harassed to the point of infertility, and if you have young, they may be killed, eaten, or taken away from you to die from neglect. No one wants to groom you, and so parasites thrive freely in your mangy coat. It's a pretty wretched life, all things considered. Predators, parasites, poor diet, grumpy peers, and the stress of low rank are all competing to take your life away. It's little wonder that you will die earlier than those above you in rank.[7]

Robert Sapolsky, a Stanford biologist who is equally at home on the Serengeti plain or in a biology laboratory, has provided much of what we know about primate dominance hierarchies, and their role in stress and health. He studies olive baboons—big, smart, long-lived social animals who live in troops ranging from 50 to 150 in size. These animals "work" about four hours a day foraging for food, leaving them, as Sapolsky puts it, with "eight hours a day to be vile to each other." They fight, gang up on one another, make silly faces behind their companions' backs, and otherwise taunt and annoy the other baboons. Life is very stressful in a baboon troop, and becomes only more so the lower down in the hierarchy you go. For harassment is handed down from higher-status to lower-status animals, and those at the bottom are everyone's doormat and punching bag.

To understand the biological effects of the harassment associated with rank, Sapolsky selects a particular baboon and puts him to sleep with a dart from a blowgun. Once the animal is unconscious, he measures his stress hormones. What Sapolsky finds is revealing. On every hormonal and physiological measure he has studied, the subordinate baboons look worse than the more dominant baboons. They have higher resting levels of stress hormones, more sluggish stress responses, lower levels of good cholesterol, and fewer T cells, all suggesting a poorly functioning immune system.[8] No wonder these animals die young.

Is this social microcosm an analogue for the effects of social class on health? Many scientists think so, but there are important differences between us and the primate troops that seem to provide a metaphor for our own lives. To begin with, among humans rank is not inevitably associated with the privations and harassment that characterize the subordinate baboon's life. A working-class man may not have the lifestyle of a millionaire, but he gets plenty of food, rarely has to worry about leopards, can have sex pretty much when he wants, and can manage daily life without fear of a random assault by some belligerent physician or attorney.

Unlike humans, nonhuman primates live in small, face-to-face groups that represent all the social classes. Dominants and subordinates live side by side, and so there is plenty of opportunity for rank-based harassment. Humans also live in groups, but often all the members in a group share the same social class. Professionals tend to spend time with those in professions, blue-collar workers with other blue-collar workers, and so forth. If you are well-to-do, impoverished people don't typically live next door; they usually live a distance away. You may never meet them except to see them on TV or drive through their neighborhoods on your way to somewhere else. In short, the harassing, continuous contact that low- and high-status primates have with one another is not, generally speaking, a fact of everyday human life.

Even within our more homogenous living situations, however, there may be ways in which we mimic the stress gradient that is so evident in primate groups. As one descends the social ladder, life is increasingly marked by a rancorous social environment distinguished by a lack of personal control and social support. The lower you are, the more people there are who can control what you do and how you do it. You are more likely to encounter violence, crime, or just plain unpleasantness. The further down you are, the more financial concerns may prey on your mind and on your relationships.

The higher up the social ladder you move, however, the more life is characterized by discretion and choice, by freedom from economic preoccupations, and by a certain pleasant quality of life: most people, from shopkeepers to the police, are pretty nice to you. I will suggest that it is this balance of positive to negative social encounters—how much tending the social environment provides—that varies with social class and that may account in large part for the health outcomes linked to social class.

How could we go about exploring this idea? First of all, we could simply ask people how much social support or conflict they have and see if those responses vary with social class. In fact, they do. The higher people's social class, the more social support they say they have, and this is true in a number of countries. The other piece of the ratio, namely social conflict, also falls into place. The lower their social class, the more social conflict people report. Social stressors such as financial insecurity, fear of crime, and unstable work are more plentiful, and these stressors also lead people to feel that they don't have much social support.[9]

Regular confrontations with difficult life circumstances may breed hostility and, indeed, the lower your income, the higher your hostility, especially if you are male. An auto mechanic describes getting a handle on his hostility:

> I yell a lot, cuss a lot. I might throw things around down here, take a hammer and hit the bench as hard as it'll go. I'm getting better though, really. I used to throw a lot of stuff. I'd just grab and throw a wrench or something. But I haven't done that in a long time now.[10]

People who vent their hostile feelings are themselves the recipients of hostility, and so they often drive off whatever social support might have been available to them. The effects of hostility and the stress it causes build up over time, piling on a little bit of health risk with every hostile, nasty, contemptuous exchange that daily life provides. And, as a result, hostility is associated with a bad cholesterol profile, high blood glucose levels, high blood pressure, obesity, and two potentially fatal diseases that show strong relationships to social class: hypertension and coronary heart disease. Does this mean that hostility is the reason why there is a class gradient in health? It is certainly a part of the picture.[11]

If social class affects how much social support and conflict you experience, this should be evident in each important area of life such as home, work, and neighborhood. What evidence is there that, the lower on the social class ladder you move, the more conflict-filled your family life becomes?

Financial trouble is one of the main triggers of family strain, abuse, and divorce. The lower a man's income, education, occupational prestige, and job security, the more likely he is to physically or verbally abuse his wife. During periods of economic hardship, marriage is one of the most common casualties. Couples get hostile and irritable with each other, increasing the likelihood that they will eventually divorce. And ultimately economic strain erodes all relationships: people on the lowest rungs of the social ladder are more likely than those further up to say that they are not currently married, have no partner, and have no best friend.[12]

Like spousal abuse, child abuse also increases when economic conditions worsen. Neglectful parenting, marked by a lack of warmth and support or by conflict and abuse, becomes much more common, and this kind of parenting has been tied to bad health in children. It does indeed appear that the quality of your immediate family life goes down the lower your social class.[13]

It isn't poverty per se that has these effects, or rather it doesn't appear to be so, as much as it is the unpredictability and chaos that low or declining social class fosters. In a remarkable study of primates that illustrates this point, researchers Leonard Rosenblum, Jeremy Coplan, and their colleagues manipulated the environments in which mother macaque monkeys raised their young, by altering how easy or difficult it was for them to find food. Their goal was to see if harsh or difficult conditions influenced the mother's caregiving toward her infants and how the infants fared as a result.

In one of the environments, food was readily available; and in these cases, the mother monkeys were attentive to their offspring, who turned out to be quite normal. In a second environment, finding the food that was present required a lot of effort. Still the mother monkeys raised their offspring with attentiveness and care. In the third environment, sometimes food was plentiful and sometimes it wasn't. Sometimes finding it took little work, other times, a lot. Under these "variable-foraging" conditions, the mothers became harsh and inconsistent in their mothering. What happened to their babies? The offspring of the variable-foraging mothers showed clear biological signs that they were under intense stress. In childhood and throughout their adult lives, they had more active HPA stress systems, and they were fearful and socially maladept as well.[14]

Why does stress foster poor parenting? Some scientists have argued that how parents treat their children is a flexible evolutionary adaptation that is heavily determined by the harshness of the environment. Warm, nurturant parenting works well if your social world is a fairly benign place, marred only by occasional stressors. It may work less well if your world is always stressful, filled with people who can cause harm to you and your children, where meeting the simplest needs of life is often a burdensome chore. Parents under this kind of stress consequently may be harsh with their children in order to keep them under control and to protect them from harm. Children raised in a stressful environment may develop a (properly) wary stance toward life, much as Rosenblum and Coplan's monkeys did. In essence, more signals from the amygdala suggest danger—"protect yourself," "get out of there," and other reactions compatible with flourishing and frequently used stress responses.[15]

The statistics on class and the toll it takes on social relationships may seem lifelessly abstract until you listen to people describe their efforts to manage the rage that festers within them. Mike LeFevre, a steelworker profiled in Studs Terkel's *Working*, confronts these demons daily as he tries to control the fury he feels about his low wages, his high-pressure working conditions, and the foreman who belittles him. The temptation to lash out at his wife, his children, even at a fellow passenger on the bus requires constant vigilance and self-control.

I work so damn hard and want to come home and sit down and lay around. *But I gotta get it out.* I want to be able to turn around to somebody and say, "Hey, fuck you." . . . 'Cause all day I wanted to tell my foreman to go fuck himself, but I can't.

So I find a guy in a tavern. To tell him that. And he tells me too. . . . He's punching me and I'm punching him, because we actually want to punch somebody else.

When I come home, know what I do for the first twenty minutes? Fake it. I put on a smile. . . . If I feel bad, I can't take it out on the kids. Kids are born innocent of everything but birth. You can't take it out on your wife either. This is why you go to a tavern.[16]

Mike LeFevre's comments bring us to work, the one aspect of life in which people in different social classes do bump up against one another, just as they do in primate troops. Most employment is organized hierarchically, and so the person just above you matters a great deal to you, much as you matter a great deal to the person just below you. Work is a profoundly important part of life, and next to family life, people say it's their work that most affects their happiness. Does work contribute to the social class gradient of health outcomes? To answer this question, we would need to be able to show that work changes the balance of positive to negative social relationships, the lower one's status at work, and that health (or at least the warning signs of deteriorating health) change along with it. Both of these conditions are borne out by the evidence.

Work is vital to health. Unemployment, or even just the threat of unemployment, harms health. During periods of economic decline, infant mortality, death from heart disease, alcohol-related problems, admissions to psychiatric hospitals, and suicide all increase. Even people who remain employed during tough times find their job demands increase while the control they have over their job decreases.[17] And, as the Whitehall studies clearly indicate, where you fall in the hierarchy at work makes a big difference to your health.

Why is this true? The very nature of work changes as you move lower in the job hierarchy. The lower your social class, the lower your pay, the greater your job insecurity, and the more likely your job is just a job, rather than a satisfying career. A newspaperman describes his early work experiences:

> Originally I was a copywriter. I sat in a room and it was very simple. I would go to the boss and he'd tell me what he wanted. I'd go back to my room and try to write it, and get mad and break pencils and pound on the wall. Then finish it and take it in to him, and change it and change it, and then I'd go back and write it over again and take it in to him and he'd change it again, and I'd take it back. This would happen thirty or forty times. . . .[18]

In contrast, the higher your social class, the more likely you are to be working, to be working full-time, to be well paid, and to be working at a job you like.

Perhaps most importantly, as your social class goes up, the likelihood that you will be in a job in which you have a lot of control also increases. What do I mean by "control" at work and why might it improve your health? Control means, in part, that you can decide on what to work, and when, and how. As your status improves, your autonomy, your ability to do your work without constantly being beholden to someone else, increases. You have opportunities to decide how to do what you need to do and to figure out better ways to accomplish it. You have greater responsibility and independence. Although you are accountable in a general sense, you are less accountable on that minute-by-minute basis that often characterizes work lower down in the work hierarchy.[19]

Control also means that you have personal discretion. You can decide whether and when to make a personal phone call, run an errand, or have a friend visit you during business hours. A welder contrasts his job with his foreman's:

> The foreman's got somebody knuckling down on him, putting the screws to him. But a foreman is still free to go to the bathroom, go get a cup of coffee. He doesn't face the penalties.[20]

In 1979, an engineer named Robert Karasek proposed that jobs with little control but high demands, what he calls "high strain" jobs, breed illness. Over the past two decades, it has become evident that he is correct. People who have jobs characterized by high demands and little control are more vulnerable to infectious disease, coronary heart disease, psychiatric disorders, hypertension, exhaustion, and alcohol and drug abuse. They are also just plain unhappier at work.[21]

Job demands alone don't have ill effects on health. People high up the social class ladder often work as hard or longer than people further down; so in terms of job strain, their work can be highly demanding. What spares them the health risks associated with the demanding lower-status jobs is control—the unfettered discretion they have to decide whether this will be a late night or not. A factory owner describes the long hours he puts in as well as the joy he takes in his work:

> I'm here at six in the morning. Five-thirty I'll leave. Sometimes I'll come here on Sunday when everybody's gone and I'll putter around with the equipment. There isn't a machine in this place I can't run. There isn't a thing I can't do. The workers say: "You're the boss, you shouldn't do this. It's not nice. You're supposed to tell us what to do, but not do it yourself." I tell 'em I love it.[22]

Clearly, then, the drama of social class and health is played out at work. People at the bottom are beholden to others in ways that people higher up are not, and it affects physical and mental health.

Is tending itself affected by these conditions? Certainly, work can be a vital source of social support. For good health at work, people need a sense that others cooperate and care about one another. They also need to have good relations with their superiors and a sense that they can talk through problems when they come up. Workers who say they have little support and limited social contacts at work have poorer health and are absent more often; among older workers, those with little social support die earlier. According to surveys of working people, social relationships are both the most frequent cause of stress in the workplace and, next to the type of work itself, also the most important source of satisfaction. More relevant to the present argument is the fact that people say they have more social support the higher they are in the employment hierarchy.[23]

Originally, when researchers became interested in social support at work, they focused primarily on opportunities to develop friendships with coworkers, and, indeed, social support with peers is good for both workingmen and -women. Quite quickly, however, it became evident that how well you are treated by your immediate supervisor makes a great difference in the quality of physical and mental health you enjoy, especially for men. It affects whether you have symptoms of illness, or a risk for coronary heart disease or heart attack, and it affects the likelihood that you will have a psychiatric disorder or an emotional problem such as depression or anxiety. To put it another way, if your supervisor is a harassing baboon, you may well get sick; if, however, your supervisor is kind and supportive, you are far more likely to stay well.[24] A blue-collar worker describes his supervisor:

This one foreman I've got, he's a kid. He's a college graduate. He thinks he's better than everybody else. He was chewing me out and I was saying, "Yeah, yeah, yeah." He said, "What do you mean, yeah, yeah, yeah. Yes, *sir*." I told him, "Who the hell are you, Hitler? What is this 'Yes, *sir*' bullshit? I came here to work, I didn't come here to crawl. There's a fuckin' difference." One word led to another and I lost.[25]

He was bumped down a grade and lost twenty-five cents an hour. Over time, such experiences will likely erode his health as well.

Work influences the kinds of social contacts you can have with others. In high-strain jobs, social contacts may be limited or highly constrained. A receptionist describes the impact her short and superficial contacts with others have on her social relationships outside of work.

I don't have much contact with people. You can't see them. You don't know if they're laughing, if they're being satirical or being kind. So your conversations become very abrupt. I notice that in talking to people, my conversations would be very short and clipped, in short sentences, the way I talk to people all day on the telephone. . . .

Even when my mother calls, I don't talk to her very long. I want to *see* people to talk to them. But now, when I see them, I talk to them like I was talking on the telephone. It isn't a conscious process. I don't know what's happened.[26]

As this woman's experiences suggest, work spills over into other aspects of social life, affecting the social support you receive. Swedish psychologist Marianne Frankenhaeuser found that people with lively, interesting jobs were more likely to create a lively social life for themselves outside of work, whereas people in more boring, constricted jobs were much less likely to do so. It was not the case that lively, interesting people simply found livelier jobs and, in turn, had a more interesting social life. By following workers over a six-year period, Frankenhaeuser was able to show that those workers whose jobs became more interesting, affording them more autonomy, increased their involvement in social and cultural activities outside of work.[27] When it comes to social life, the rich do indeed get richer.

LET'S LOOK AT another aspect of life, namely where you live, to see if the social class of your neighborhood affects your social life. A good place to begin is with crime. We might expect to see that crime varies with social class, and, on the whole, the statistics bear this out. The lower your income, the greater your chances of being a victim of violent crime, a risk that increases pretty steadily as income goes down. Murder, assault, and rape all show a social class gradient. Theft, however, does not. True, poor people are the most likely to be victims of theft, a perversely unfair outcome if ever there was one, and your risk of theft decreases as your income increases, but only to a point. Above a certain level of income, you have good stuff to steal, and so your income no longer protects you, and your risk of being a victim of theft rises again.[28]

From a health standpoint, though, violent crime has the greatest effect. The stress systems of violent crime victims do not look normal. Sometimes these victims appear to be in a state of constant stress, somewhat like Sapolsky's low-status baboons; other times, their biological responses to stress are flat, suggestive of posttraumatic stress disorder (PTSD). Indeed, the main causes of PTSD are having been a victim of violence or having been exposed to violence.[29] With stress-regulatory systems out of whack, the groundwork for disease is laid.

Just as you are more likely to be a victim of violence the lower your income, you are more likely to be a witness to violence as well. Living in a violent neighborhood, even if you are never a victim yourself, is an extraordinary stressor that takes a daily toll. You are constantly on the alert for possible trouble, never knowing from where it may come. Comedian Chris Rock gives an account of what it was like to live in this kind of neighborhood. "We couldn't go outside. We ate on the floor, slept on the floor . . . watched TV on the floor . . . I spent my formative years nose to nose with a beagle."[30] Your stress systems stand guard, keeping you wary and vigilant.

Busing has brought many low-income kids to the affluent west side of Los Angeles for schooling. I was waiting at a stoplight one day next to one of these schools when the children were outside on the playground. The car in front of me suddenly let out a very loud backfire that startled everyone within a block. When I glanced over at the playground, virtually every black and brown child had hit the pavement. Their bewildered white companions, who were unaccustomed to the sound of gunfire, were still standing. Even if one is unaware of the need to monitor the environment constantly for threat, the body may be on alert nonetheless.

It doesn't take the extreme case of violent crime for your neighborhood to affect the quality of your life and your health. Nice neighborhoods foster better relationships and better health than ugly run-down neighborhoods do. What exactly is a nice neighborhood and what benefits does it give its residents? Sociologists have answered these questions by going into neighborhoods that differ in social class, and these are a few of the differences they have found.[31]

The nicer your neighborhood, the more parks and recreational opportunities there are. You are more likely to have access to a track, pond, cycling area, golf course, putting green, swimming pool, tennis court, soccer or football field, walking path, and other opportunities to exercise safely. There are more shopping centers nearby. Schools are better. There is more and better public transport. There are more churches and community organizations, and there are more and better health-care services. You have a wider choice of physicians, dentists, opticians, pharmacies, and orthodontists. If you are a home owner, the value of your home is more likely to remain constant or increase. You are less likely to have a nuclear power plant or chemical plant close by and less likely to live near a toxic waste site. Your streets are less likely to have broken glass, dog feces, or beer cans lying in the gutters, because they get cleaned promptly. Your street lighting is better and better maintained. Police answer calls more quickly.

The lower the average income of your neighborhood, the harder it will be to find a Laundromat, a dry cleaner, a restaurant, or convenient food shopping. You will have more trouble finding healthy food, and your food will cost you more. Cockroaches and graffiti are more likely to be part of your life. You will have higher levels of air pollution and nitrates in your drinking water. The lower the average income of your neighborhood, the less likely you are to have convenient transportation, banking services, shops, and churches. (Finding a bail bondsman, a pawn shop, or a liquor store will not be a problem, however.) The poorer your neighborhood, the higher the crime rate and the lower the ratio of police to crimes. The chance of a major fire increases, and the number of available firefighters decreases. So where do you think you'd like to live? Perhaps it is easier to understand why the higher the average income a neighborhood has, the better tended its residents are.

As FURTHER EVIDENCE that social support and conflict are vital to health, consider two little aberrations in the effects of the social gradient on health. They concern African Americans and women who are at the very top of the income and educational ladders. By any account, they're rich, they're smart, and they're the best in their professions. They have defied every expectation and all the odds for achievement. So they should enjoy the very best health, shouldn't they? The fact is, they don't. Although the social class and health gradient for white men reaches all the way to the top, for women and African Americans, it levels off just above the middle class and actually heads downward for those at the top. Very well educated women and African Americans who are well-to-do and employed in prestigious occupations do not enjoy the good health and long life that they should be getting from their social position.[32] Why not?

The phrase "It's lonely at the top" may come to mind. Those who have studied the health of women and African Americans suggest that, once you move into professions, neighborhoods, and communities where there aren't a lot of people like you, you no longer have so much social support. People may resent you, express coolness toward you, or exhibit a reluctance to get to know you very well, all of which further isolates you. Experiences of outright discrimination add insult to your privileged status, such as when an African American executive is late for a meeting because he couldn't get a taxi, or a woman's contributions to a business meeting go unnoticed. In short, the balance of support and hassle may be less favorable at the top for African Americans and women, as compared with the white men who more commonly populate these elite ranks. The combination of social isolation and lack of support, coupled with more hostility and resentment, may keep women and African Americans at the top of the social ladder from getting the good health they could otherwise expect.

WE'VE SEEN THAT relationships of all kinds are affected by position in the social gradient. Marriages suffer with economic strain, raising the likelihood of conflict, hostility, and abuse. Parenting deteriorates as economic troubles worsen. Work provides fewer opportunities for social support, the lower you are in the hierarchy, and control over your work passes from you to someone else. Neighborhoods are more crime-ridden, stressful, and rancorous, the lower your neighborhood's social class. And now we ask one last blunt question about social class, social conflict, and social support: With whom are you spending your time?

Most of us get our support from our family and friends, who are typically about the same social class as we are. If you are high in social class, you are enjoying the company of other people like yourself with money, time, and discretion over what they do. You and your friends may share theater tickets, leftovers from catered dinner parties, and elegant clothes that no longer fit. You go to restaurants together and play tennis and golf. Your friends may invite you to their summer cottage for a few days, and you may reciprocate by taking their children along on your family ski trip. You and your friends are likely to be healthy and self-sufficient, and each of you benefits from the other's nice life.

The lower you are on the social class ladder, the more likely your friends and family are to be under the same kind of stress that you suffer. Nor will your stressors protect you from being affected by their stressors. You may need to give your friend a ride to the repair shop when his car breaks down, or let your sister and her family move in with you when her husband loses his job. You may need to help bail out your nephew or find a drug-treatment program for your cousin. Chances are, your friends and relatives will share all the same problems associated with a poor neighborhood, work insecurity, and the difficulty of getting the simplest daily tasks done. The lower your social class, the more likely your friends and relatives are to have substance abuse problems such as alcoholism, and the more likely they are to be ill. And the lower your social class, the more likely your friends and relatives are to die young.

Low social class doesn't just give you less social support than higher social class gives to others; it gives you less of what is likely to be intrinsically poorer social support.[33] In essence, then, the balance of support versus sheer hassle that you receive from your social support network is less favorable.

Economic hardship and the social conflicts that accompany it creep into your life in ways that make it recurrently stressful and exhausting. Over time, your body accumulates the costs of these stresses and social conflicts, at first invisibly. And then at midlife, one or more full-blown diseases of wear-and-tear emerges: Your blood pressure is too high, your arteries are clogged, a malignancy snuck in while your immune system was napping, and the stage is set for one or more chronic diseases. Can we turn this process around? I believe we can. We can work toward creating a tending society.

CHAPTER 11

The Tending Society

Tending is a powerful force. The benefits it provides to children, especially those with genetic or acquired risks, are substantial. The fact that social ties can hold off potent flu viruses or retard the progress of chronic diseases speaks to its power as well. Indeed, this force seems literally to hold society together, a fact made clear by the staggering death and disease rates of Eastern Europe. And when nations are under assault from outside forces, our abilities to nurture one another are needed and tested. Yet as the last chapter showed, forces that underscore the divisions within a society also undermine the abilities of people to tend to one another's needs. If we were to try to design a society based on tending, what would distinguish it?

As a beginning, we would need to recognize that tending is intrinsic to our nature, at least as vital as the selfishness and aggression that more commonly shape its portrait. Our beliefs about human nature provide us with a lens that guides not only how we interpret our own actions and those of others, but what actions we even notice and consider to be significant. When the image we form is of an individualistic person who acts primarily with selfish self-interest, we cannot help but be affected.

Princeton psychologist Dale Miller has argued that the prevailing view of self-interest as a dominant human motivation has led to a self-fulfilling prophecy that is reflected in all our institutions—our schools, the workplace, our government bodies, and other social institutions. People think they should be selfish, they think other people are selfish, and so they construct social institutions that incorporate these assumptions. A bold and sweeping assessment, indeed, but Miller has a lot of evidence to back up his assertions.[1]

In a remarkable and somewhat chilling example of this point, economist Robert Frank and his colleagues assessed the impact of simply taking a course in economics on students' views about human nature. Economics is marked by the idea that people act in their own selfish interest, and so the research team wanted to know if merely taking a course would change the students' views in a more cynical, self-interested direction. They asked the students what they would do in several hypothetical situations, such as finding a wallet with $100 in it or detecting a billing error in their favor. Would the students give altruistic reasons for returning the wallet before the economics course ("He'll need his ID and the money." "It's the right thing to do.") and more selfish reasons after taking the course ("I wouldn't want someone to think I'd stolen it." "Someone might have seen me pick it up.")?

They found that taking a course in economics had a far more devastating impact on students' altruism than they had imagined. It wasn't merely that the students accepted the cynical viewpoint that self-interest lies behind most or all human behavior. They came out of the course believing that an honest and forthright action, such as returning a lost wallet, was a fool's errand, and that rational self-interest should lead them to keep the money! Nor is the dismal science without impact on its own practitioners. A recent study comparing charitable giving rates among professionals from different fields found that economists were at the bottom of the giving list, far below what would be expected on the basis of their income.[2]

Like economics, the field of political science represents the person as driven by self-interest, an assessment that heavily influences how historians and social scientists interpret political behavior. Yet the evidence suggests that this characterization is a half truth at best. Political scientist David Sears has spent his career patiently accumulating evidence that, in fact, people's political activities—their patterns of voting, the organizations to which they contribute money, the campaigns they work for, the causes they support—are heavily influenced by their concern for others, rather than their concern for self. This is not to say that self-interest has a trivial impact on behavior. Rather, Sears has found, as have others, that people often undertake political actions that favor what they believe is best for society, and these actions can be directly counter to their personal interests. They support school bonds long after their children have left school. They vote to increase benefits for civic workers even though the funds will come from their taxes. On issues ranging from health care and war to energy shortages and crime, people follow their consciences. Sears's evidence is extremely persuasive. Yet the attacks on his carefully documented position are vociferous and strident, as if something about the idea that caring might dictate political behavior sticks in the craw of his critics.[3]

We make excuses for our altruism. People often engage in acts of great compassion, yet when they are asked why they did it—volunteering their time, for example—they give pragmatic reasons for their actions: "It got me out of the house," or "It gave me something to do," or other acceptable explanations to avoid being labeled a "do-gooder" or a "bleeding heart." When people leave the voting booth and are asked by pollsters how they voted, they typically provide a self-interested explanation: "This will benefit my children," or "This candidate will put more dollars in my pocket." But when voting behavior and actual self-interest are compared against each other, they sometimes show little relation. Even our charities now feel obliged to give something back—a chocolate bar for a school donation, a CD of listener favorites for $50 to the local classical radio station, a Jerry Garcia coffee mug for a $100 donation to PBS, and so on. Didn't we used to give generously without these incentives?

Even when we know our own behavior isn't motivated by self-interest, we assume other people's behavior is.[4] When a group of wealthy Americans came out against the repeal of the estate tax a couple years ago, people were stunned. The explanations these wealthy Americans provided, not without some embarrassment, was that America had given them so much, they felt the government was entitled to take some of it back. Not everyone was persuaded, however, and newspaper articles and commentators tried to ascertain what these seemingly altruistic Americans stood to gain from their stance.

We look at every act of unselfishness with a suspicious eye. When we recognize that tending is an intrinsic part of our nature—that unbridled selfishness does not inevitably rule over our behavior—we will have made a good beginning. Changing an expectation of selfishness to an expectation of cooperation will lead us to look at our institutions and one another's behavior in an enlightened way.

A SECOND APPROACH to creating a tending society involves tackling our hierarchies head on. Simply put, social class hierarchies unravel the social fabric. Every relationship is put under strain and suffers as a result, from ties between parents and children to relations between coworkers and friends. When people simply do not have what they need to get by—and, at least as important, observe that others do—then social institutions and relationships become yet another source of strain, rather than the supportive resources they would otherwise be. These problems worsen as the gap between rich and poor widens, and people pay a high price to live in a society that tolerates these gaps. Sociologist Richard Wilkinson has shown that beyond a certain basic income, your health is influenced more by the gap between rich and poor than by your absolute income.[5]

One way to see this is by comparing the death rates of countries that have small gaps between the rich and poor with those that have large gaps. For example, Cuba and Iraq are both poor nations with an equivalent gross domestic product (per capita) of $3,100, but the gaps between rich and poor are much smaller in Cuba than in Iraq. Accordingly, people in Cuba live a full 17.2 years longer than people in Iraq. The United States is a much wealthier nation than Costa Rica, yet in Costa Rica, where income gaps are small, life expectancy is higher.[6]

Where income differences are large, people perceive the social environ- ment to be more hostile, and tending suffers. Civic participation drops. People belong to fewer social groups, such as community groups, fraternal organizations, choruses, and sports teams. Fewer people vote, and fewer people serve in local government or volunteer for political campaigns. And income inequality erodes tending as well. The bigger the income gap, the more violent crime a state has, the higher the homi- cide rate,[7] the higher the divorce rate, and the higher the infant mortal- ity rate. Epidemiologist Ichiro Kawachi and his colleagues maintain that in countries or states where income inequality is greatest, even the fun- damental bonds of social cohesion and trust break down. For example, in their studies, they ask people which of the following statements they believe: "Can most people be trusted or would most people try to take advantage of you if they got the chance?" As income inequality increases, so does the number of people who endorse the second option.[8]

When we make our hierarchies extreme and inflexible, we corre- spondingly erode tending. Obviously, we will never eliminate hierarchy altogether—it seems to be in our nature, as we have seen—but we can mute its impact. Any time we as a social group do something that increases people's educational achievement or income, we make a dent in these inequalities. Any time we say no to outrageous compensation packages, we make a dent. Any social policy we pursue that increases a person's standard of living makes another dent. Any effort to increase autonomy at work will make a dent. Any time we reach across social classes to solve a problem collectively, whether drunk driving, age dis- crimination, or air pollution, we make a dent. There is no magic bullet that will suddenly propel everyone to the top of the social class ladder and improve their health. But after enough dents, perhaps the gradient will begin to flatten, and the strain that erodes our tending will begin to ease.

GRADUALLY, WE'RE COMING to recognize the importance of tending in our institutions as well. These creeping insights have come in part from the entry of women into fields that were traditionally the province of men. As women have moved into these positions, the visibility of tending skills and their relation to effective performance have become more clear. Two examples make this point well.

Eight percent of the nation's police officers are women, and as their numbers have risen, so has our recognition of the value their tending skills bring to the job. In most respects, men and women in the police force look much the same, but in potentially volatile situations, women's abilities to manage situations that might escalate or turn violent have proven very useful. Women handle domestic violence, disputes between neighbors, and rape cases especially well. They are far less likely than male officers to have complaints filed against them by members of the community they serve.

Let's put these observations into economic terms. In the 1990s, the city of Los Angeles paid out $53.8 million to settle lawsuits brought against police officers for use of excessive force. Male police officers accounted for $50.8 million of that total. Although men outnumber women in the force by 4:1, payouts in brutality cases involving male officers exceeded those of female officers by 23:1, payouts involving male officers killing a suspected perpetrator exceeded payouts for female officers by 43:1; and for assault and battery, 32:1. Male officers also had judgments of $10.4 million brought against their departments for sexual abuse, sexual molestation, and domestic violence, whereas not one penny was paid out on these grounds for women officers. The tending skills that women have brought to police work have been vital to turning around community perceptions of the police.[9]

The business world provides another object lesson. For decades, corporate America has seemingly been a stronghold of the self-interested position, and yet nowhere is the value of social and empathetic skills more in evidence. Of the social skills that account for success in the marketplace, persuasion—that is, the ability to get others to buy in to one's ideas—is perhaps the most vital. The ability to convince others that an idea is exciting and to use skills for building consensus are essential to developing the cooperative mission so critical to any business success. What companies increasingly value over technical talents are emotional and social competencies, such as being adaptable, trustworthy, and able to work with others.

When women first began entering the upper echelons of business, pessimistic articles proclaimed their inevitable failure and solemnly maintained that their lack of experience on sports teams would preclude their effective cooperation with others. I remember hooting with laughter at the time. From an early age, girls and women have somewhat better social and emotional skills than boys and men, and they get a lot of practice using them. To be sure, they don't get much experience crashing around on a football field, but they do spend a lot of time talking with others, finding out what others are thinking about, and working to soothe hurt feelings and restore good ones. As people began to realize the significance of social skills in the workplace, it was virtually inevitable that the effectiveness of women in management would be noticed as well. Much of this evidence has accumulated recently, when consulting companies that were evaluating business management stumbled on the fact that women were doing very well indeed.

Business Week recently reviewed the results of several independent surveys on issues unrelated to gender and discovered that they converged on the same findings. Whereas men and women were equivalent in strategic planning skills and issue analyses, women consistently outperformed men in motivating others, fostering communication, and listening to others. In one study, for example, interviewers evaluated fifty-two management skills, and women scored higher than men on forty-two of them. Among the findings: Women thought through decisions better than men, were more collaborative, and sought less personal glory. Women also outperformed men on overall work quality, recognizing new trends, and developing new ideas. One consultant commented that, with respect to the skills he sees as most vital to success in business, women excel at most of them, including personal scrutiny, coaching, networking, public speaking, team building, communication, and flexibility.[10]

What are the men doing wrong? This question was posed to a consultant who had conducted one of the studies. His immediate reaction was that men were trying to live up to an outmoded stereotype of what a male leader should be like—aggressive and controlling, dictating solutions to problems, instead of building consensus.

The case I want to make by using these examples is not about bringing women into traditionally male occupations. It is about bringing in the skills that the inclusion of women has made especially salient. The skills once labeled as "feminine" have been found to be so advantageous that programs to train business leaders in these skills have sprung up around the country. The top-down military style is giving way to a consensus-building style.

Firms now refer to "relationship capital," the wealth that is embedded in the relationships they have with their clients. Paradoxically, because consumer choices are so vast and because business is often no longer done on a face-to-face basis, relationships are now more important than ever, because otherwise there is no contact, no loyalty, none of the personal qualities that traditionally keep people coming back to the same company. The value of social skills for maintaining relationship capital is undeniable.[11]

The importance of social and emotional skills becomes especially evident when people lack them, as the following example suggests. For many years, the medical establishment enjoyed a certain immunity from lawsuits; patients were grateful for any efforts to treat their disorders. In the 1950s, that picture began to change, and insurance companies began to see an abrupt rise in the number of malpractice suits being filed. Researcher Richard Blum set out to understand this increasing trend toward litigation and studied the records of the legal cases to see what accounted for it. Blatant cases of malpractice were easily explained, and so Blum focused his efforts primarily on what he identified as discretionary malpractice cases, those cases in which a patient might or might not file a claim. Why did some patients act on their sense of maltreatment and outrage and others not?

As he looked through the records, he began to see that some physicians were especially "suit prone," that is, they had an unexpectedly high number of discretionary legal actions filed against them. Blum zeroed in on what distinguished these suit-prone physicians. His findings were very clear. Patients described these physicians as uninvolved and unemotional, indifferent to their pain and incapable of showing an emotional response to their plights. They were considered to be uncaring, condescending, and derogatory in manner. Patients said their medical complaints were rudely dismissed, their requests for explanations were ignored, and their phone calls were not returned. Quite simply, these suit-prone physicians lacked emotional and social skills. And so the patients retaliated by filing suits when their treatments left them less than satisfied.[12]

Recognizing the benefits of tending in all aspects of society ought to prompt a reassessment of its worth. Even a brief glimpse reveals how little societies reward tending occupations. The fields of nursing and elementary school teaching are suffering chronic shortages, as the women who used to fill these positions discover they can make better incomes doing almost anything that has traditionally been regarded as men's work. Infant and toddler care pays so poorly that it is not a viable living for many of the women who populate its ranks. Two of our chief tending occupations—motherhood and caregiving to spouse and relatives—are unpaid, and recent economic studies of both document the economic costs of this neglect.[13]

Women have moved into many areas of life that were previously the province of men, yet there has been little movement in the other direction. Men's occupational patterns, for example, are virtually unchanged. The world's tending jobs are undervalued and pay so poorly that men have little incentive to move into caregiving roles. As long as tending is not rewarded, these patterns will remain stagnant or grow worse.

PEOPLE VARY IN their capacities for tending and in the resources they bring to it. Here, too, a tending society would intervene. Tending begins in the womb, and so we can begin by taking better care of mothers. The United States is one of the few countries of the world that has no national health program. Women who become pregnant are left to arrange their own prenatal care; those with insurance get it, and those without insurance make do with whatever clinic services are available. Young, low-income mothers who lack good health care are most at risk, and their babies are most vulnerable. Their babies are often born early with the congenital weaknesses that a harsh environment only aggravates.[14]

By intervening with these high-risk mothers, we can offset some of this potential damage. Visits from a midwife, nurse, or social worker who provides emotional support and useful information about how the pregnancy is progressing have been successful in lowering pregnancy-related complications. Assistance such as providing food or vitamins can improve birth outcomes as well. Even regular phone calls to check on a mother's progress and to discuss problems that have developed show discernible effects on birth outcomes. In one British study, for example, women who had been in such an intervention gave birth to bigger babies and were less likely to have a preterm delivery. When you recall that poor tending often interacts with problems that can develop during pregnancy or birth, thus producing damaging trajectories of poor mental and physical health across a lifetime, it becomes clear how important early intervention is.[15]

Knowing how to parent is one of the more vital skills people need, and yet we invest more resources in teaching people how to drive than we do in teaching them how to care for children. We give high-risk babies back to young girls who are themselves still children. We let neglectful parents make whatever child-care arrangements they can afford, without much thought to the emotional well-being of their children. The solution is not to snatch these children away from their ignorant parents, but to educate the parents, to teach them the difference between good and bad parenting, and to let them know what the true and lifelong emotional and physical risks of neglectful or harsh parenting really are.

Interventions that teach parents how to parent better hold considerable promise. There is no question that children at risk—children of young, inexperienced mothers, children of abusive or neglectful parents, children with genetically based risks, or children who otherwise are not getting enough nurturance—profit from efforts to enrich and "warm up" the early environment. When risky family conditions are mild or moderate, we can succeed in getting parents to be more nurturant with their children, spend more time with them, read to them, and have fun with them. Parents who are taught how to be supportive and warm become better parents.[16]

If any further inducement is needed to protect children from risky families, it is this: People treat their own children as they were themselves treated. From vervet monkeys to humans, one of the clearest influences on how a mother treats her young is how she was treated during her own childhood. In monkeys, mothers who were themselves mistreated or deprived in infancy never mother their own offspring as well as nurtured monkeys do. Men and women who were physically abused as children are quite likely to become abusive parents themselves. And as we've seen, it doesn't take full-fledged abuse to produce these effects. Harsh or neglectful families produce much of the same damage. We live with the legacy of risky families for a long time.[17]

Another way we can intervene is by raising the status of the world's tenders. The United Nations' efforts to improve the quality of life throughout the world have focused on several key points, one of which is improving women's educational opportunities. These efforts to promote women's literacy and educational attainment have had more impact on the health of a society than many other more direct interventions. In countries where women are better educated, infant mortality rates are lower and children's health is better. In countries where women are educated, even men live longer. When the world's tenders have resources, everyone is healthier.[18]

What can we do to improve the ability of communities to offset the stressors that children face? As we saw in Chapter 10, many of our neighborhoods, especially the low-income ones, have grown toxic, exposing children to crime, violence, drug use, and other chronic debilitating stressors. Building "social capital"—the infrastructure of a community that brings people together—is widely recommended as a point of intervention. Britain's prime minister recently formed a commission led by Sir Donald Acheson to come up with specific interventions to reduce social class inequalities in health. Chief among its recommendations were efforts to build social capital—youth organizations, neighborhood centers, health clinics, and other community institutions.[19]

Scientists have long been intrigued by resilience—how people overcome what would seem to be punishing conditions in early life and go on to unexpected accomplishments in economic, intellectual, and social life. We still know little about resilience from a scientific standpoint, but one factor stands out. Children or adults with a mentor—one person committed to their welfare—are more likely to show this resilience. The grandmother who taped vocabulary words to the mirror for her grandson to memorize each morning, the pastor who raised scholarship money for a talented student who would otherwise not go to college, the veteran who inspired a youth ready to drop out of school, the teacher who tutored a young, unmarried woman through high school—these are the parents of resilience.

More than 2,000 studies of mentoring have documented an array of benefits in mentoring interventions of all kinds. Many of these benefits involve skill improvements, but most of them also produce changes in commitment and attitudes on the part of the protégés. The most striking aspects of protégés' accounts are the psychological and social benefits they report, as some of the following examples attest.

- A mentoring intervention with low-income pregnant girls produced fewer preterm and low-birth-weight babies, compared to community statistics. A similar intervention with young mothers found a higher rate of completed and on-time immunizations and fewer signs of neglect or disorganization in the home.[20]
- A mentoring program with at-risk adolescents led to fewer school absences, better relations with parents, and improvements in academic performance.[21]
- Army nurses who participated in a mentoring program had greater job satisfaction and were more likely to plan to stay in the profession.[22]
- Mentoring proved instrumental to the success of women lawyers in terms of earnings, promotion opportunities, and career satisfaction.[23]

Although most of the formal studies of mentoring involve minorities and women, studies of naturally occurring mentoring indicate that men benefit as well. Men who say they had a mentor in their early career recount specific gains that mentoring helped them achieve, such as more rapid advancement, and also report more satisfaction with their career paths.[24]

Indeed, perhaps the most common outcome of studies on mentoring is the enhanced satisfaction the protégés experience in their chosen professions or activities. These benefits are sometimes seen many years after the mentoring has taken place. Mentoring is a stunning example of our abilities to minister to strangers, to turn unfamiliar people into friends, and to ameliorate the course of a life that could otherwise go wrong.

ARE WE READY to absorb the lessons of tending? Many social critics would argue that precisely the opposite is true at the present time, that, instead, we are in the midst of a sea change in which, rather than making the most of the tending that is so much a part of our nature, we are becoming more like the individualistic, self-interested people we so often tell ourselves we are. Certainly, there is an argument to be made for this position.

The fact that our social connectedness has waned is startlingly evident. In *Bowling Alone*, Harvard professor Robert Putnam documents in full and unnerving detail our declining participation in virtually every aspect of social and civic life. From local politics to just having friends over to dinner, our social ties have weakened. Instead of heading off to the local tavern, we watch TV. Instead of talking with one another, we go online. Instead of playing ball in a vacant lot with friends, our children play video games. Increasingly, our activities are solitary. We play video games against the computer, not with a real opponent. We roam the Internet instead of sending a letter. We laugh at the antics of our favorite TV characters, but they don't smile back.[25]

These trends are accompanied by disturbing increases in psychological and social pathology that have been linked in part to declining social ties. For example, in the last thirty years, we have seen a two- to three-fold increase in suicide, especially among young men. While women are not killing themselves in the same numbers, depression among women has risen to extraordinary levels: one in seven women may expect to experience a major depression during her lifetime. A recent study compared national rates of anxiety in the U.S. population, first in 1952 and again in 1993. In both children and adults, anxiety has soared during the intervening forty years.[26]

To try to understand these trends, psychologist Jean Twenge of Case Western Reserve University examined several possible contributors to the increased rates of psychological distress. One of her early hypotheses was that simply trying to make a decent living is now a more harrowing and difficult job than it once was. But fairly quickly Twenge ruled out economic concerns as the cause underlying this change. Instead, she found that the most anxious people were those who had suffered adverse social changes in their lives, such as getting divorced, being the child of a divorce, witnessing crime, or being a victim of crime. A decline in the sense of social connectedness and a perception that the social landscape has become more dangerous are chiefly responsible for the epidemic of distress.[27]

The stubbornly high divorce rate is also evidence of our compromised tending. As would be expected from the evidence I've provided so far, chronic marital conflict, separation, and divorce are major stressors that adversely affect physical and mental health. Separated and divorced people get sick more and for longer periods than married people. They make 30 percent more visits to physicians than married people, and they are more likely to become and remain chronically ill and disabled. They are more vulnerable to infectious diseases, especially fatal ones. Separated and divorced people are especially vulnerable to depression and are six times more likely to seek psychiatric help than people who remain married.[28]

Nor do we have any right to be sanguine about the impact of divorce on children. While it is certainly true that exposure to constant conflict and hostility is worse for a child than an amicable divorce, the evidence concerning the impact of divorce on children gives no basis for optimism about its effects. Even into adulthood, people from divorced families experience a greater risk of illness and early death.[29]

Clearly, it will do little good to tell people not to get divorced or to exercise more sense and caution about whom they marry. We do, however, need to be clear-eyed about the adverse effects on personal health and the health of children by recognizing that the breaking of such bonds comes at enormous cost.

What these social trends suggest is that friendships will become an ever more important part of the social landscape. Many of us no longer live close to parents, siblings, and other relatives who provided the social ties that sustained us throughout our early history. When families began to disperse across a wide geographic area in response to industrial development, we lost a major set of sustaining ties. The high rates of separation and divorce among couples have eroded these sustaining ties further. Friendship is the bond most likely to fill these voids.

A recent *New York Times Magazine* devoted to intimate relationships made it clear just how vital friendships are coming to be. One columnist argued that a "tribal" phase of life, marked by close ties with a small group of friends, will bridge the gap between living with parents and marriage.[30] This has already become common and meets many of the same needs that have typically been met by family. Nonetheless, it puts a lot of responsibility on friendships, bonds that are not cemented by kinship, sexual ties, or formal commitment. Do friendships have the ability to fill this gap? Women have known for centuries that their bonds with other women sustain them and have drawn on them to meet this need throughout their lives.

Striking evidence for this point was recently driven home to me when my colleagues, Regan Gurung, Teresa Seeman, and I recently looked at social relationships among the married elderly to see which ties were perceived to provide the most support. The typical older man in our study said that his main source of social support was his wife. The typical older woman in our study said that her main sources of support were her children, her relatives, and her friends. Since all the people were married, this is a telling difference.[31]

Friendship may well become the mainstay of social life. It already is for the never married or divorced. Once we recognize and fully appreciate its significance, the motivation to use it more effectively may come about. On the whole, women seem to be better at providing the emotional and health benefits of friendship, yet men do have this capacity.

In a study by Ladd Wheeler and associates (which I described in Chapter 5), college students who spent their time with women friends better avoided the loneliness and distress of social isolation during the December holidays, whereas those who spent their time with men friends did not. However, when the men and women in Wheeler's study indicated how "meaningful" their contact with others had been, the picture changed: the meaningful contacts with men were as successful at reducing loneliness as simply being with women friends.[32]

Need we accept the harsh assessment that we are now a country of social isolates? Certainly, the decline in civic and political participation is very real. And, without question, certain types of ostensibly asocial activities have seen a correspondent rise, such as television viewing and Internet surfing. But even as society is becoming less connected, there are trends that work in the other direction. We've become a nation of cell phone users, carrying our social support network around with us to help us make even the smallest transition ("We're on the ground, I'll call you from the baggage claim").

When I went to college, I talked to my parents on Sundays (because the rates were lower); after ten minutes, my father would say, "Well, we're wasting your inheritance" and hang up. My own children are in college now, and I hear from them nearly every day, either via e-mail or free long distance. To be sure, a lot of these exchanges consist of "Gotta go. Calculus test" or "What temperature do you cook fish at?," but it makes us an ongoing part of one another's lives in ways that my weekly calls did not do to nearly the same degree. My students tell me they have friends from high school whom they e-mail every day, even several times a day. We may indeed watch too much TV and eschew our civic obligations, but we're certainly not out of touch.

I think we should stop assuming that the impact of our current culture necessarily undermines what is good about our social relationships. Instincts have the ability to express themselves in very unlikely ways. Use of the Internet may rob us of some of our time with others but it does not deprive us of a feeling of connectedness. Those who go online regularly often report an exhilaration in their feelings of being tied to others.[33] Even the characters so many of us enjoy on television do some of the same things our friends do—they make us laugh, help us to see that our difficulties may not be as great as we imagine, and distract us from our problems for a while. In the psychology courses I teach, I have been struck by how television characters find their way into conversations about relationships, ranging from why people connect in the first place, to how breakups are handled, to whether certain characters will ever get together romantically. After a few minutes of spirited conversation—everyone has these "friends" in common, after all—there will be a moment of embarrassed laughter, as it dawns on the students that they have just vigorously debated the motives and actions of people who do not actually exist. Should we be surprised that fictional characters are social contacts, even sources of social support? Not if we recall that social support is often at its best when it's invisible, present only as a protective but unused resource.

Can this kind of support actually reduce stress the way real support can? Consider a futuristic study by La Trobe University psychologist Einar Thorsteinsson and his colleagues. They brought people into their laboratory and asked them to perform a demanding computer task that was highly stressful. Half of the participants saw an accompanying videotape in which a same-sex person made socially supportive remarks—"you're doing well," "that's good"—while the other half of the participants performed the same task without benefit of this support. Those who saw the videotape of supportive comments (which was preprogrammed and had nothing to do with them personally) nonetheless responded to the task with lower heart rate and cortisol levels (an indicator of HPA stress responses) than did those who did not.[34] It's remarkable the comfort that an imaginary friend can provide.

I do not want to push this point too far, because imaginary friends are a very minor substitute for real social contact. What about our real contacts? Are men and women ready to develop and use tending skills? According to *Fortune*'s study of the millennial generation, we may indeed be witnessing a shift on these very issues. Perhaps because they have seen the fallout of self-absorption firsthand in their parents' generation, young adults born since the early 1980s say that relationships are key to their thinking about the future—marriage, time with children, relationships with coworkers, friendships. Moreover, these bonds are important to men and women alike. Whether a newfound commitment to relationships is rising to replace an entrenched commitment to individual self-interest remains to be seen.[35]

NURTURANCE AND CARING are wired in to our nature. As the creature with the big brain, we acquire vital emotional knowledge early in life. When the initially strange and threatening becomes reassuringly familiar, we acquire the ability to discern the intentions and motives of others, sometimes using this knowledge to further our own ends, but often using it to meet the needs of others, to give solace, and provide companionship. Our nurturance and caring lives right alongside our selfish indifference and aggression. Sometimes the selfish side overwhelms the nurturing side, but often our caring gains control, and even if it does not eliminate the more base or violent tendencies, it can at least subdue them.

Certainly, as we've seen, harsh treatment in childhood fuels a daunting array of physical and mental health risks in adulthood. But are those risks inevitable or irreversible? It is unlikely. Adults are not inevitably prisoners of their childhoods. Resilience, as I've noted, is also ubiquitous in the human spirit, and tending in adulthood, such as that found in a close friendship, a strong marriage, or a supportive mentoring relationship, represents the key to resilience.

The animal cross-fostering studies, in which a pup with a genetic risk is fostered to an unrelated mother, have revealed eye-opening, even eye-popping, results. The genetic risk seems to vanish under certain rearing conditions. Not only do these studies reverse the "natural" behavior, they create a new behavior that is transmitted to future generations. This process, bearing the complicated name nongenomic intergenerational transfer of behavior, is one of the most profoundly optimistic lessons to be learned from the study of genes and the environment. This plasticity of genetic trajectories speaks more persuasively than perhaps any other kind of evidence to the potential for interventions to profoundly affect the environmental conditions that influence the expression of genetic risks.[36]

The concepts of plasticity in the neurocircuitry and resilience in psychology are mirrored in behavior by the concept of flexibility. I've noted several times that humans have a big neocortex that enables us to do a lot of things that we wouldn't ordinarily do. Women and men have little if any trouble doing tasks that are traditionally performed by the other sex. The older you get, the more you appreciate just how flexible these roles can be.

What is striking about human behavior is how, despite our many differences, the qualities that make people good leaders, mentors, parents, and friends are the same. Caring and tending to others have long been considered the talents and responsibilities of women, but as is evident in fathering, in mentoring, and in the profiles of our enduring leaders, men have these same capabilities; when they use them, they profit as well.[37] Social ties are the cheapest medicine we have. When we erode our social and emotional ties, we pay for it long into the future. When we invest in them instead, we reap the benefits for generations to come.

Notes

Chapter 1: The Power of Tending

1. Widdowson (1951).
2. See Bell (2001) for a discussion of how caregiving has been relatively ignored in work on evolutionary theory. Unlike other "instincts," which are possessed by individuals, tending assumes the form of reciprocal, complementary relationships between individuals that are evoked by need or signals of distress, maintained by attachment or bonding, and sustained by a common or overlapping biology, with the primary function of regulating, especially reducing, physiological and neuroendocrine responses to stress. This tending affects brain development, genetic expression, the development of social and emotional skills, stress responses, and health. These effects are especially evident in the mother-infant interaction but continue throughout life and are affected by all tending relationships and their absence as well.
3. Moore (2001).
4. See Baumeister and Leary (1995); Caporeal (1997).
5. Dettwyler (1991); Silk (1992).
6. In arguing that there is an affiliative neurocircuitry that underlies social relationships of all kinds, I do not mean to suggest that the *same* hormones are involved in all social relationships. There is considerable differentiation based on what the relationships are. Nonetheless, there do seem to be some overlap and commonalities in the underlying biological structure. For perspectives on these issues, see Panksepp (1998) and Carter, Lederhendler, and Kirkpatrick (1999).

7. Sanders and Gray (1997). For a general discussion of the important role that environ-mental and behavioral influences play in regulating gene activity, see Gottlieb (1998).
8. For biological perspectives on infanticide, see Hrdy (1999); Van Schaik and Dunbar (1990).

Chapter 2: The Origins of Tending

1. Stress responses may be thought as of adaptive mechanisms that allocate energy among different bodily functions including immunity, growth, reproduction, muscle action, and cognition. Conditions of threat lead to reallocation of resources from the normal steady state to prepare the body to meet a challenge. For a discussion of the historical origins of the fight-or-flight response, see Cannon (1932) and Selye (1956). For a per-spective on how the fight-or-flight metaphor has guided research on stress and coping, see Taylor (1999). For an early account of the centrality of social relationships to cop-ing in my work, see Taylor (1989).
2. See Taylor, Klein, Lewis, Gruenewald, Gurung, and Updegraff (2000) for an analysis of the gender composition of stress studies; see Rodin and Ickovics (1990) for a discussion of the underrepresentation of women in clinical trials. In a particularly remarkable example, 100 percent of the testing of the active agent in weight-loss pills (phenyl-propanolamine) was done on men, despite the fact that 90 percent of the users of weight-loss pills are women (Hamilton, 1989).
3. Scientists believe that during our early prehistory, humans opted for fewer offspring spaced far apart. Because each child requires so much care, births may have been spaced up to four years apart or more so that women could provide a continual source of nutri-tion through lactation and manage foraging demands while simultaneously caring for an infant. With the development of agriculture, these demands on the mother subsided somewhat, making larger families with more offspring spaced closely together possible (see Hrdy, 1999, for a discussion of these issues).

   Parasympathetic regulation plays an important role in these processes, which I will largely relegate to the footnotes. The parasympathetic system is an important counter-regulatory influence on the sympathetic activation of fight or flight. Any time we see an animal's or human's stress responses compromised by long-term exposure to stress, we need to entertain the hypothesis that parasympathetic functioning, in addition to sym-pathetic regulation, may have been altered in response to these stressors.
4. See Repetti (1989, 1997, 2000) and Repetti and Wood (1997). For another perspective on this issue, see studies on work spillover effects; specifically, these studies show that men are more likely to bring their stress home from work into the family environment than women are (see Bolger, DeLongis, Kessler, and Schilling, 1989; Stets, 1995).
5. Luckow, Reifman, and McIntosh (1998). Note that there is substantial cross-cultural evidence for this finding as well (Edwards, 1993; Whiting and Whiting, 1975).
6. Early life experiences literally craft HPA functioning. Meaney and his associates have found that early life stimulation in the form of gentle stroking attenuates behavioral and neuroendocrine responses to stressors across the life span, but in contrast, early life exposure to protracted stress (usually separation from the mother) leads to exaggerated

stress responses (Anisman, Zaharia, Meaney, and Merali, 1998; Liu et al., 1997; Meaney et al., 1996; see also Ladd, Owens, and Nemeroff, 1996; Suchecki, Rosenfeld, and Levine, 1993). The most common research paradigm used for studying stress in infancy in animal models and its impact on development is the maternal separation paradigm in which infants are removed from the nest for specified periods of time and then returned. This is a highly stressful process not only for infants but for mothers as well and leads to dramatic increases in stress hormones for both (e.g., Levine, Wiener, and Coe, 1993). Susceptibility to illness during infancy may be affected as well. Bailey and Coe (1999), for example, found that maternal separation disrupted the integrity of the intestinal microflora in infant rhesus monkeys, rendering them potentially susceptible to opportunistic bacterial infections. Separation from the mother also increases vulnerability to a broad array of potential causes of death including cancer and susceptibility to the adverse effects of toxins (Ader and Friedman, 1965; Schreibner, Bell, Kufner, and Villescas, 1977). For extensions of this reasoning to human offspring, see Chorpita and Barlow (1998); Flinn and England (1997); Hertsgaard, Gunnar, Erickson, and Nachmias (1995).

7. Many studies have now shown that maternal contact leads to reduced distress in the mother and infant upon being reunited (see, for example, Coe, Mendoza, Smotherman, and Levine, 1978; Mendoza, Coe, Smotherman, Kaplan, and Levine, 1980). Studies suggesting that an offspring's stress responses are enhanced by maternal separation and/or reduced by maternal attention following a threatening event include Gunnar, Gonzalez, Goodlin, and Levine (1981); Kuhn, Pauk, and Schanberg (1990); Mendoza, Smotherman, Miner, Kaplan, and Levine (1978); Pihoker, Owens, Kuhn, Schanberg, and Nemeroff (1993); Reite, Short, Seiler, and Pauley (1981); Stanton, Gutierrez, and Levine (1988); Wang, Bartolome, and Schanberg (1996). The extent to which these calming and soothing processes are dependent on physical contact is not fully known, especially with respect to humans, but the importance of physical contact for development is driven home by Tiffany Field's creative research on premature babies. Field and her colleagues demonstrate that premature babies who receive massage therapy (three fifteen-minute sessions for five to ten days) gain between 31 and 47 percent more weight than those not receiving the massage intervention (Field, 2001). The importance of physical contact in appropriate animal infant development has also been demonstrated in the groundbreaking work of Harry Harlow and his colleagues on infant monkeys (Harlow and Harlow, 1962). Studies of orphans who received little attention and who were deprived of physical contact (Carlson and Earls, 1997; Spitz and Wolff, 1946) clearly imply that early tactile deprivation has permanent adverse effects that may parallel those seen in experimental studies with animals, including a reduced number of glucocorticoid receptor binding sites in the hippocampus and the frontal cortex.

For discussions of the relation of oxytocin to maternal behavior and to reduced stress responses, see Carter, Williams, Witt, and Insel (1992); Drago, Pederson, Caldwell, and Prange (1986); Fahrbach, Morrell, and Pfaff (1985); Gibbs (1986); Martel, Nevison, Rayment, Simpson, and Keverne (1993); McCarthy, Chung, Ogawa, Kow, and Pfaff (1991); McCarthy, McDonald, Brooks, and Goldman (1996); Panksepp,

Nelson, and Bekkedal (1999); Uvnas-Moberg (1996; 1997); Windle, Shanks, Lightman, and Ingram (1997); Witt, Carter, and Walton (1990). The exact role that oxytocin plays in maternal behavior, including human maternal behavior, is not yet known. Oxytocin facilitates a rapid conditioning association to maternal odor cues but not to nonsocial stimuli (Nelson and Panksepp, 1998), suggesting its significance to maternal tending. In animal studies, oxytocin appears to affect the initiation of maternal behavior, but not its maintenance. For example, if a female rat receives an oxytocin antagonist (that blocks the usual effects of oxytocin), she will fail to show maternal behavior; but if she has already engaged in maternal behavior, an oxytocin antagonist has no impact on maternal behavior (Witt and Insel, 1991). A dilemma with borrowing too heavily from animal models for understanding the effects of oxytocin, however, is that its effects are highly dependent upon where the receptors for these hormones are (Insel, Winslow, Wang, and Young, 1998).

8. Kendrick, Keverne, and Baldwin (1987); Kendrick and Keverne (1989).

9. Evidence from animal studies for the significance of endogenous opioid peptides in maternal and protective behavior toward infants includes Kendrick and Keverne (1989); Martel, Nevison, Rayment, Simpson, and Keverne (1993); and Panksepp, Nelson, and Bekkedal (1999). The activation of the beta-endorphin system during late pregnancy and suckling may promote positive affect arising from maternal bonds, and the pharmacological reduction of opioid activity may promote a state comparable to that which occurs when the safety of the offspring is threatened. For example, in one study, the administration of an opioid receptor blocker (naltrexone) to rhesus macaque mothers or infants increased their affiliative behavior and clinging after separation and reunion (Kalin, Shelton, and Lynn, 1995). Similarly, the administration of the opioid blocking agent naloxone to juvenile macaques resulted in their seeking contact with their mothers and soliciting grooming (Martel, Nevison, Simpson, and Keverne, 1995; Schino and Troisi, 1992).

10. In animals, hormones are more important for the initiation of maternal behavior than for its maintenance, although these patterns are species-specific. In human mothers, there are reliable changes in hormones that occur during pregnancy and birth, but psychological responses of caregiving do not track hormonal changes. The physiological and hormonal events of pregnancy and the period immediately postbirth may facilitate the onset of maternal responsiveness by sensitizing the mother to a complex array of infant stimuli. Once the mother begins caring for the infant, maternal behavior may be maintained by the caregiving experience itself, the mother's own preferences, and the characteristics of her infant, including the signals that the infant sends that evoke caregiving. Specifically, both mother and child (as we see in Chapter 3) typically form attachment bonds that begin in pregnancy and strengthen following birth, which are implicated in the complex interactive behavioral program that evolves between child and caregiver. Maternal behavior depends also on distress vocalizations (crying or other sounds emitted by the baby) (see, for example, Zeskind and Collins, 1987). For general references to the maternal caregiving system, see Corter and Fleming (1990), Fleming, Ruble, Krieger, and Wong (1997); Maestripieri (1999), and Rosenblatt (1990).

Is oxytocin necessary for the initiation of maternal behavior? Russell and Leng (1998) conducted studies in transgenic mice in which the oxytocin gene had been knocked out and examined the impact on maternal behavior. Both parturition and maternal behavior proceeded without oxytocin (OT). The authors expressed surprise, given the wide range of evidence suggesting that OT influences parturition, maternal behavior, lactation, sexual behavior, and gonadal function. They speculated that one of the reasons may be redundancy in the mechanisms that elicit and maintain these behaviors.

11. In at least some animals, oxytocin may be important for social recognition, that is, for recognizing that one has met a particular partner before. Ferguson and colleagues (2001) used a knock-out oxytocin gene mouse model to study this issue and found that mice in whom the oxytocin gene had been knocked out failed to display any signs of social recognition to partners whom they had previously encountered. However, when exogenous oxytocin was administered prior to an initial encounter, it led to social recognition, even in the oxytocin knock-out mice. The authors argued that oxytocin receptor activation in the medial amygdala is necessary as well as sufficient for social recognition in the mouse.

12. Adler, Cook, Davidson, West, and Bancroft (1986); Altemus, Deuster, Galliven, Carter, and Gold (1995); see also Chiodera and colleagues (1991); Dunn and Richards (1977); Light, Smith, Johns, Brownley, Hofheimer, and Amico (2000); Lightman and Young (1989); Suh, Liu, Rasmussen, Gibbs, Steinberg, and Yen (1986); Uvnas-Moberg (1996).

13. Jezova, Jurankova, Mosnarova, Kriska, and Skultetyova (1996). See Taylor et al. (2000).

14. See, for example, Clarke-Stewart (1978); Spelke, Zelazo, Kagan, and Kotelchuck (1973); Yogman (1990). For a primate perspective, consider Suomi (1977).

15. Wynne-Edwards and her colleagues have found that both men and women have high concentrations of prolactin and cortisol in the period just before birth and lower postnatal concentrations of sex hormones (testosterone or estradiol) (Storey, Walsh, Quinton, and Wynne-Edwards, 2000; Wynne-Edwards, 2001), which suggests some hormonal commonalities in the biology underlying mothering and fathering. See Mota and Sousa (2000) and Ziegler and Snowdon (2000) for primate perspectives on fathering and its relation to prolactin.

16. Carter (1998); Panksepp (1998).

17. For references to fathering, the reader is referred to Clarke-Stewart (1978); Lamb (1977); Pedersen (1980); Pedersen, Rubenstein, and Yarrow (1979); Spelke, Zelazo, Kagan, and Kotelchuck (1973); Yogman (1990). For a primate perspective, consider Suomi (1977). Mothers who reside in secure households characterized by the presence of a mate or kin are more able and willing to provide high-quality child care. Those without a mate or kin may exhibit poorer parenting. Significantly, the findings of Repetti (2000) (that when working women came home they were highly nurturant with their children) extended primarily to mothers in intact families. When she looked at the behavior of low-income single mothers, she was more likely to find withdrawal than affectionate maternal care following a stressful day at work.

18. In referring to fatherhood as a backup system, I don't wish to offend devoted fathers, especially single fathers. In the United States, the number of single-parent families headed by fathers has risen dramatically over the past twenty years, up from approximately 600,000 to more than 2.2 million at the present time. Single-father households make up 2.1 percent of all American households (by comparison, single-mother households are 7.2 percent). These statistics represent a significant trend in the United States, although the extent to which they are mirrored worldwide is questionable (Fritsch, 2001).

Chapter 3: The Tending Brain

1. Adolphs (1999); Baron-Cohen et al. (1999); Brothers (1990); Dunbar (1998). Scientists believe that social intelligence is quite separate from general intelligence and that it draws on different parts of the brain, including the amygdala, especially the left amygdala, which identifies complex emotional information from faces; and areas in the prefrontal cortex that help with short-term memory for social information (Baron-Cohen et al., 1999). In 1990, Brothers proposed that a network of neuroregions in the orbitofrontal cortex, superior temporal gyrus (STG), and amygdala compose the social brain. Using fMRI technology, Simon Baron-Cohen and his colleagues (1999) subsequently were able to show that the STG, the amygdala, and certain areas of the prefrontal cortex showed increased activation when people were doing tasks requiring social intelligence. They interpreted their results as supportive of Brothers's social brain hypothesis.
2. Darwin (1871/1952), p. 566.
3. Darwin (1871/1952), p. 566.
4. Kaplan, Hill, Hawkes, and Hurtado (1984). See Boehm (1999); Hrdy (1999) for discussions of this issue.
5. Doing several tasks at once *may* be a significant difference between men and women. Some scientists have speculated that this skill—multitasking—has been important enough to women's survival that it may be reflected in sexually dimorphic brain development. Women's brains are less lateralized (that is, women are especially likely to draw on both hemispheres for certain tasks), and the hemispheres have a thicker tissue connection (in the corpus callosum) than is true for men. For example, women engage both sides of their brain when talking with others, compared to men. Might this be a reason why women typically pick up more incidental information about social situations, such as nonverbal communication? Fisher (1999) has suggested that women's contextual abilities and skills for doing several things at once may be hardwired in the brain, reflected in differences like these.
6. Field, Woodson, Greenberg, and Cohen (1982). By twelve to eighteen months, infants spontaneously check a speaker for intentional cues such as gaze direction, emotional expression, gestures, and body posture to help interpret the speaker's actions and verbalizations. For example, following an emotional outburst by an adult, infants less than two years of age will spontaneously follow the person's gaze to see what aspect of the environment might have provoked the emotional response (see

also Baldwin, 2000; Meltzoff and Moore, 1977). Face perception seems to be a special aspect of social cognition. People use different brain regions for face recognition than they do for other kinds of objects (for example, see Farah, Wilson, Drain, and Tanaka, 1998; Kanwisher, McDermott, and Chun, 1997).

Play, especially with the mother early in life, is thought to be one vehicle by which emotional and social skills develop (Stern, 1983). Pellis and Iwaniuk (2000) found that 60 percent of the variance in playtime across primates is accounted for by degree of prenatal brain growth, consistent with the argument that play is important to postnatal development.

7. Both studies with monkeys (Harlow and Harlow, 1962) and studies with humans (Spitz and Wolff, 1946) have revealed that close contact with a mother or live caregiver is important to normal adult behavior. For example, monkeys raised with an artificial mother (i.e., a terrycloth mother) and isolated from other monkeys during the first six months of life showed disruptions in their social behavior in adulthood. They failed to interact normally with other monkeys, their sexual responses were inappropriate, and they showed either highly fearful or abnormally aggressive behavior. They were also less likely to groom other monkeys, and females who had children became poor mothers, at least with their firstborns (Harlow and Harlow, 1962). Work by psychoanalyst John Bowlby in the 1950s and 1960s identified attachment as the mechanism underlying phenomena like these. He defined attachment as an evolved biobehavioral system designed to regulate behavior in a potential caregiver. Because infants are born immature and require a long period of vigilant care, they signal to a caregiver through crying, reaching, clinging, and other behaviors what their needs are. This system, according to Bowlby, has evolved in order to facilitate survival. Like the Harlows, Bowlby suggested that the inability to form a secure attachment to one or more people in the early years of life interferes with the ability to develop close relationships in adulthood (Bowlby, 1969; 1988).

One of the most revealing examples of the underlying coordination between mother and infant occurs when the mother, acting under instructions from a researcher, holds herself with a still face, looking at the baby, but not showing any indication of emotion or responsiveness to the baby's expressions. At first, the baby makes efforts to communicate, expressing distress and gesturing actively; then it avoids the mother's expression; and finally these efforts give way to harsh protesting, such as crying and other gestures, that attempt to entice the mother back into this synchronous interaction.

8. Psychologist Nalini Ambady and colleagues (1993) have found that people are remarkably accurate at making complex judgments on the basis of brief observations of "thin slices" of nonverbal behavior, mere seconds in length. In one study, Ambady and Rosenthal (1993) showed college students approximately thirty seconds of a professor's nonverbal behavior (without sound) and found that those ratings predicted the professor's teaching ratings at the end of the semester very well.

9. Size of the neocortex in primates correlates with the length of the juvenile period, but not with length of gestation, amount of time spent nursing, or the reproductive life span. This point is suggestive evidence that the "software programming" of the social learning of the juvenile period influences brain development (Dunbar, 1998).

10. To clarify some terminology: The frontal cortex refers to everything in front of the central sulcus (a major vertical dividing line in the brain) and is often used interchangeably with the term "neocortex," referring to its presence only in phylogenetically modern species like humans and monkeys—therefore it is the "new" cortex. The prefrontal cortex is the front half of the frontal cortex.

11. Damasio (1994), pp. 57–58.

12. Carlson and Earls (1997). See Gunnar (2000) for evidence regarding long-lasting damage. Some researchers have suggested that the rocking, head-banging, self-mutilation, and cutting that may be seen in some of these deprived youngsters are distorted manifestations of a self-soothing system, related to the capacity of pain to activate the brain's opioid systems (Perry and Pollard, 1998). Low levels of norepinephrine in the brain may also be associated with self-injurious and repetitive behaviors. Interestingly, mother-deprived monkeys display similar odd behaviors, including rocking, hugging themselves, sucking on their fingers, biting themselves, banging their heads, and other activities, like those seen in the Romanian orphans.

13. See Taylor, Peplau, and Sears (1999) for a discussion of evaluation in impression formation. Additional evidence for the importance of the friend-foe distinction includes the fact that threatening, angry faces draw attention quickly and are more accurately detected than friendly or neutral faces. The threat advantage can be attributed to its survival value (Ohman, Lundqvist, and Esteves, 2001; see also Taylor, 1991, for a review of the initial advantage that negative information enjoys).

14. See Taylor (1991). Extensive research on automatic cognitive processes has documented a pervasive tendency to nonconsciously classify most, if not all, incoming stimuli as either good or bad. This occurs very rapidly without any cognitive effort or even awareness of the process and leads to corresponding tendencies to approach or avoid the incoming stimulus as a result (Chen and Bargh, 1999).

15. See Adolphs (1999). My presentation of emotion regulation in the human brain is oversimplified as a dialogue between the prefrontal cortex and the amygdala. In fact, as noted, human emotion is regulated via a complex circuit consisting of the orbitofrontal cortex, the amygdala, the anterior cingulate cortex, and several other interconnected regions (Davidson, Putnam, and Larson, 2000).

16. Le Doux (1996) suggested that the brain is fundamentally an emotional organ. Scientists now believe that even moral reasoning, once thought to depend entirely on the capacity for rational thinking, is now critically dependent on emotions. Evidence for this assertion includes the fact that areas of the brain implicated in emotional processing show activation when people are pondering moral dilemmas (Helmuth, 2001).

17. University of Wisconsin psychologist Richard Davidson and his colleagues, for example, have amassed extensive evidence that the prefrontal cortex modulates the time course of emotional responding, evidenced, in part, by extensive reciprocal connections between the amygdala and the prefrontal cortex. Their findings suggest that the prefrontal cortex normally inhibits the amygdala, shortening the time course of emotional responding, especially the amount of time required to recover from a strong emotional state. These patterns are consistent with a general model that maintains that higher order cortical processes of the sort that are learned early in life help to

moderate what would otherwise be strong emotional and stress responses to novel and especially threatening stimuli (Davidson, 1998).

18. Mere exposure to a person (or any stimulus, for that matter) leads to a more positive reaction to it on a next exposure. This positive effect of familiarity is found in many species, ranging from chickens to humans (Zajonc, 1965; 1968; 2001) and probably reflects the damping down of threat responses that occurs in the presence of a familiar stimulus. Indeed, familiarity seems to be a basic determinant of how incoming information is processed. When people sense that incoming information is familiar to them, they are more likely to process that information nonanalytically with automatic heuristically based strategies that require little thought. In contrast, when incoming information is unfamiliar, people switch to a more analytic, systematic way of processing information (Garcia-Marques and Mackie, 2001).

19. Stress hormones released during emotionally arousing situations also modulate memory processes (see also McGaugh, Cahill, and Roozendaal, 1996).

20. Liu and colleagues (1997); Meaney et al. (1996).

21. See Repetti et al. (2002) for a review of this literature; see also Perry and Pollard (1998). The emotion skills that result from early parent-child interactions and on which so much subsequent social behavior depends have been grouped under the umbrella term "emotional intelligence" (Goleman, 1997). Emotional intelligence is defined as the ability to monitor one's own emotions and others' emotions, to discriminate among various emotional states, and to use the information to guide one's own thinking and actions toward others (Mayer and Salovey, 1993).

22. Repetti et al. (2002).

23. Repetti et al. (2002); Eisenberg, Fabes, Shepard, Guthrie, Murphy, and Reiser (1999).

24. Repetti et al. (2002). Much of the work that has related family interaction to the development of emotional and social skills involves going into the home and looking at how parents and children relate to one another and then assessing those children's behaviors in other environments outside the home such as in school. A wealth of studies shows the significance of family interactions for emotional development. For example, Dunn, Brown, and Beardsall (1991) found that three-year-old children's conversations about feelings states with their mothers and siblings predicted their later ability to recognize emotions expressed by others. Feldman, Greenbaum, and Yirmiya (1999) found that children who experienced synchronous affective states with their mothers during play had greater self-control two years later, after controlling for other predictors of self-control such as temperament, maternal style, and IQ. Manifold studies demonstrate that children who live with a depressed parent or who witness or experience domestic violence are at risk for developing poor strategies for managing their emotions, and several authors have suggested specific interventions to help at-risk children develop emotion regulation skills (see Repetti et al., 2002, for a review). The evidence relating the ability to control negative emotions to social competence is manifold as well. Children who are better able to manage their emotions are judged to be more socially competent in peer interactions (Fabes et al., 1999). Eisenberg and colleagues (1996), for example, found that children who demonstrated sympathy for others and related empathetic qualities were perceived by teachers to be more socially competent.

Adding fuel to the argument that social and emotional skills are vital to managing stressful situations are animal studies exploring this relation. For example, Gust, Gordon, Hambright, and Wilson (1993) found that rhesus monkeys who had greater social skills with respect to affiliative behavior and evaluations of potential threats had lower cortisol (HPA) responses to these events than monkeys with poorer such skills. Sapolsky (1990; see also Sapolsky, 1998) found a relation between greater social skills and lower cortisol responses to stress among olive baboons.

25. See Repetti et al. (2002) for a review; see Davies and Cummings (1995) for an example. Psychopathology in the mother (such as depression) can disrupt early social and emotional development in the infant, which, in turn, may lead to parallel disturbances in biological systems prognostic for emotional distress (Dawson, Hessl, and Frey, 1994).

Chapter 4: *Good and Bad Tending*

1. The ideas in this chapter draw heavily on three previous papers: Repetti, Taylor, and Seeman (2002); Taylor, Repetti, and Seeman (1997); and Taylor, Sage, and Lerner (2002).

2. Nearly 3 million children are abused each year in the United States, 1,400 of whom die each year at the hands of a parent or other family member. Another 18,000 live with permanent disabilities from abuse, and nearly 40,000 more children need immediate medical attention (such as setting a broken bone) to avoid a permanent impairment (U.S. Department of Health and Human Services, 1999). Scientists who study abuse believe that these statistics underestimate the extent of death and permanent injury. Child abuse is associated with markedly elevated rates of major depression and other psychiatric disorders in adulthood. Early stress, as from abuse, also alters the development of the HPA axis and the serotonergic system, among other neurobiological changes (Kaufman, Birmaher, et al., 1998; Kaufman, Plotsky, Nemeroff, and Charney, 2000). SNS and HPA hyperactivity, presumably due to CRF hypersecretion, are persistent consequences of childhood abuse (Heim et al., 2000; see Cicchetti and Carlson, 1989).

3. Repetti, Taylor, and Seeman (2002). Jane Goodall observed a similar pattern in the chimpanzees she studied at Gombe (1999). Mothers who were playful, affectionate, tolerant, and supportive raised offspring who as adults had relaxed temperaments and good relations with community members. Mothers who instead were more harsh, less caring, and less playful raised offspring who as adults tended to be tense and ill at ease.

What determines whether a parent will be a good or a bad one? This issue will be only implicitly covered in this book, so I address it directly here with references for those readers who are interested in exploring the issue further. Basically, warm parental care with minimal neglect or abuse comes from parents who have secure (nonneurotic, not anxious) personalities, who grew up in families marked by good caregiving, who had some experience with play mothering (as through caring for younger siblings or baby-sitting), who had relatively stress-free pregnancies and early postbirth periods (in part, because problems during pregnancy and birth can aggravate a child's temperament), who have children with good temperaments, and who parent in an environment that is low in stress and high in social support (see Belsky, 1984). In contrast, neglectful or abusive parenting most often occurs when a parent is insecure or neurotic, had a growing-up experience that was marked by poor tending, had a stressful pregnancy and postpartum period, and lives in a highly stressful environment with little or no social support (see Maestripieri, 1999). I will focus a bit on the role of the stressful environment (this chapter, Chapter 10), and on learning from one's own parents (Chapter 11), but less on the other factors. It is clear, though, that there are reliable temperamental differences that affect parenting. Even in rats, there are strains in which mothers are high lickers and groomers and those in which mothers are low lickers and groomers (see, for example, Liu et al., 1997). See Ladd and colleagues (2000); Sapolsky (1998) for related observations in animal studies.

4. Evidence relating gaps in emotional development to subsequent psychopathology is manifold (Izard and Harris, 1995; see Repetti et al., 2002, for a review). Disobedience, noncompliance, and aggression appear to be fostered by coercive, negatively demanding, and physically punishing patterns of parenting (Martin, 1981; Patterson, 1986). This appears to be true not only in contemporary Western society, but throughout the world (Rohner, 1975). (See Dodge, Pettit, and Bates, 1994.)

   Ladd and colleagues (2000) demonstrated that the quality of the primary caregiver–infant bond influences an individual's ability to adapt to challenges throughout life. Their model, though based entirely on studies with rats, features emotion-regulation-like processes (specifically, anxiety, depression-like symptoms) as important intervening variables. They found consistently that separation from the mother in early life influences anxiety and fearlike behavior that lasts well into adulthood and that the interaction between a genetic vulnerability or acquired vulnerability in early life, coupled with adverse early life events, is the genesis of many of these disorders. It is rare to see such a fully developed animal model in which the evidence so closely parallels human data, and the experimental precision of the animal model, coupled with evidence of the same relations in humans, lends strength to the viability of these arguments.

5. I am going to talk about a warm, nurturant (though not overprotective) parenting style as a "good" mothering style. From the standpoint of mental and physical health, such a judgment is defensible. From an evolutionary standpoint, such a characterization is meaningless, however. Generally, there are trade-offs in mothering style. Mothers who are more rejecting can produce more offspring, but mothers who are more protective have increased infant survival (Fairbanks, 1996).

6. Taylor, Repetti, and Seeman (1997).

7. Felitti, Anda, Nordenberg, Williamson, Spitz, Edwards, Koss, and Marks (1998); see also Russek and Schwartz (1997); Walker, Gelfand, Katon, Koss, Von Korff, Bernstein, and Russo (1999). In a survey of 1,225 women, Walker and colleagues (1999) compared women with and without histories of maltreatment as children with respect to physical health status, functional disability, health risk behaviors, common physical problems, and physician diagnoses. Women who had experienced maltreatment as children had a wide range of adverse physical health outcomes including poorer overall

health, greater physical and emotional disability, more distressing physical symptoms, and a large number of health risk behaviors. Women who had multiple types of mal-treatment showed the greatest health problems.

8. See Repetti et al. (2002) for a consideration of these methodological issues and a review of these observational studies.

9. Taylor, Sage, and Lerner (2002).

10. Harris (1995; 1998).

11. See, for example, O'Connor, Deater-Deckard, Fulker, Rutter, and Plomin (1998). Johnson, Cohen, Brown, Smailes, and Bernstein (1999) found that people with docu-mented child abuse or neglect were more than four times as likely as those not abused or neglected to be diagnosed with personality disorders in adulthood. These relations persisted after parental psychiatric disorders were controlled statistically, thus reduc-ing the viability of the alternative explanation that shared genetic variance accounted for the psychopathology in the children.

12. See Repetti et al. (2002) for a review. There is abundant evidence that caregiver psy-chopathology, such as depression or hostility, can adversely affect the infant's mental development, and growing evidence that patterns of emotional interaction in early life may be a powerful mediator of these effects (Trevarthen and Aitken, 1994).

Weaknesses that are aggravated by adverse early parenting can also come from problems experienced during pregnancy or birth. An example comes from a study of 4,000 boys in the United States who were studied first at birth and again eighteen to twenty-two years later by Adrian Raine and his colleagues (Raine, Brennan, and Med-nick, 1994; Raine, Brennan, Mednick, and Mednick, 1996). They looked, first, to see which boys had been exposed to a biological risk during pregnancy (a bacterial infec-tion in the uterus, for example) and at-birth complications (such as low birth weight). They also looked at the newborn's environment including whether the family life was stable, whether the mother or father had a criminal record, and the like. Finally, they interviewed the mother about her attitudes toward her baby, focusing on whether she had wanted her baby or whether she had contemplated abortion or tried to put her baby up for adoption. They then looked at the criminal records up to age twenty-two for four groups of boys: those with birth complications only, those with adverse social conditions only, boys with neither a biological nor a family risk, and boys who had both a biological risk and a rejecting early environment. They found that boys who had suffered complications during pregnancy or birth and boys whose mothers had rejected them at birth were both more likely to have engaged in a violent crime by the age of eighteen than boys who had neither of these risks. But the boys who had *both* the biological risk *and* an unloving home environment were more than twice as likely to have a record of theft or violent crime by age eighteen. When their parents had a harmonious marital life and the home environment was nurturant, even boys who were biologically at risk did pretty well.

13. Single genes do not determine most human behaviors; instead, most behavior depends on an interplay between environmental factors and multiple genes (McGuf-fin, Riley, and Plomin, 2001). Phenotypes evolve to maximize their fitness in different environments, reflecting their adaptive plasticity. Phenotypic plasticity is the ability

of an organism to express different phenotypes depending on characteristics of the environment. It has long been known that chemistry, physiology, development, morphology, and behavior influence phenotypes in response to environmental cues (see Agrawal, 2001; Losick and Sonenshein, 2001). See Plomin, DeFries, McClearn, and Rutter (1997) for a discussion of gene-environment interactions.

14. Children with more difficult temperaments are typically more reactive, and the same amount of maternal attention will not have the same effect on a highly reactive child as on a less reactive child. This means that maternal nurturance may be especially important with children who have difficult temperaments, but simultaneously more difficult to provide, especially if the mother shares a similar temperament (see, for example, Easterbrooks, Cummings, and Emde, 1994, for a discussion of this issue).

The evidence that excessively harsh, abusive, or neglectful families contribute to emotional disorders and substance abuse, independent of shared genetic factors, was recently given additional weight by Johnson et al. (2001), who controlled for family pathology in their environments. See also O'Connor, Deater-Deckard, Fulker, Rutter, and Plomin (1998).

The idea that a risky family environment interacts with genetically based or acquired weaknesses also suggests that genetic factors may confer hardiness or resilience, leading to protection against some of the more deleterious stressors of life. Anisman and his associates (1998) conducted a study that is suggestive on this point. They identified mice from strains that were prone either to be highly reactive to stress (from a neuroendocrinological standpoint) or less reactive to stress. When the highly reactive mice were cross-fostered to dams of a strain that was less reactive to stress, the maternal attention from the less reactive mother was protective, as others have found. (For example, in adulthood these mice were less reactive to stress and showed better HPA functioning.) More interesting was the fact that when young mice from the less reactive strain were cross-fostered to dams high in stress reactivity, the mice did not show the adverse effects of being raised with a reactive mother. They appeared to be protected by their genetic predisposition.

15. Kagan (1997); Kagan, Snidman, and Arcus (1992). Jerome Kagan and his associates are in the vanguard of research on behavioral reactions to unfamiliar events. They have identified an inherited form of extreme shyness characterized by a lower threshold for arousal in limbic sites, most notably the amygdala, that contributes to shyness in childhood and to extreme degrees of social avoidance in adulthood (Kagan, Reznick, and Snidman, 1988). Shyness is also associated with greater relative right frontal EEG activity (Schmidt, 1999). Kalin and associates (1998) noted that cortisol levels and relative right asymmetric frontal activity in the brain are correlated, which suggests that extreme asymmetrical frontal electrical activity, cortisol levels, and trait-like fear may co-occur, at least in the animal studies they have conducted.

16. Steven Suomi reports from his laboratory at Emory University that rhesus monkeys who are genetically predisposed to extreme shyness but reared by especially tolerant foster mothers have above average relationships with their peers, demonstrating much the same effect as Emily's mother had on Emily's behavior (Dess, 2001). More generally, when monkeys who have high HPA reactivity to stressors are cross-fostered to

mothers who are less reactive to stress, they are typically low in stress reactivity as adults. When cross-fostered to a mother also high in HPA reactivity, however, the expression of genetically based reactivity is readily seen (Suomi, 1987; 1997).

17. Higley and colleagues (Higley, Mehlman, Higley, Fernald, Vickers, Lindell, Taub, Suomi, and Linnoila, 1996; Higley, Mehlman, Poland, Taub, Suomi, and Linnoila, 1996) found that high serotonin turnover rate and corresponding low levels of circulating serotonin were associated with aggression, risk taking, and premature death among rhesus monkeys. Mehlman and associates (1995) found that male monkeys with high concentrations of a serotonin metabolite (CSF 5-HIAA) exhibited more social competence and emigrated from their social groups at a later age, whereas males with low concentrations were less competent and emigrated at an earlier age (see also Lesch et al., 1996; Fahlke, Lorenz, Long, Champoux, Suomi, and Higley, 2000). Aggression and violence appear to represent faulty emotion regulation, influenced, in part, by the prefrontal cortex, which receives a major serotonergic projection. Abnormal patterns of prefrontal activation are found in individuals who show impulsive violence (Davidson, Putnam, and Larson, 2000). For studies relating serotonin and aggression in humans, see Brown et al. (1982); Brown, Goodwin, Ballenger, Goyer, and Major (1979); Coccaro, Kavoussi, Trestman, Gabriel, Cooper, and Siever (1997); Coccaro, Kavoussi, and Hauger (1995); Manuck, Flory, McCaffery, Matthews, Mann, and Muldoon (1998); Pine et al. (1997).

18. References for the clustering of problem behaviors and for the theory that strong interrelationships among adolescent problem behaviors exist because they have common causes and influences include Biglan, Metzler, Wirt, Ary, et al. (1990) and Jessor and Jessor (1977). See also Barnes, Reifman, Farrell, Dintcheff (2000); Barrera, Chassin, and Rogosch (1993); Campo and Rohner (1992); Caspi et al. (1995); Denton and Kampfe (1994); DiBlasio and Benda (1990); Duncan, Duncan, and Strycker (2000); Fisher and Feldman (1998); Miller, Forehand, and Kotchick (1999); Newcomb, Maddahian, and Bentler (1986); Shedler and Block (1990); Small and Luster (1994); Spoth, Redmond, Hockaday, and Yoo (1996); Turner, Irwin, Tschann, and Millstein (1993); Wills and Cleary (1996). Researchers have suggested that the appearance of the behavioral cluster may be related to the changes in the brain that occur during adolescence. Among the prominent brain transformations of early adolescence are alterations in the prefrontal cortex, limbic brain areas, and their dopamine input, systems that are sensitive to stress and form part of the neural circuitry that modulates the motivational value of drugs and other reinforcing stimuli. These developmental transformations of the brain may predispose adolescents to substance abuse (Spear, 2000a; 2000b). Whether the adolescent succumbs to the risks incurred by these changes, however, appears to be modulated by the early family environment.

Moss and colleagues (1999) developed a model for intergenerational transmission of substance abuse liability. Specifically, they argued that offspring who were raised with a parent who had a substance use disorder coped with this situation over time by developing HPA (specifically cortisol) underresponsivity and that HPA hyporeactivity, as an adaptation to chronic stress, may in turn have disposed them to substance abuse.

19. To assess the impact of early social skills on the ability to develop and sustain romantic relationships later in life, psychologist Rand Conger and his colleagues (2000) studied nearly 200 children, first when they were in seventh grade and then again when they were age twenty. They found that those who had grown up in nurturant, involved families were more likely to have strong romantic relationships nearly a decade later, compared with those who did not, largely because the former group had better skills for managing stress, conflict, and insecurities.

20. Peterson (1998), reported in Capaldi, Crosby, L., and Stoolmiller (1996); Wills and Cleary (1996).

21. People raised in conflict-ridden or otherwise harsh environments may develop long-term changes in brain serotonergic functioning. Evidence from animal studies suggests that reduced serotonergic responsivity is tied to aggression and impulsivity as well as to an increase in the reinforcing properties of nicotine and alcohol (e.g., Higley et al., 1996a; 1996b; see Stanford, Greve, and Dickens, 1995, for related human evidence). Taken together, these findings suggest that alterations in serotonergic functioning may be one pathway whereby individuals from risky families are at risk for both behavior problems and problems with substance abuse (Matthews, Flory, Muldoon, and Manuck, 2000).

22. See Coplan et al. (1998) for a relevant animal model for these processes; animal evidence relates maternal deprivation to numbers of serotonin receptors in the hippocampus and cortex (Vazquez, Lopez, Van Hoers, Watson, and Levine, 2000). See also Koob, Sanna, and Bloom (1998). There is significant evidence relating smoking, alcohol abuse, and drug abuse to enhancement of serotonergic activity (Balfour and Fagerstrom, 1996; Jaffe, 1990; Ribeiro, Bettiker, Bogdanov, and Wurtman, 1993; Stahl, 1996; Valenzuela and Harris, 1997). Abuse of substances may function, in part, to alleviate feelings of depression or hostility that arise in conjunction with serotonergic dysfunction (e.g., Stahl, 1996).

23. Abuse-related posttraumatic stress disorder is related to dysregulation of daily levels of norepinephrine, epinephrine, dopamine, and cortisol (Heim, Newport, Miller, and Nemeroff, 2000; Lemieux and Coe, 1995).

24. Much of my characterization of the impact of stress on these biological systems has come from the work of Bruce McEwen and his associates on allostatic load (McEwen, 2002; McEwen, 1998; McEwen and Seeman, 1999; McEwen and Stellar, 1993; Seeman, Singer, Rowe, Horwitz, and McEwen, 1997; Seeman, McEwen, Rowe, and Singer, 2001). McEwen's viewpoint is that the many events of daily life that elevate our physiological systems create wear and tear on the body, reflecting not only the effects of stressful life experiences, but their interaction with genetic predispositions, individual habits (such as diet, exercise, and substance abuse), and developmental experiences that set lifelong patterns of behavioral and physiological reactivity. All contribute to the buildup of wear and tear, leading to premature aging. Research by Cohen and colleagues (2000) has shown that stress responses show a moderate to high degree of stability and that cardiovascular, immune, and endocrine reactivities are intercorrelated, providing evidence of a relatively unified stress response.

25. Abrupt increases in heart rate or blood pressure, as are experienced in repeated bouts of stress, may lead to injury of the endothelium of the arteries, infiltration of plasma lipoproteins into the intimal area of the arteries (as a result of enhanced permeability of regenerating endothelial cells), and a release of mitogenic substances that foster proliferation of intimal smooth muscle cells, all of which promote atherosclerosis (Clarkson, Manuck, and Kaplan, 1986).

People who have more reactive biological systems, either by virtue of genetic or acquired vulnerabilities, show greater reactivity to stress; however, eventually these systems can lose their elasticity, giving way to hyporesponsive systems instead (Cacioppo et al., 1995; McEwen, 1998).

26. Allen, Matthews, and Sherman (1997).

27. Stress can alter the activity of several important cortical neurotransmitters, and neurotoxic exposure to adrenal steroid hormones, particularly early in life, can induce permanent changes in these transmitter systems in the corticolimbic regions, such as the hippocampus and the cingulate gyrus, both of which have a high density of glucocorticoid receptors (e.g., Benes, 1994). Through this mechanism, exposure to severe stress in the early, postbirth period could induce alterations in the circuitry of the anterior cingulate cortex and hippocampus, which can interfere with normal attention and learning. Kaufman and colleagues (1998) found evidence of HPA axis dysregulation in depressed, abused children that paralleled the pattern of HPA dysregulation reported in animal studies of chronic stress. See also Gold, Goodwin, and Chrousos (1988a; 1988b).

28. Evidence for the neurotoxicity of glucocorticoids in primate brains comes from studies by Uno and colleagues (1994; Benes, 1994; see also Sapolsky, 1992a). The glucocorticoid cascade hypothesis of hippocampal aging has substantial research to support it (McEwen, 1999; McEwen, de Leon, Lupien, and Meaney, 1999).

29. Some overweight middle-aged people are heavy through the hips, whereas other people carry their weight in their abdomen; i.e., they have big guts or "beer bellies," as many men like to call them. Scientists refer to these two types of people as "pears" and "apples" respectively, because of their distinct shapes. It is not particularly healthy to be either a pear or an apple, but between the two, being an apple is worse. Men and women who carry their excess weight through the midsection are at greater risk for health problems, especially coronary heart disease. A high waist-to-hip ratio (which is the measure of "apple-ness" scientists use) is tied to impaired glucose tolerance, impaired insulin resistance, high "bad" cholesterol, low "good" cholesterol, and high levels of fibrinogen in the blood. All of these factors increase risk for coronary heart disease and for late-life onset of diabetes (Epel, McEwen, Seeman, Matthews, Castellazzo, Brownell, Bell, and Ickovics, 2000; Larsson, Svardsudd, Welin, Wilhelmsen, Bjorntorp, and Tibblin, 1984).

30. Catecholamines affect immune-related changes (Benschop, Rodriguez-Feuerhahn, and Schedlowski, 1996). Abnormal infant rearing of infant rhesus monkeys was found to be related to long-lasting effects on the immune system, likely to have health consequences later in life (Coe, Lubach, Schneider, Dierschke, and Ershler, 1992; Lubach, Coe, and Ershler, 1995).

31. Sephton, Sapolsky, Kraemer, and Spiegel (2000) found that a flattened or abnormal diurnal cortisol rhythm predicted early mortality in breast cancer patients. Sapolsky and Donnelly (1985) found that if a tumor of a certain type is induced to grow in a rat, it will grow faster if the rat is repeatedly stressed, probably because of the glucocorticoids that are secreted during stress. To test this hypothesis, they infused young rats with extra glucocorticoids at the end of each stressful event in a way that mimicked the shut-off problem of old rats, and the young ones grew tumors faster as well. (See Cole, Naliboff, Kemeny, Griswold, Fahey, and Zack, 2001, for a perspective on stress reactivity and the progression of the HIV virus).

32. Chalmers and Capewell (2001); the co-occurence of somatic and psychiatric illness is well established in the adult literature (Cohen, Pine, Must, Kasen, and Brook, 1998). See Repetti et al. (2002) for a review. There is also a high degree of comorbidity between borderline personality disorders and substance use disorders, as would be expected from this analysis (Trull, Sher, Minks-Brown, Durbin, and Burr, 2000). (See also Kessler et al., 1994; Knopman and colleagues, 2001; Vanhanen and Soininen, 1998.)

33. Seeman, McEwen, Rowe, and Singer (2001). The health effects of maternal nurturing may be seen very early in life. For example, nurturant behavior on the part of the mother can affect the levels of certain bacteria in the intestines (Bailey and Coe, 1999). Inasmuch as infectious diarrhea is one of the major causes of death in infants, maintaining a proper balance in the microflora of the intestine is important. Other research has shown that the mother-infant interaction is so close and synchronized that, when the mother is under stress, wheezing in children at risk for asthma increases (Wright, Cohen, Carey, Weiss, and Gold, in press).

Chapter 5: A Little Help from Friends and Strangers

1. Hobel, Dunkel-Schetter, and Roesch (1998); see also Hobel, Dunkel-Schetter, Roesch, Castro, and Arora (1999); Sandman, Wadhwa, Chicz-DeMet, Dunkel-Schetter, and Porto (1997).

2. For animal studies of these issues, see Coe, Lubach, Karaszewski, and Ershler (1996); Reyes and Coe (1997); Roughton, Schneider, Bromley, and Coe (1998); Schneider, Coe, and Lubach (1992). As an example of the substantial impact the mother's emotional state has on her developing infant, see Lundy et al. (1999) regarding the impact of a mother's depression on her neonate.

3. Meijer (1985).

4. Catalano and Serxner (1992); Erickson and colleagues (2001). Wadhwa, Culhane, Rauh, and Barve (2001).

5. Dunkel-Schetter, Gurung, Lobel, and Wadhwa (2001); Feldman, Dunkel-Schetter, Sandman, and Wadhwa (2000). See also Collins, Dunkel-Schetter, Lobel, and Scrimshaw (1993); Kennell, Klaus, McGrath, Robertson, and Hinkley (1991); Oakley, Rajan, and Grant (1990); Sosa, Kennell, Klaus, Robertson, and Urrutia (1980).

6. Holden (2000), p. 580.

7. See, for example, Brooks-Gunn, Duncan, Klebanov, and Sealand (1993); Klebanov, Brooks-Gunn, and Duncan (1994); Kupersmidt, Griesler, DeRosier, Patterson, and

Davis (1995); Malmstrom, Sundquist, and Johansson (1999); Mayer and Jencks (1989). Children who live in physically unsafe neighborhoods also have fewer friends than those who live in safer neighborhoods, because their parents may keep them inside as a protective effort. Nonetheless, such efforts may strain social development (Lavrakas, 1982; Medrich, Roizen, Rubin, and Buckley, 1982).

8. E.g., Berkman, Leo-Summers, and Horwitz (1992); House, Landis, and Umberson (1988); House, Robbins, and Metzner (1982). Most of us understand that "friends are good medicine," but the degree to which this is true may not be fully appreciated. The importance of social isolation or lack of social ties as a risk factor for disease is equivalent to that of high blood pressure, obesity, and lack of exercise, and approximates that of smoking (House and colleagues, 1988). Memberships in affiliative networks do not, in general, buffer the impact of stressful life events on mental health, and their effects on physical health are modest. Emotional support and the perceived availability of support, however, do have strong positive effects on both mental and physical health (e.g., Kessler and McLeod, 1985). (See also Knox and Uvnas-Moberg, 1998.)

9. Berkman and Syme (1979); see also Holahan and Moos (1981); House, Landis, and Umberson (1988); Seeman (1996). In Berkman and Syme's study, the relationship between social ties and mortality was independent of self-reported physical health status at the start of the study, socioeconomic status, and health practices such as smoking, alcoholic beverage consumption, obesity, physical activity, and use of health services, as well as a cumulative index of practices known to affect health.

10. Cohen, Doyle, Skoner, Rabin, and Gwaltney (1997).

11. Sugiyama (1988); Boesch (1991).

12. See Diamond (2001) for a beginning effort to understand the physiological and neuroendocrine underpinnings of bonding. The ideas that adult caregiving and responses to strangers rely on attachment bonds not unlike those experienced between parent and child is gaining support in the psychological community (Feeney and Collins, 2001; see also Mikulincer and Shaver, 2001).

The capacity to develop bonds with strangers is not unique to humans, but it is probably one of our more distinctive qualities. Many of our primate relatives do not have this capacity to nearly the same extent. For example, monkeys who are separated from their mothers will be spared the substantial increase in stress responses that occurs during separation if they are placed in a social group, but only if they already know the other animals. If the animals are strangers, their presence merely aggravates the stress responses of the distressed monkey further (Levine, Weiner, and Coe, 1993). Although many human infants go through a period when they are terrified of strangers, it can quickly subside. In societies where children are raised by many adults, this early period of stranger anxiety may be virtually absent. Even young children bond very quickly with new caregivers or teachers and with unfamiliar children, with only short-term distress.

13. Spiegel and Bloom (1983); Spiegel, Bloom, Kraemer, and Gottheil (1989). See also Ell, Nishimoto, Mediansky, Mantell, and Hamovitch (1992); Goodwin, Hunt, Key, and Samet (1987); Reynolds and Kaplan (1990); Turner-Cobb, Sephton, Koopman, Blake-Mortimer, and Spiegel (2000). Support groups are, by no means, a cure-all for

illness, however, especially advanced and potentially fatal diseases. Recently, Goodwin et al. (2001) were unable to replicate the Spiegel and Bloom (1983) findings with metastatic cancer patients. This failure to replicate does not negate the earlier findings, but rather points out that social support is only one of many factors that influence the course of disease. Sometimes, even often, social support may not be sufficient to overcome other, more potent, influences on disease course.

14. I draw here on a published paper with my colleagues (Taylor, Dickerson, and Klein, 2001). See also Seeman and McEwen (1996); Roy, Steptoe, and Kirschbaum (1988); Uchino, Cacioppo, and Kiecolt-Glaser (1996).
15. Carter, Williams, Witt, and Insel (1992); Insel (1997); Popik, Vetulani, and Van Ree (1992); Uvnas-Moberg (1997; 1998; 1999).
16. See, for example, Epel, McEwen, and Ickovics (1998); Malarkey and colleagues (1994).
17. Taylor, Dickerson, and Klein (2000). See, for example, Jamner, Alberts, Leigh, and Klein (1998); Martel, Nevison, Simpson, and Keverne (1995); McCubbin (1993); Verrier and Carr (1991) for both animal and human evidence regarding the relation of EOPs and social support.
18. Biondi and colleagues (1986); Taylor, Dickerson, and Klein (2000); see Insel and Winslow (1998) for a discussion of serotonin and social behavior in animal studies.
19. Seeman, Berkman, Blazer, and Rowe (1994).
20. Uchino, Holt-Lunstad, Uno, Betancourt, and Garvey (1999).
21. Bolger, Zuckerman, and Kessler (2000); see also Taylor and Turner (2001).
22. Broadwell and Light (1999).
23. Fontana, Diegnan, Villeneuve, and Lepore (1999); Glynn, Christenfeld, and Gerin (1999); Kirschbaum, Klauer, Filipp, and Hellhammer (1995); Seeman, Berkman, Blazer, and Rowe (1994).
24. Wheeler, Reis, and Nezlek (1983).

Chapter 6: Women Befriending

1. See Hrdy (1999) for a discussion of these issues.
2. See Baumeister and Sommer (1997) and Belle (1987) for reviews. See also Laireiter and Baumann (1992); McFarlane, Neale, Norman, Roy, and Streiner (1981).
3. McClintock, personal communication (May 8, 1998); LeFevre and McClintock (1991) also found that isolation accelerated reproductive senescence in female rats.
4. DeVries and Carter (unpublished data, cited in Carter, 1998).
5. Hennessy, Mendoza, and Kaplan (1982); Saltzman, Mendoza, and Mason (1991).
6. This assertion is not as blatantly sexist as it may sound. My anthropologist friend is referring to the fact that women's groups tend to be informal, whereas men more commonly create formal and organized groups for political, social, and military purposes. Nonetheless, popular wisdom has long maintained that women do not naturally bond with one another, and studies of nonhuman primates have inadvertently conspired in this mythology (Parish and De Waal, 2000).
7. Caporeal (1997); Dunbar (1996).
8. De Waal and Lanting (1997); De Waal (1982); Taylor et al. (2000). About 30 million

years ago, Old World primates split into two lines, one of which includes baboons and macaque monkeys, the other of which includes humans. The human and ape line shows several splits, with gibbons peeling off the main trunk some 22 million years ago; orangutans, 16 million years ago; and gorillas, about 7 million years ago. Humans split off from chimpanzees about 6 million years ago, and bonobos from chimps about 3 million years after that. We share a great deal of our genetic makeup with all our primate relatives, but we are most closely related to chimps and bonobos.

9. De Waal (1996).

10. Baldwin (1985); see also De Waal (1996); Dunbar (1996); Mason and Epple (1969); Parish (1996); Parish and De Waal (2000). Caution should be used in generalizing from studies of primate groups. There are more than 130 different primate species, and there is substantial variability in whether and how female groups develop. While it would be unwise to draw direct links from primate behavior to humans, it would be foolish to claim that there is nothing to be learned from primate behavior merely because there is variability among primate species.

11. Dunbar (1996).

12. De Waal (1996); see also Silk (2000) and Wrangham (1980).

13. Hrdy (1999); Keverne, Nevison, and Martel (1999). Allomothering by related and unrelated females occurs in a number of primate species and may constitute up to 50 percent of the caregiving the infant receives (McKenna, 1981).

14. Dunbar (1996).

15. Dunbar (1996), pp. 20–21.

16. Bernstein and Ehardt (1986); Boesch (1991); Fossey (1983); Goodall (1986); Smuts (1987); Smuts and Smuts (1993); Sugiyama (1988); Wrangham (1980).

17. De Waal (1996), p. 205.

18. Boinski (1987; cited in De Waal, 1996).

19. Hrdy (1999).

20. E.g., Boehm (1999); Kaplan, Hill, Hawkes, and Hurtado (1984); Hrdy (1999).

21. Hrdy (1999). One of the reasons why adolescent girls may have been involved in child care is that they were not yet good at other tasks. Efficient and effective foraging takes a lot of effort and practice, and adolescent girls can be short on both. Consequently, until they have children of their own, adolescent girls in foraging societies typically do lighter work than the foraging that occupies their mothers and grandmothers, and child care is one of these lighter tasks.

Is "baby-sitting" experience vital socialization for the next generation of mothers? This may well be the case. When young female monkeys are deprived of maternal social contact early in life, they become inadequate mothers, and their inadequacies may include abuse and infanticide. Providing these socially deprived females with social contact and opportunities to provide maternal care subsequently improves the care of their own infants, but their care is never as good as that of females raised in the wild (Ruppenthal, Harlow, Eisele, Harlow, and Suomi, 1974).

22. Hrdy (1999). In the case of foraging societies, older women's adept and efficient foraging techniques may have provided them with more food than they needed for their own use, and so they likely shared it with relatives.

23. See Hrdy (1999) for a discussion of this issue. Corter and Fleming (1990) maintained that in most present-day cultures and probably in all hunter-gatherer societies, primary nurturant responsibilities resided with the biological mother. The fact that girls and women are still overrepresented in tending occupations is abundantly clear. Recent national surveys indicate that 85 percent of teenage baby-sitters are female. Women are nine times more likely than men to be involved in nursery school or kindergarten care of children (e.g., Digest of Education Statistics, 1996). More than 97 percent of child-care workers are women (Bureau of Labor Statistics, 2001).

24. Dunbar (1996); see also Silk, Seyfarth, and Cheney (1999). Mihalyi Csiksentmilhayi has found that, compared to boys, girls experience more positive affect and have higher self-esteem when they are talking on the telephone (personal communication, October 26, 2001).

25. Murphy and Murphy (1985), p. 134.

26. Daly and Wilson (1988; 1996); Goodman, Koss, Fitzgerald, Russo, and Keita (1993); Koss, Goodman, Browne, Fitzgerald, Keita, and Russo (1994); Malamuth (1998); Straus and Gelles (1986).

27. Counts (1990a). See Holtzworth-Munroe, Bates, Smutzler, and Sandin (1997).

28. Counts (1990a).

29. Mitchell (1990), p. 148.

30. Nash (1990).

31. Counts (1990 a, b).

32. Wolf (1975), p. 124.

33. Luckow, Reifman, and McIntosh (1998).

34. Biernat and Herkov (1994).

35. Clancy and Dollinger (1993); Cross and Madson (1997); Kashima, Yamaguchi, Choi, Gelfand, and Yuki (1995); Niedenthal and Beike (1997).

36. See Belle (1987; 1989) for reviews; Copeland and Hess (1995); Edwards (1993); McDonald and Korabik (1991); Ogus, Greenglass, and Burke (1990); Ptacek, Smith, and Zanas (1992); Veroff, Kulka, and Douvan (1981); Wethington, McLeod, and Kessler (1987); Whiting and Whiting (1975). A study by Dunbar and Spoors (1995) found that men and women had roughly the same size networks, but women have more females and more kin in their networks than men do. Interestingly, each sex exhibits a strong preference for members of their own sex (see also Booth, 1972; Rands, 1988).

37. Schachter (1959).

38. Lewis and Linder (unpublished data).

39. See, for example, Fontana and colleagues (1999); Kamarck, Manuck, and Jennings (1990); Kirschbaum and colleagues (1995); Glynn, Christenfeld, and Gerin (1999); see also Seeman and colleagues (1994), Snydersmith and Cacioppo (1992) for related evidence. There is one qualification concerning this pattern, however. When a woman feels that her performance under stress is being evaluated by her friend or a same-sex stranger, the benefits of social support from other women are not seen (e.g., Kors, Linden, and Gerin, 1997). In nonevaluative contexts, however, women experience support and reduced stress responses from other women, but less often from men,

even if the man is her own boyfriend. Realize that the implications of this evidence are quite startling: *Any* supportive woman, even a stranger, may be more soothing to another woman (biologically speaking) in times of stress than her own partner (at least for some stressful circumstances).

40. Newman (1999); Stack (1975).
41. Newman (1999), p. 197.
42. Newman (1999), p. 219.
43. Newman (1999), p. 70.
44. Belle (1987). From our family-centered Western vantage point, it is easy to assume that our way is the usual way, namely that men and women live together in couples with their own children, sometimes close to their kin, but often not. In such a world, reliance on female kin and friends seems ambiguous. In fact, nearly half of the world's families are headed by women who live in close proximity to their relatives. Many of them are very poor, and networks of women can be critical to survival.
45. Keverne, Martel, and Nevison (1996).
46. See Carter, Lederhendler, and Kirkpatrick (1999) and Panksepp (1998) for general sources on this issue. Other evidence that does not directly test this idea nonetheless provides suggestive relevant evidence. For example, social contact is enhanced, and aggression diminished, following central oxytocin treatment in estrogen-treated female prairie voles (Witt, Carter, and Walton, 1990), and the exogenous administration of oxytocin in rats causes an increase in social contact and in grooming (Argiolas and Gessa, 1991; Carter, De Vries, and Getz, 1995; Witt, Winslow, and Insel, 1992). With reference to humans, Carter (1998) suggested that oxytocin may be at the core of many forms of social attachment, including not only mother-infant attachments but also adult pair bonds and friendships (see also Drago, Pederson, Caldwell, and Prange, 1986; Fahrbach, Morrell, and Pfaff, 1985; Panksepp, 1998).
47. Keverne, Nevison, and Martel (1999).
48. Jamner, Alberts, Leigh, and Klein (1998).

Chapter 7: Tending in Marriage

1. For references concerning the desire to marry, see Glenn and Weaver (1988); Lauer and Lauer (2000). Hochschild (1989) reported a figure of 97 percent in her survey of Berkeley undergraduates. For a perspective on the development of monogamy in primate species, the reader is referred to Van Schaik and Dunbar (1990).
2. Some readers may wonder why I refer to these relationships as "marriage." Wouldn't cohabitating couples experience the same benefits? Wouldn't gay and lesbian couples do so as well? The answers to these questions are largely unknown because scientists haven't explored these relationships as fully as marriage. Although there is some evidence that female companions buffer their male partners' stress responses in laboratory stress tasks, the reverse is not true, mirroring the effects for married couples. To my knowledge, there has been no study of the effects of a gay or lesbian partner in terms of buffering responses to stress. It should be noted, however, that in the psychological well-being literature, it is clear that marriage, and not necessarily cohabitation,

has the beneficial effects. Compared with married people, cohabitors are more depressed, and so cohabitation may not afford all of the same protections that marriage does (Brown, 2000). It should also be noted that in many parts of the world, polygyny is still a strong norm. Whether men get the same advantages in multiwife situations that they do from a single tender is not currently known.

3. Berkman and Syme (1979); Helsing, Szklo, and Comstock (1981); House, Robbins, and Metzner (1982); Litwak and Messeri (1989); Ross, Mirowsky, and Goldsteen (1990); Stroebe and Stroebe (1983); Umberson (1992); Wiklund, Oden, Sanne, Ulvenstam, Wilhelmsson, and Wilhelmsen (1988). Marriage also preserves men's mental health, e.g., Stansfeld, Bosma, Hemingway, and Marmot (1998).

4. Tucker and Mueller (2000); Umberson (1987; 1992); Wickrama, Conger, and Lorenz (1995). If wives do indeed regulate their husbands' stress responses in ways that are beneficial to health, one would expect to see that men's health deteriorates dramatically following the death of a spouse, but that the same pattern is not true for women. This is indeed the case. Mortality rates among widowed men are higher than for widowed women, and widowed men who remarry are much less likely to die than those who do not remarry; among widowed women, however, remarrying or not has no effect on age of death (Helsing, Szklo, and Comstock, 1981; see also Stroebe and Stroebe, 1983).

5. Bird (1999); Hochschild (1989); see also Levine et al. (2001). Arlie Hochschild was one of the first sociologists to pull together the substantial literature demonstrating the increased work burden of women as compared with men. Time use diaries kept in an exhaustive study of how people use their time by Szalai and his colleagues (1972) also found a nearly three-hour time difference in the work performed by men and women across a broad array of countries.

Levine and his colleagues studied several thousand individuals living in the Ivory Coast and in Nepal (2001) and found that the total work burden for women exceeded that of men by 2.9 hours a day. Women spent less time at leisure and in nonwork activities than men, just as is true in the United States. Do these differences take a toll on women? On average, women perform household labor beyond the point of maximum psychological benefit whereas men do not. Inequity in the division of household labor has a greater impact on distress than does the total amount of work. Men report performing 42.3 percent of the housework compared to 68.1 percent reported by women (Bird, 1999).

6. Frankenhaeuser, Lundberg, Fredrikson, Melin, Tuomisto, Myrsten, Hedman, Bergman-Losman, and Wallin (1989). See also Brisson, Laflamme, Moisan, Milot, Masse, and Vezina (1999); Frankenhaeuser (1993); Goldstein, Shapiro, Chicz-DeMet, and Guthrie (1999). See also Lundberg and Palm (1989); Marco, Schwartz, Neale, Schiffman, Catley, and Stone (2000).

7. Tannen (1990); in fact, men's capacity for empathy may be somewhat limited, at least when it comes to understanding emotions. What is the evidence for such an extreme statement? Researchers often videotape marital interactions between husbands and wives, both their pleasant exchanges and their contentious ones, and sometimes, in a surprise move, they will play back portions of the tapes and ask husbands and wives to

guess what each was thinking. Wives are much better at discerning their husbands' feelings than husbands are at figuring out what their wives were feeling.

8. When men are asked where their emotional support comes from, most men name their wife as their main source of social support, and most say that she's *the only person* to whom they confide their personal problems or difficulties. See Glaser and Kiecolt-Glaser (1994); New England Research Institutes (1997); Phillipson (1997).

9. Ross and Holmberg (1990).

10. Putnam (2000).

11. Conger, Lorenz, Elder, Simons, and Ge (1993); Sorenson, Pirie, Folsom, Luepker, Jacobs, and Gillum (1985).

12. Chun and Lee (2001). Previous efforts to explain why married men earn more had focused on the fact that women may select men with good earning prospects; however, analyses that controlled for factors related to prospects found no support for this explanation.

13. Kiecolt-Glaser and Newton (2001). A mere thirty minutes of discussion of marital conflict is associated with changes in cortisol, adrenocorticotropic hormone, and norepinephrine in women but not in men (Kiecolt-Glaser, Glaser, Cacioppo, MacCallum, Snydersmith, Cheongtag, and Malarkey, 1997). Marital conflict has been linked to high blood pressure (Ewart, Taylor, Kraemer, and Agras, 1991), elevated plasma catecholamine levels (Malarkey, Kiecolt-Glaser, Pearl, and Glaser, 1994), and sympathetic nervous system arousal more generally (Levenson, Carstensen, and Gottman, 1993). In most of these studies, women show the effects more adversely, with one exception; men who score high in hostility also show adverse physiological effects in discussion of marital conflict (Smith and Allred, 1989; see also, Davidson, Putnam, and Larson, 2000). For studies that show men's reactions to discussions of marital conflict, see Ewart, Taylor, Kraemer, and Agras (1991); Frankish and Linden (1996); Kiecolt-Glaser, Malarkey, Chee, Newton, Cacioppo, Mao, and Glaser (1993); Mayne, O'Leary, McCrady, Contrada, and Labouvie (1997); Morell and Apple (1990); Thomsen and Gilbert (1998); women show such responses more reliably and their responses are greater (e.g., Baker et al., 1999; Broadwell and Light, 1999; Burnett, 1987; Carels, Sherwood, and Blumenthal, 1998; Ewart, Taylor, Kraemer, and Agras, 1991; Fehm-Wolfsdorf, Groth, Kaiser, and Hahlweg, 1999; Hagestad and Smyer, 1982; Harvey, Wells, and Alvarez, 1978; Huber and Sitze, 1983; Jacobson, Bottman, Waltz, Rushe, Bobcock, and Holtzworth-Munroe, 1994; Kiecolt-Glaser et al., 1997; Kiecolt-Glaser et al., 1996; Kiecolt-Glaser et al., 1993; Kiecolt-Glaser, Glaser, Cacioppo, and Malarkey, 1998; Kiecolt-Glaser, Newton, Cacioppo, MacCallum, Glaser, and Malarkey, 1996; Kirschbaum, Klauer, Filipp, and Hellhammer, 1995; Kirschbaum, Wust, and Hellhammer, 1992; Malarkey, Kiecolt-Glaser, Pearl, and Glaser, 1994; Mayne, O'Leary, McCrady, Contrada, and Labouvie, 1997; Morell and Apple, 1990).

14. Matthews, Gump, and Owens (2001); Weidner (2000).

15. See Kiecolt-Glaser and Newton (2000), for a review.

16. Cushing and Carter (1999).

17. Insel and Hulihan (1995); Insel, Winslow, Wang, and Young (1998); Cushing and Carter (1999); Panksepp (1998). Insel and Winslow (1998) suggest that pair bonding

in the female prairie vole involves oxytocin and dopamine receptors via estrogen-dependent mechanisms whereas in the male, vasopressin and serotonin interact in an androgen-dependent fashion. An oxytocin injection facilitates females' developing a preference for the partner in the absence of mating, and administration of an oxytocin antagonist blocks formation of partner preference (Insel and Hulihan, 1995).

18. Hrdy (1999); Panksepp (1998). Parallels between romantic relationships and infant-caregiver attachment bonds have long been noted (see Hazan and Shaver, 1987; Hazan and Diamond, 2000). Hrdy (1999) refers to oxytocin as the endocrinological equivalent of "candlelight, soft music, and a glass of wine," p. 154. Other neurotransmitters are implicated in female pair bonding as well, including dopamine (Gingrich, Liu, Cascio, Wang, and Insel, 2000).

19. Hrdy (1999), p. 139.

20. Carter (1998); Panksepp (1998); Winslow, Hastings, Carter, Harbaugh, and Insel (1993). Pitkow, Sharer, Xianglin, Insel, Terwilliger, and Young (2001) have recently been able to increase bonding in prairie voles by transferring a receptor gene for vasopressin into their brains, findings that reinforce the idea that monogamy in male prairie voles and the formation of pair bonds is enhanced by vasopressin. Note as well that a vasopressin antagonist blocks the development of partner preference, suggesting that it may underlie the normally intensely monogamous male prairie vole's commitment. Vasopressin antagonists also block selective aggression against potential rivals. Partner preference and aggression appear to be linked, inasmuch as the administration of vasopressin leads to intense signs of monogamous bonding in the form of both partner preference and aggression against potential rivals. A vasopressin antagonist administered prior to mating eliminates both partner preference and selective aggression against potential rivals; after mating, however, the bonds appear to be in place. Thus, much as oxytocin appears to influence the initiation but not the maintenance of partner preference in female prairie voles, vasopressin likewise is implicated in the initial partner preference but not in its maintenance (Winslow, Hastings, Carter, Harbaugh, and Insel, 1993).

21. Bobak and Marmot (1996); Cockerham (1997); Stone (2000). See also Dehne, Khodakevich, Hamers, and Schwartlander (1999); Stegmayr et al. (2000); Strasser (1998).

22. *The Economist* (1994, April 23); Erlanger (2000). As would be expected from the theory I have developed, another problem the Eastern European countries faced was increases in child abuse and neglect (Sicher et al., 2000).

23. Bobak and Marmot (1996); Cockerham, 1997; *The Economist* (1994, April 23); Stone (2000).

24. Bobak and Marmot (1996); Stone (2000).

25. See Stone (2000); see also Bobak and Marmot (1996); Hajdu, McKee, and Bojan (1995).

26. Bobak, Pikhart, Hertzman, Rose, and Marmot (1998); Bobak, McKee, Rose, and Marmot (1999). See also Mittag and Schwarzer (1993) for a perspective on alcohol consumption risk among migrants and refugees from East Germany. See Bobak and Marmot (1999), and Simpura, Levin, and Mustonen (1997) for perspectives on Russian alcohol consumption.

27. Hertzman (1995).

28. See, for example, Carlson (1998); Cockerham (1997). Watson (1995) suggests that the very burdens that take a physiological toll on women act as a source of protection. The argument goes like this: Women have to both work outside the home and do all the housework and child care, but that keeps them going. Their lives depend less on a single vision of success, namely viable economic employment, than is true for men. Instead many aspects of their lives provide them with a sense of meaning and purpose. For example, children are a source of great pride and purpose for women, more so than is true for men. Setbacks in one life domain, such as unemployment, may be buffered by gratifying experiences in other life domains, such as raising children.

    The evidence for this argument is research from the United States showing that women who both work outside the home and have family responsibilities are more satisfied with their lives and less likely to be stressed than women who have only work or family responsibilities. But the relevance of the U.S. studies is questionable. The so-called protective effects of women's employment occur primarily for women of at least middle-class means and for whom the total burden of employment, house, work, and child care is not overwhelming (see Taylor, 1999, for a review and discussion of this issue; see also Stephens, Franks, and Townsend, 1994; Gove and Zeiss, 1987; Lundberg, Mardberg, and Frankenhaeuser, 1994; Williams, Suls, Alliger, Learner, and Wan, 1991). Women who say that they get enough help at home, either through hired help or a partner helping, are most likely to report the benefits of combining work and family life. Working-class and poor women often say, instead, that they are exhausted by trying to combine both roles. This latter situation is more likely to be true for the majority of women in Eastern Europe.

29. Bobak, Pikhart, Hertzman, Rose, and Marmot (1998).

30. See Stone (2000); Weidner (1998). For example, Schwarzer, Hahn, and Schroder (1994) conducted a longitudinal study of East German migrants to West Germany and found that migrants who formed new social ties typically adjusted well. Following the move women migrants reported receiving more support and said there was more support available to them than men did. Women's new ties tended to be heavily, though not exclusively, with other women.

31. Stone (2000).

Chapter 8: Men's Groups

1. The title of Maccoby's book describing these trends is *The Two Sexes: Growing Up Apart, Coming Together*. Studies of social networks suggest that the coming together may be quite limited, however, inasmuch as adults typically exhibit a preference for members of their own sex in their social networks (Dunbar and Spoors, 1995; see also Young and Willmott, 1957).

2. It is important to note that competitive striving for leadership among males may not have characterized simple foraging societies but did characterize the more complex hunter-gatherer societies that followed them. Simple foraging societies appear to have been more egalitarian (see, for example, Tooby and DeVore, 1987, for a discussion of this issue).

3. Maccoby and Jacklin (1974).
4. See Sapolsky (1998) and Aureli and De Waal (2000) for discussions related to this issue. See especially Preuschoft and van Schaik (2000).
5. Sapolsky (1998).
6. See also Preuschoft and van Schaik (2000). Once primatologists began to look for this kind of behavior in primate groups, they began to see it. More than 100 papers on twenty-seven different primate species have documented social skills like these in both wild and captive groups of primates.
7. Sapolsky (1998).
8. Tiger (1970).
9. Manuck, Kaplan, Adams, and Clarkson (1988). More egalitarian work conditions have been tied to lower levels of cardiovascular disease (Marmot and Davey Smith, 1997).
10. Tiger (1970).
11. Slotow, van Dyk, Poole, Page, and Klocke (2000). Evidence from primate studies suggests that dominance position affects testosterone as well. If you place four male squirrel monkeys together in a cage—two dominant monkeys, and two less so—the two dominant ones will gain weight, have higher levels of testosterone, and show the seasonal variation in testosterone expected in males that helps them mate and reproduce. The low-status males will be smaller, have lower levels of testosterone, and show less seasonal variation. Place a dominant and a subordinate male together in a cage, and the dominant male's level of testosterone will rise and stay there. If a female is brought into the cage, only the dominant male will show a rise in testosterone (Coe and Levine, 1983; see also Coe, Mendoza, and Levine, 1979).
12. Sapolsky (1998).
13. Goodall (1986).
14. Jensen, Grogan, Xenakis, and Bain (1989); Draper and Harpending (1982) suggest that father absence sets in a reproductive strategy characterized by a stressful rearing environment, precocious sexuality, unstable pair bonding in adulthood, and a limited investment in child rearing. Boys from families in which parents have divorced or where fathers are otherwise absent frequently engage in exaggeratedly and stereotypically masculine behavior during childhood. (See also Belsky, Steinberg, and Draper, 1991; Bereczkei and Csanaky, 1996.)
15. Flinn and England (1997).
16. Van den Berg, Hol, Van Ree, Spruijt, Everts, and Koolhaas (1999). At one time, researchers believed that play fighting in male animals was rehearsal for adult combat. However, the evidence now suggests that this is probably not the case. Play fighting is quite distinctive and different from combat and involves little overlap in skills. Rather, play appears to help animals to distinguish playfulness from true aggression (Pellis and Pellis, 1998; 1996). Although this knowledge is not necessarily critical in early childhood, it assumes substantial importance as animals become sexually mature and stronger and begin competing for dominance in a social group (Pellis and Pellis, 1996).
17. Geary (1999).
18. Dabbs (1998); see Dabbs and Dabbs (2000) for a perspective on testosterone and behavior. Even watching a sports event can have these effects. A study of male fans

watching the World Cup soccer match found that those who supported the winning team had higher levels of testosterone than those who had supported the losing team (Bernhardt, Dabbs, Fielden, and Lutter, 1998).

There is now substantial evidence that testosterone is associated with dominance behavior and with aggression related to dominance. Studies range from those conducted with boys in early adolescence (Tremblay, Schaal, et al., 1998) through adulthood (see Dabbs and Dabbs for a readable summary on the literature on testosterone).

Having seen that men regulate one another's testosterone levels through their aggressive contests striving for dominance, the question may arise as to whether women regulate each other's biology, too, and if so to what end? The answer is yes. The initial observation was made by Martha McClintock (1971), who showed that groups of women living together in dormitories achieved menstrual synchrony in their close living conditions. Subsequently, Stern and McClintock (1998) investigated how this effect was mediated. They found that pheromones, airborne chemicals released by an individual into the environment, affect the physiology and behavior of other members of the same species. By exposing one woman to an odorless compound extracted from another woman's armpits in the late follicular phase of the menstrual cycle, they were able to accelerate the preovulatory surge of luteinizing hormone of the recipient woman and shorten her menstrual cycle. Later in the cycle, however, the synchrony was not achieved.

19. Mazur and Booth (1998). Risk for aggression, as we've seen, does not come solely from testosterone. Serotonin levels are clearly implicated as well (Simon, Cologer-Clifford, Lu, McKenna, and Hu, 1998). The combination of high testosterone and low serotonin appears to be particularly problematic, leading to the impulsive aggressive behavior that commonly gets males of all species in trouble (see, for example, Suomi, 2000). Vasopressin also contributes to aggressive behavior (Panksepp, 1998; Stribley and Carter, 1999).

20. Insel and Winslow (1998); Suomi (1997; 2000). Dominance hierarchies are maintained by coalitions, grooming, third-party interventions into squabbles, spontaneous submission, and the use of infants as buffer zones between potentially quarreling parties (De Waal, 1991; 2000).

21. Raleigh, McGuire, Brammer, Pollack, and Yuwiler (1991). Consistent with Raleigh et al. (1991) results, Smuts (1987) has suggested that in nonhuman primates, females are often able to affect how males control and coerce others in small societies.

The orbitofrontal cortex is implicated in social affiliative behavior and is of interest in part because of certain subtypes of serotonin receptors, the density of which correlates with an animal's social status (Adolphs, 1999).

At least some of the neuroendocrine protection that is afforded to high-status males is available *only* to those who have social skills. Sapolsky and Ray (1989) demonstrated that dominant males consistently have lower basal concentrations of cortisol than do subordinate males, but only if they have social skills. Dominant males who lacked these social skills had cortisol levels as high as those of subordinate males. (See also Sapolsky, 1992b.)

22. Geary (1999).

23. Tiger (1970). The physiological underpinnings of bonding in male groups have not, to my knowledge, been studied. Investigators have, however, examined the effects of vasopressin and oxytocin on stress responses in veterans suffering from posttraumatic stress disorder incurred during personal combat injury. A group of forty-three such veterans was randomized to receive either vasopressin, a placebo, or oxytocin, and their stress responses to combat imagery were assessed (heart rate, skin conductance, and EMG responses). The results indicated that vasopressin enhanced stressful responses relative to a placebo, but oxytocin reduced them (Pitman, Orr, and Lasko, 1993). Whether vasopressin enhances the stress response during actual combat, whereas oxytocin incurred during bonding may come into play once one is out of the stressful circumstance, remains to be seen. Given oxytocin's role in affiliative behavior, the study is suggestive regarding a potential point of investigation.

24. Elder and Clipp (1988).

25. Manchester (1980), p. 451 (quoted in Elder and Clipp).

26. Muirhead (1986), pp. 106–7 (quoted in Elder and Clipp).

27. Gray (1956), p. 46 (quoted in Elder and Clipp).

28. Quote from a WWII veteran interviewed on *NBC Evening News* (June 6, 2000).

29. Elder and Clipp (1988).

30. Tiger (1970).

Chapter 9: Where Altruism May Reside

1. Brown and Harden (1982) and Meyer and Kurtz (1982) (of *The Washington Post*) are excellent sources on the Air Florida crash. There are more than 1,000 Web site references to Arland Williams.

2. Huston, Ruggiero, Conner, and Geis (1981); Huston, Geis, and Wright (1976).

3. Moen, Robison, and Fields (1994). Approximately 26 million people provide unpaid health-care services in homes throughout the United States, most of them women. As people have lived longer, caregiving has become a more significant part of a woman's life. Moen et al. (1994) found that nearly one in four women became a caregiver between ages thirty-five and forty-four, and 36 percent by ages fifty-five to sixty-four. Another survey found that only 45 percent of women born between 1905 and 1917 became caregivers to aged parents or husbands, whereas 64 percent of those born between 1927 and 1934 did. I did an informal count of my friends born a couple decades later than these women, and more than 50 percent have already been involved in caregiving, in some cases for as long as ten years. Furthermore, as was true in both this study and my informal network, being employed full-time in no way lessened the likelihood of taking on caregiving. See Web sites for the National Institute on Disability and Rehabilitation Research (www.disabilitydata.com), for the National Alliance for Caregiving (www.caregiver.org), and www.dsaapd.com.

   The difference in women's and men's propensity for caregiving is especially clear toward the end of life. Whereas women are likely to keep their husbands at home if they become disabled, men are more likely to institutionalize their wives. Part of the reason is that wives are typically younger and healthier than their husbands, and so the husbands may be at a point where caregiving is difficult for them (see Taylor, 1999, for a discussion of these issues).

Commercial care is also increasing because as the population ages, more people are in need of care, and because women, the traditional supply of unpaid caregivers, are increasingly working outside the home. The care industries, however, are a poor substitute. Those who work in them typically receive little pay and have little training. About 40 percent of nursing homes repeatedly fail health and safety inspections (Rothschild, 2001).

4. Fairbanks (2000). See Web sites for the National Institute on Disability and Rehabilitation Research (www.disabilitydata.com) and for the National Alliance for Caregiving (www.caregiver.org) and www.dsaapd.com.

5. Dettwyler (1991); Silk (1992). It is likely that boys and men were the most common recipients of this caregiving because a combination of the tasks in which they were involved (such as hunting and warfare) and hormonal propensities toward aggressive behavior suggest that their injury rates would have been higher. Certainly this is true today—a visit to the Centers for Disease Control and Prevention Web site (www.cdc.gov/ncipc/factsheets/adoles.htm) reveals that males are more likely than females to experience or die of almost every kind of injury across every stage of the life span.

6. See Fairbanks (2000); Hrdy (1999) for a discussion of this issue.

7. Beach and Schulz (2000); Cacioppo, Burleson, and colleagues (2000); King, Oka, and Young (1994); Spitze, Logan, Joseph, and Lee (1994); Wu, Wang, Cacioppo, Glaser, Kiecolt-Glaser, and Malarkey (1999). See also Nancy Folbre's *The Invisible Heart* (2001) for an excellent analysis of the economics of caregiving. Genetic expression occurs not only in early childhood but throughout life, and the research on caregiving by Wu et al. (1999) suggests that some of the problems experienced by those providing spousal caregiving occur at the level of gene expression.

8. See Crognier (2000) for a thoughtful account of how individual adaptation can find its way into adaptive advances of the species as a whole. See also Boehm (1999).

9. Altruism is evident in our primate relatives as well (see, for example, de Waal and Berger, 2000). Building on Hamilton's (1963) ideas, in 1971, biologist Robert Trivers (Trivers, 1971) put forth the concept of reciprocal altruism, a powerful principle that provides some insight into the evolutionary dilemma of altruism. Trivers maintained that altruists do not dispense their altruism at random but rather are likely to aid genetically related others and behave altruistically toward other altruists when there is some expectation of reciprocation. Through such behavior, altruism in the species may evolve: in relationships where sacrifices and benefits are exchanged evenly over time, cooperators gain reproductive success over those who fail to cooperate, because the potential costs of giving help to others are offset, from an evolutionary vantage point, by the benefits of receiving help from others. Together, these contributions (Hamilton and Trivers) have formed the backbone of evolutionary biology's approach to the paradox of altruism.

Not everyone is satisfied with this tit-for-tat resolution to the paradox of altruism. Anthropologist Christopher Boehm (1999) is among the scientists who think we should take a second look at group survival. He argues that under certain environmental conditions, which may have been prevalent during significant times in human evolution, the balance of forces may have shifted from individual selection to group selection.

10. Genes can have multiple phenotypic effects, and consequently the same genes that promote parental investment and helping of very close kin may also allow nonkin, at least those with whom social bonds have been formed, to be treated in a similar favored manner (see Boehm, 1999, for a discussion of this issue).

11. Axelrod and Hamilton (1981), for example, offer a game theory framework to identify conditions under which cooperation based on reciprocity can evolve. They show that, under certain conditions, reciprocal cooperation is a stable strategy.

12. See Sapolsky (1998) and Aureli and de Waal (2000) for related discussions.

13. See Dawkins (1976), for an early discussion of this hypothesis and Batson (1991) for a recent perspective on empathy and altriusm.

Chapter 10: The Social Context of Tending

1. Adler, Boyce, Chesney, Folkman, and Syme (1993); Adler, Boyce, Chesney, Cohen, Folkman, Kahn, and Syme (1994); House, Lepkowski, Kinney, Mero, Kessler, and Herzog (1994); Kaplan, Pamuk, Lynch, Cohen, and Balfour (1996); Williams and Collins (1995). Indeed, an editorial in the *Journal of the American Medical Association* stated that lower socioeconomic status is probably the "most powerful single contributor to premature morbidity and mortality not only in the United States but worldwide" (Williams, 1998, p. 1745).

The social gradient is related to some unusual causes of death. In October of 1912, the British luxury liner *Titanic* set sail from Southampton, England, to make its maiden voyage to the United States. Touted as one of the greatest ships ever made, it was said to be iceberg-proof, and so to get its passengers to New York in the promised time, it sped its way through the treacherous ice-filled waters of the North Atlantic. On the evening of October 14–15, the *Titanic* hit an iceberg off the coast of Newfoundland, and in short order it became evident that the ship would sink. Equally clear was the fact that there were only enough lifeboats for one-third of the 2,200 passengers and crew aboard. Women and children were given priority in the lifeboats, but as records subsequently show, some did better than others. Of the first-class passengers, only 3 percent died in the tragedy. Sixteen percent of second-class passengers did not make it out, and a full 45 percent of third-class passengers lost their lives. Even accidental death shows a clear relationship to social status (Yu and Williams, 1999).

The question arises as to whether stressors related to socioeconomic status (SES) produce poor physical and psychological health or whether those in poor health experience declining SES, a hypothesis referred to as "social selection" or "downward drift." Investigators have largely ruled out social selection and downward drift as major contributors to the social class and health gradient. Although people clearly experience worsening SES as their health declines, this movement explains only a small portion of the gradient (see, for example, Eaton, Muntaner, Bovasso, and Smith, 2001; Lynch, Kaplan, and Shema, 1997).

2. Marmot and Davey Smith (1997); Marmot, Rose, Shipley, and Hamilton (1978). A recent study of 70,365 men and women in Scotland who were born in 1920 examined death and economic data in 1997 when respondents were seventy-seven years old. About half the group had died. Relation of death to socioeconomic status was very strong. Of particular interest was the fact that the researchers used the same metaphor as has independently been used by researchers studying biological processes related to stress, namely that those with the higher death rate seemed to be on a different clock. The less affluent people had the same patterns of disease and mortality as the more affluent people but developed their disorders, on average, seven years earlier (Chalmers and Capewell, 2001).

The social gradient is related not only to most major causes of death but to risk factors for chronic disease including obesity, presence of metabolic syndrome, high blood pressure, and plasma fibrinogen (Brunner, Marmot, Nanchahal, Shipley, Stansfeld, Juneja, and Alberti, 1997; Carroll, Smith, Sheffield, Shipley, and Marmot 1997).

3. Adler et al. (1993).

4. Marmot and Davey Smith (1997).

5. Williams and Collins (1995).

6. Ross (1994), p. 81.

7. Sapolsky (1998).

8. Sapolsky (1998); Sapolsky does not dart females, first because if they are pregnant, the procedure could harm them, and second, because when you dart a female, other females rush over to protect her, making it impossible to get close enough to assess her stress hormones! (Sapolsky, 2001).

9. Klebanov, Brooks-Gunn, and Duncan (1994); Matthews, Raikkonen, Everson, Flory, Marco, Owens, and Lloyd (2000); Stansfeld, Head, and Marmot (1998).

10. Terkel (1997), p. 550.

11. Barefoot, Peterson, Dahlstrom, Siegler, Anderson, and Williams (1991); Williams, Barefoot, and Shekelle (1985). Matthews, Flory, Muldoon, and Manuck (2000) found that low SES is associated with reduced central serotonergic responsivity, which they credited to the stressful environments to which individuals from low socioeconomic backgrounds are exposed. This is an especially intriguing set of findings because reduced serotonergic responsivity has been related to impulsivity and aggression, which are also related to socioeconomic status. The blunted serotonergic response persisted, however, even when controlling for participants' scores on aggression and impulsivity. These findings may also be directly related to health. Serotonin (5-HT) depletion increases food intake, body weight, and central adiposity (particular signs of weight gain around the middle) and also increases the reinforcing properties of nicotine and alcohol. Reduced serotonergic function is also associated with increased sympathetic and reduced parasympathetic activation. Overall, this pattern of findings—possible increases in aggression, the accompanying hostile affect, changes in sympathetic functioning, and potential alteration in health habits and in risk

factors—represents pathways that may promote the development of hypertension and atherosclerosis, and thus this pathway may be significant in accounting for the SES gradients for these diseases. (See also Pine et al., 1997.)

The idea that family environment influences the development of hostility toward others has received fairly wide empirical support. Woodall and Matthews (1989), for example, found that children from families characterized by less supportive and involved interactions had children who were assessed as more angry and hostile. Boys from these families had more pronounced heart rate responses to laboratory stressors.

12. Bolger, DeLongis, Kessler, and Schilling (1989); Conger and Elder (1994); Conger, Elder, Lorenz, Conger, Simons, Whitbeck, Huck, and Melby (1990); Conger, Rueter, and Elder (1999); Holtzworth-Munroe et al. (1997); Lavee, McCubbin, and Olson (1987); Liker and Elder (1983); McKendy (1997); Stets (1995); U.S. Department of Justice (1997); Wacquant and Wilson (1989). Estimates are that between 30 and 60 percent of wives in the United States have been abused by their husbands, with 14 percent suffering severe and chronic abuse (Straus and Gelles, 1986). Work stressors are often implicated in the etiology of wife abuse (Straus, Gelles, and Steinmetz, 1980). The wife abuse literature suggests that men who are violent may have had more attachment and dependency problems in childhood and experienced more violence in their families while growing up. This background can lead to few social and communication skills, especially in marital interaction, and a high level of marital distress (often accompanied by alcohol problems). Consequently, the literature on violent husbands provides evidence for the pathways from early childhood through poor social and emotional skills to problems containing anger, of hostility, alcohol abuse, and corresponding violence (Holtzworth-Munroe et al., 1997).

13. Justice and Justice (1990); thanks to Gary Evans of Cornell University for his help in locating evidence relating the social-class gradient to abuse of wives and maltreatment of children in families.

14. Coplan, Andrews, Rosenblum, Owens, Friedman, Gorman, and Nemeroff (1996). As adults, those raised under variable-foraging-demand conditions had the most dominance struggles and the lowest levels of grooming. Infants raised in the variable-foraging conditions showed the most sustained clinging to the mother, the lowest levels of social play and exploration, and the highest levels of affective disturbance. Variable foraging was also related to elevated levels of serotonin and dopamine metabolite concentrations in grown offspring (Coplan, Trost, et al., 1998), suggesting some disruption in these systems as well. The authors concluded that when mothers are psychologically unavailable to their infants, due to the stress of their environment, attachments are less secure, normal development is disrupted, and psychopathology in the offspring is more likely to develop (Rosenblum and Paully, 1984).

15. Belsky (1980); Belsky, Steinberg, and Draper (1991); Chen and Matthews (in press); Geary (1999).

16. Terkel (1997), pp. xxxv, xxxii–xxxiii.

17. Catalano and Serxner (1992); Ferrie, Shipley, Marmot, Stansfeld, and Smith (1998);

Mattiasson, Lindgarde, Nilsson, and Theorell (1990); Schnall, Pieper, et al. (1990); Turner, Kessler, and House (1991).

18. Terkel (1997), p. 76.

19. Falk, Hanson, Isacsson, and Ostergren (1992); Jonsson, Rosengren, Dotevall, Lappas, and Wilhelmsen (1999).

20. Terkel (1997), p. 161.

21. Alfredsson, Karasek, and Theorell (1982); Bosma, Marmot, Hemmingway, Nicholson, Brunner, and Stansfeld (1997); Greenberg and Grunberg (1995); Karasek (1979); Karasek, Baker, Marxer, Ahlbom, and Theorell (1981); Karasek, Theorell, Schwartz, Schnall, Pieper, and Michela (1988); Landsbergis et al. (1992); Mausner-Dorsch and Eaton (2000); for studies relating job strain to adverse physical or mental health, see Schnall, Pieper, et al. (1990); Schnall, Schwartz, Landsbergis, Warren, and Pickering (1992); Schlussel, Schnall, Zimbler, Warren, and Pickering (1990); Stansfeld, Bosma, Hemingway, and Marmot (1998); Storr, Trinkoff, and Anthony (1999).

22. Terkel (1997), p. 196.

23. Falk, Hanson, Isacsson, and Ostergren (1992); Hammar, Alfredsson, and Johnson (1998); Loscocco and Spitze, 1990.

24. Buunk (1989); Repetti (1993).

25. Terkel (1997), p. xxxiii.

26. Terkel (1997), p. 30.

27. Frankenhaeuser (1993).

28. U.S. Department of Justice (1992). Crime is more likely to occur in neighborhoods with high population density, high housing density, high levels of family disruption, and high levels of community change and population turnover. Sampson, Raudenbush, and Earls (1997) argue that, in neighborhoods marked by high density but rapid turnover, there may be little opportunity to develop formal and informal networks of community social control. As a result, the neighborhood may be unable to supervise and control teenage peer groups, among other adverse effects.

29. E.g., King, King, Gudanowski, and Vreven (1995).

30. *Lethal Weapon 4*.

31. Istre, McCoy, Osborn, Barnard, and Bolton (2001); Macintyre, Maciver, and Sooman (1993); Sampson, Raudenbush, and Earls (1997); Troutt (1993); Wallace and Wallace (1990). See Ross and Mirowsky (2001) for a discussion of the contribution of neighborhood disadvantage to health. In one study (Troutt, 1993) comparing low- and middle-income neighborhoods, disparities were found in the degree to which a number of basic needs could be met: weekly shopping needs (28 percent for low-income versus 92 percent for middle income), food shopping within the neighborhood (23 percent versus 82 percent), available banking services (46 percent versus 71 percent), Laundromats (69 percent versus 80 percent), dry cleaners (46 percent versus 90 percent), and restaurants (40 percent versus 69 percent).

32. Gutierres, Saenz, and Green (1994); Koskinen and Martelin (1994); Mackenback et al. (1999); Matthews, Manor, and Power (1999); Stronks, van de Mheen, Van Den Bos, and Mackenback (1995); Williams and Collins (1995).

33. See, for example, Yu and Williams (1999).

Chapter 11: The Tending Society

1. Miller (1999); Miller and Ratner (1998).
2. Frank, Gilovich, and Regan (1993); Marwell and Ames (1981).
3. Sears and Funk (1991).
4. Miller (1999). Can being nice hold its own in an environment marked by aggression? Consider the following study by primatologists Frans de Waal and Denise Johanowicz (1993). They picked two different monkey species, rhesus and stumptails, who differ greatly in both their propensity for aggression and their peacemaking skills. Rhesus monkeys are intolerant and aggressive and don't do a very good job of reconciling after fights. Stumptails, on the other hand, are less aggressive and have good peacemaking skills. De Waal and Johanowicz put young monkeys of both species together for five months. Then, they put them back with monkeys of their own kind and observed what happened. Exposure to the peaceful stumptails greatly increased the rhesus monkeys' reconciliation skills, which they subsequently employed with their own species. They became somewhat less aggressive as well. Fortunately, the stumptails stayed pretty much as they had always been—peaceful and conciliatory. An important implication of this study is that reconciliation is clearly a malleable skill, rather than a wired-in behavior. Since humans' learning capacities are far greater, one assumes that the capacity to learn peacemaking skills is true of humans as well.
5. Wilkinson (1996). Note that Wilkinson's conclusions with respect to income inequality and health have not gone unchallenged (Mackenbach, 2002).
6. Kaplan, Pamuk, Lynch, Cohen, and Balfour (1996) found that variations between states in the inequality of income distribution were significantly associated with a broad array of health outcomes and with mortality.
7. Wilkinson (1996) relates income inequality to the amount of violent crimes society experiences and its homicide rate.
8. Kawachi and Kennedy (1997); Kennedy, Kawachi, and Prothrow-Stith (1996); Fiscella and Franks (1997); Shi, Starfield, Kennedy, and Kawachi (1999). There is a relationship between a state's per capita expenditures for public welfare and its divorce rate (Zimmerman, 1994): family life is less stable in states that give less to support family life. This finding is important, because it is widely believed that government social programs undermine family life and foster breakups.
9. Feminist Majority Foundation (2000); Women's Justice Center (2001).
10. In another study (a survey of 58,000 managers), women outranked men on 20 of 23 skills measured. A third study of 2,482 executives found women outranking men on 17 of 20 skills that were evaluated (Sharpe, 2000); see also Fisher (1998). A study by Fondas and Sassalos (2000) found that having women on boards of directors for organizations has a positive impact on performance. Specifically, boards with more female directors had more influence over management decisions than all-male boards. The authors speculated that because women have tended to be outside rather than inside directors, they often bring a broader perspective to the table. They also have had to pass higher hurdles in order to get on the boards and may therefore be

especially capable or motivated to make a contribution. See also Welbourne (in press) for a discussion of the relative success of women's initial public offerings (IPOs).

11. For a perspective on the idea that "relationships rule" the new business environment, see Tapscott, Ticoll, and Lowy (2000). See also Fisher's (1999) *The First Sex* for a provocative discussion of women's current and potential contributions to society.

12. Blum (1957).

13. *The Invisible Heart: Economics and Family Values* (2001) by Nancy Folbre and *The Price of Motherhood* (2001) by Ann Crittenden. For example, U.S. Bureau of Labor Statistics records for the year 2000 (Bureau of Labor Statistics, 2000) show that the median weekly earnings for a child-care worker is $265, for a teacher $711, and for a registered nurse $790. In contrast, firefighters earned median weekly earnings of $690, truck drivers $1,104, police $802, and airline pilots $1,052. For a perspective on the fact that men are making little to no movement into traditionally female jobs and roles, see *The Economist* (September 28, 1996).

14. Geronimus (1996); Dunkel-Schetter (1998).

15. Albee and Gullotta (1997); Black, Dubowitz, Hutcheson, Berenson-Howard, and Starr (1995); McLoyd (1998). For example, a program of home visitation by nurses undertaken with pregnant women was associated fifteen years later with fewer instances of running away, fewer arrests, fewer convictions and violations of probation, fewer lifetime sex partners, fewer cigarettes smoked, and fewer days of alcohol consumption in their offspring. In addition, the parents reported fewer behavior problems. The authors concluded that prenatal and early childhood visitation by nurses can reduce serious antisocial behavior and emergent use of substances in high-risk adolescents over the long term. This study is notable because the mothers received only nine visits on average during pregnancy and about twenty-three visits over the subsequent two years (Olds and colleagues, 1998).

16. See Black and Krishnakumar (1998); Newman (1999); Wandersman and Nation (1998). A number of animal studies have now demonstrated intergenerational transfer of parenting behavior (see Fairbanks, 1989, and Francis, Diorio, Liu, and Meaney, 1999, as examples). Comparable studies have not been conducted with humans, although the robust finding that child-abusing parents were frequently themselves abused by their parents is largely credited to this same intergenerational transfer mechanism.

Not surprisingly, when non-parental child care has been formally evaluated, it has fared dismally. In one study, 56 percent of providers were called "adequate" and another 35 percent were rated as "inadequate." Less than 10 percent of child care was rated as "good" (Mehren, 1994). Moreover, there is not enough of it. For example, only 14 percent of children eligible in a New York area for subsidized child care received it (Newman, 1999).

The 1994 Carnegie report (Carnegie Task Force on Meeting the Needs of Young Children, 1994) documented many of the effects of a child's environment on healthy development and called for universal health care and education as parts of the solution. The "ho-hum" attitude that greeted the appearance of the Carnegie report, however, was disturbing. For example, *Fortune* magazine entitled its article "The Carnegie

Solution: Yet Again" (Seligman, 1994), implying that we are so aware of the problems facing children in our country that we have become inured to their plight and cannot muster the resources needed to treat these problems.

17. Fairbanks (1989); Francis, Diorio, Liu, and Meaney (1999).

18. Family Planning and Service Expansion and Technical Support (SEATS) and World Education (1999); Kawachi, Kennedy, Gupta, and Prothrow-Stith (1999); UNICEF (2001). Under the Taliban in Afghanistan, for example, women's life expectancy declined to age forty-five, lower than men's at age forty-six. An important contributor in this case was the fact that women were not permitted to seek medical treatment.

19. Acheson (1998); Sampson, Raudenbush, and Earls (1997).

20. De Anda (2001).

21. Barron-McKeagney, Woody, and D'Souza (2001).

22. Prevosto (2001).

23. Wallace (2001).

24. Johnson, Lall, Holmes, Huwe, and Nordlund (2001). One article reported that mentoring programs for men are typically called "coaching" because men often have an aversion to traditional therapeutic endeavors, even to the point of rejecting formal mentoring programs. The idea of a short-term career and personal guidance from a "coach" is more acceptable (Carey, 2001).

25. Putnam (2000). Nuclear families have dropped to less than 25 percent of households (Schmitt, 2001). One in every two marriages ends in divorce. In the 1990s, the number of unmarried partners grew by almost 72 percent, nearly five times as fast as the number of households or growth in households. The number of Americans living alone has doubled, surpassing 27 million. Households headed by single mothers increased more than 25 percent during the 1990s. Two percent of Americans live together without marrying, but these numbers, too, are rising (Fields, 2001).

26. Twenge (2000); National Center for Health Statistics (1998). There are disturbing signs that physical health in the midyears is declining as well. Disability rates of those in their twenties to their fifties have actually risen in the last decade, largely from increases in obesity, diabetes, and asthma (Koretz, 2001).

27. Twenge (2000).

28. There is substantial evidence that marital strain and disruption increase risks for physical and mental health problems (see Kiecolt-Glaser and Newton, 2001, for a review; e.g., Bloom, Asher, and White, 1978; Kiecolt-Glaser, Fisher, Ogrocki, Stout, Speicher, and Glaser, 1987; Spanier and Thompson, 1984; Weiss, 1975).

29. See, for example, Amato and Booth (2001); Clarke-Stewart, Vandell, McCartney, Owen, and Booth (2000); Glenn and Kramer (1987); Spigelman, Spigelman, and Englesson (1994); Tucker and colleagues (1997).

30. Watters (2001).

31. Gurung, Taylor, and Seeman (2001).

32. Wheeler, Reis, and Nezlek (1983).

33. Odell, Korgen, Schumacher, and Delucchi (2000); Weiser (2000). When the Internet was first invented, most of the users were male and their activities involved searching

for information and playing competitive games. Once women began to use the Internet, the patterns of usage changed dramatically. Outside of work, women use the Internet heavily to keep in touch with friends and relatives.

34. Thorsteinsson, James, and Gregg (1998).

35. O'Reilly (2000).

36. Francis, Diorio, Liu, and Meaney (1999); Floeter and Greenough (1979); Laviola and Teranova (1998). See also Anisman et al. (1998).

37. DePaulo (1992); Hall (1978). For example, Lisa Feldman Barrett and colleagues (2000) found that women consistently displayed more complexity and differentiation in their articulation of emotional experiences than did men, even when their verbal advantage was statistically controlled.

References

Acheson, D. 1998. *Independent inquiry into inequalities in health: Report*. London: The Stationery Office.

Ader, R., and S. B. Friedman. 1965. Social factors affecting emotionality and resistance to disease in animals: V. Early separation from the mother and response to a transplanted tumor in the rat. *Psychosomatic Medicine*. 27:119–22.

Adler, E. M., A. Cook, D. Davidson, C. West, and J. Bancroft. 1986. Hormones, mood and sexuality in lactating women. *British Journal of Psychiatry*. 148:74–79.

Adler, N., T. Boyce, M. Chesney, S. Cohen, S. Folkman, R. Kahn, and L. Syme. 1994. Socioeconomic status and health: The challenge of the gradient. *American Psychologist*. 49:15–24.

Adler, N., T. Boyce, M. Chesney, S. Folkman, and L. Syme. 1993. Socioeconomic inequalities in health: No easy solution. *Journal of the American Medical Association*. 269(24):3140–145.

Adolphs, R. 1999. Social cognition and the human brain. *Trends in Cognitive Sciences*. 3:469–79.

Advisory Board of the National Center for Women and Policing. 1995. More women police, better response to domestic violence are goals of the new center [Online]. Available: http://www.feminist.org/research/71_wompol.html [October 15, 2001].

Agrawal, A. A. October 12, 2001. Phenotypic plasticity in the interactions and evolution of species. *Science*. 294:321–26.

Albee, G. W., and T. P. Gullotta, eds. 1997. *Primary prevention works*. Thousand Oaks, Calif.: Sage Publications.

Alfredsson, L., R. Karasek, and T. Theorell. 1982. Myocardial infarction risk and psychosocial work environment: An analysis of the male Swedish working force. *Social Science Medicine*. 16:463–67.

Allen, M. T., K. A. Matthews, and F. S. Sherman. 1997. Cardiovascular reactivity to stress and left ventricular mass in youth. *Hypertension*. 30:782–87.

Altemus, M. P., A. Deuster, E. Galliven, C. S. Carter, and P. W. Gold. 1995. Suppression of hypothalamic-pituitary-adrenal axis response to stress in lactating women. *Journal of Clinical Endocrinology and Metabolism*. 80:2954–959.

Amato, P. R., and A. Booth. 2001. The legacy of parents' marital discord: Consequences for children's marital quality. *Journal of Personality and Social Psychology*. 81:627–38.

Ambady, N., and R. Rosenthal. 1993. Half a minute: Predicting teacher evaluations from thin slices of nonverbal behavior and physical attractiveness. *Journal of Personality and Social Psychology*. 64:431–41.

Anisman, H., M. D. Zaharia, M. J. Meaney, and Z. Merali. 1998. Do early-life events permanently alter behavioral and hormonal responses to stressors? *International Journal of Developmental Neuroscience*. 16:149–64.

Ardrey, R. 1961. *African genesis: A personal investigation into the animal origins and nature of man*. London: Collins.

Argiolas, A., and G. L. Gessa. 1991. Central functions of oxytocin. *Neuroscience and Biobehavioral Reviews*. 15:217–31.

Aureli, F., and F. B. M. deWaal, eds. 2000. *Natural conflict resolution*. Berkeley, Calif.: University of California Press.

Axelrod, R., and W. Hamilton. 1981. The evolution of cooperation. *Science*. 211:1390–396.

Bachrach, L. L. 1975. *Marital status and mental disorder: An analytical review*. Washington, D.C.: U.S. Printing Office.

Bailey, M., and C. Coe. 1999. Maternal separation disrupts the integrity of the intestinal microflora in infant rhesus monkeys. *Developmental Psychobiology*. 35:146–55.

Baker, B., K. Helmers, B. O'Kelly, I. Safinofsky, A. Abelsohn, and S. Tobe. 1999. Marital cohesion and ambulatory blood pressure in early hypertension. *American Journal of Hypertension*. 12:227–30.

Baldwin, D. A. 2000. Interpersonal understanding fuels knowledge acquisition. *Current Directions in Psychological Science*. 9:40–45.

Baldwin, J. D. 1985. The behavior of squirrel monkeys (*Saimiri*) in natural environments. In *Handbook of squirrel monkey research*, edited by L. A. Rosenblum and C. L. Coe. New York: Plenum.

Balfour, D. J. K., and K. O. Fagerstrom. 1996. Pharmacology of nicotine and its therapeutic use in smoking cessation and neurodegenerative disorders. *Pharmacological Therapeutics*. 71:51–81.

Barefoot, J., B. Peterson, W. Dahlstrom, I. Siegler, N. Anderson, and R. Williams. 1991. Hostility patterns and health implications: Correlates of Cook-Medley hostility scale scores in a national survey. *Health Psychology*. 10:18–24.

Barkow, J. H., L. Comides, and J. Tooby, eds. 1992. *The adapted mind: Evolutionary psychology and the generation of culture*. Oxford: Oxford University Press.

Barnes, G. M., A. S. Reifman, M. P. Farrell, and B. A. Dintcheff. 2000. The effects of parenting on the development of adolescent alcohol misuse: A six-wave latent growth model. *Journal of Marriage and the Family.* 62:175–86.

Baron-Cohen, S., H. A. Ring, S. Wheelwright, E. T. Bullmore, M. J. Brammer, A. Simmons, and S. C. R. Williams. 1999. Social intelligence in the normal and autistic brain: An fMRI study. *European Journal of Neuroscience.* 11:1891–898.

Barrera, M., L. Chassin, and F. Rogosch. 1993. Effects of social support and conflict on adolescent children of alcoholic and nonalcoholic fathers. *Journal of Personality and Social Psychology.* 64:602–12.

Barrett, L. F., R. D. Lane, L. Sechrest, and G. E. Schwartz. 2000. Sex differences in emotional awareness. *Personality and Social Psychology Bulletin.* 26:1027–1035.

Barron-McKeagney, T., J. D. Woody, and H. J. D'Souza. 2001. Mentoring at-risk Latino children and their parents: Impact on social skills and problem behaviors. *Child and Adolescent Social Work Journal.* 18:119–36.

Batson, C. D. 1991. *The altruism question: Toward a social-psychological answer.* Hillsdale, N.J.: Erlbaum.

Baumeister, R. F., and K. L. Sommer. 1997. What do men want? Gender differences and two spheres of belongingness: Comment on Cross and Madson. 1997. *Psychological Bulletin.* 122:38–44.

Baumeister, R. F., and M. R. Leary. 1995. The need to belong: Desire for interpersonal attachments as a fundamental human motivation. *Psychological Bulletin.* 117(3): 497–529.

Beach, S., and R. Schulz. 2000. Mortality among elderly caregivers: Reply, American Medical Association, US. *Journal of the American Medical Association.* 283:2106.

Bell, D. C. 2001. Evolution of parental caregiving. *Personality and Social Psychology Review.* 5:216–29.

Belle, D. 1987. Gender differences in the social moderators of stress. In *Gender and stress,* edited by R. C. Barnett, L. Biener, and G. K. Baruch. New York: The Free Press.

Belle, D. 1989. Gender differences in children's social networks and supports. In *Children's social networks and social supports,* edited by D. Belle. New York: Wiley.

Belsky, J. 1980. Child maltreatment: An ecological integration. *American Psychologist.* 35:320–35.

Belsky, J. 1984. The determinants of parenting: A process model. *Child Development.* 55:83–96.

Belsky, J., L. Steinberg, and P. Draper. 1991. Childhood experience, interpersonal development, and reproductive strategy: An evolutionary theory of socialization. *Child Development.* 62:647–70.

Benes, F. M. 1994. Developmental changes in stress adaptation in relation to psychopathology. *Development and Psychopathology.* 6:723–39.

Benschop, R. J., M. Rodriguez-Feuerhahn, and M. Schedlowski. 1996. Catecholamine-induced leukocytosis: Early observations, current research, and future directions. *Brain, Behavior, and Immunity.* 10:77–91.

Bereczkei, T., and A. Csanaky. 1996. Evolutionary pathway of child development: Lifestyles of adolescents and adults from father-absent families. *Human Nature.* 7(3):257–80.

Berkman, L. F., L. Leo-Summers, and R. I. Horwitz. 1992. Emotional support after myocardial infarction. *Annals of Internal Medicine*. 117:1003–1009.

Berkman, L. F., and L. S. Syme. 1979. Social networks, host resistance, and mortality: A nine-year follow-up study of Alameda county residents. *American Journal of Epidemiology*. 109:186–204.

Bernhardt, P. C., J. M. Dabbs, Jr., J. A. Fielden, and C. D. Lutter. 1998. Testosterone changes during vicarious experiences of winning and losing among fans at sporting events. *Physiology and Behavior*. 65(1):59–62.

Bernstein, I. S., and C. Ehardt. 1986. The influence of kinship and socialization on aggressive behavior in rhesus monkeys (*Macaca mulatta*). *Animal Behaviour*. 34:739–47.

Biernat, M., and M. J. Herkov. 1994. Reactions to violence: A campus copes with serial murder. *Journal of Social and Clinical Psychology*. 13:309–34.

Biglan, A., C. W. Metzler, R. Wirt, D. V. Ary, et al. 1990. Social and behavioral factors associated with high-risk sexual behavior among adolescents. *Journal of Behavioral Medicine*. 13:245–61.

Biondi, M., P. Pancheri, D. Falaschi, A. Teodori, G. Paga, R. Delle Chiaie, G. DiCasare, and A. Proietti. 1986. Social support as a moderator of the psychobiological stress response. *New Trends in Experimental Clinical Psychiatry*. 2:173–83.

Bird, C. E. 1999. Gender, household labor, and psychological distress: The impact of the amount and division of housework. *Journal of Health and Social Behavior*. 40:32–45.

Black, M. M., and A. Krishnakumar. 1998. Children in low-income, urban settings: Interventions to promote mental health and well-being. *American Psychologist*. 53:635–46.

Black, M. M., H. Dubowitz, J. Hutcheson, J. Berenson-Howard, and R. H. Starr. 1995. A randomized clinical trial of home intervention for children with failure to thrive. *Pediatrics*. 95:807–14.

Blass, E. M. 1997. Infant formula quiets crying human newborns. *Journal of Developmental and Behavioral Pediatrics*. 18:162–65.

Bloom, B. L., S. J. Asher, and S. W. White. 1978. Marital disruption as a stressor: A review and analysis. *Psychological Bulletin*. 85:867–94.

Blum, R. H. 1957. *The psychology of malpractice suits*. San Francisco: California Medical Association.

Bobak, M., and M. Marmot. 1999. Alcohol and mortality in Russia: Is it different than elsewhere? *Annual Epidemiology*. 9(6):335–38.

Bobak, M., and M. Marmot. 1996. East-West mortality divide and its potential explanations: Proposed research agenda. *British Medical Journal*. 312:421–25.

Bobak, M., M. McKee, R. Rose, and M. Marmot. 1999. Alcohol consumption in a national sample of the Russian population. *Addiction*. 94(6):857–66.

Bobak, M., H. Pikhart, C. Hertzman, R. Rose, and M. Marmot. 1998. Socioeconomic factors, perceived control and self-reported health in Russia. A cross-sectional survey. *Social Science and Medicine*. 47(2):269–79.

Bobak, M., Z. Skodova, Z. Pisa, R. Polendne, and M. Marmot. 1997. Political changes and trends in cardiovascular risk factors in the Czech Republic, 1985–92. *Journal of Epidemiology and Community Health*. 51:272–77.

Boehm, C. 1999. *Hierarchy in the forest: The evolution of egalitarian behavior.* Cambridge, Mass.: Harvard University Press.

Boesch, C. 1991. The effects of leopard predation on grouping patterns in forest chimpanzees. *Behaviour.* 117:220–42.

Bolger, N., A. DeLongis, R. C. Kessler, and E. A. Schilling. 1989. Effects of daily stress on negative mood. *Journal of Personality and Social Psychology.* 57:808–18.

Bolger, N., A. Zuckerman, and R. C. Kessler. 2000. Invisible support and adjustment to stress. *Journal of Personality and Social Psychology.* 79:953–61.

Booth, A. 1972. Sex and social participation. *American Sociological Review.* 37:183–92.

Bosma, H., M. G. Marmot, H. Hemmingway, A. C. Nicholson, E. Brunner, and S. A. Stansfeld. 1997. Low job control and risk of coronary heart disease in Whitehall II (prospective cohort) study. *British Medical Journal.* 314:558–65.

Bowlby, J. 1969. *Attachment and loss, vol. I: Attachment.* New York: Basic Books.

Bowlby, J. 1988. *A secure base: Parent-child attachment and healthy human development.* New York: Basic Books.

Brisson, C., N. Laflamme, J. Moisan, A. Milot, B. Masse, and M. Vezina. 1999. Effect of family responsibilities and job strain on ambulatory blood pressure among white-collar women. *Psychosomatic Medicine.* 61:205–13.

Broadwell, S. D., and K. C. Light. 1999. Family support and cardiovascular responses in married couples during conflict and other interactions. *International Journal of Behavioral Medicine.* 6:40–63.

Brooks-Gunn, J., G. J. Duncan, P. K. Klebanov, and N. Sealand. 1993. Do neighborhoods influence childhood and adolescent development? *American Journal of Sociology.* 99:353–95.

Brothers, L. 1990. The social brain: A project for integrating primate behavior and neurophysiology in a new domain. *Concepts in Neuroscience.* 1:27–51.

Brown, C., and B. Harden. 1982. The scene; Ice hampers rescue attempts; Night falls as rescue crews attempt to find victims. *The Washington Post,* pp. A1 et al., January 14.

Brown, G. L., M. H. Ebert, P. F. Goyer, et al. 1982. Aggression, suicide, and serotonin: Relationships to CSF amine metabolism. *American Journal of Psychiatry.* 139:741–46.

Brown, G. L., F. K. Goodwin, J. C. Ballenger, P. F. Goyer, and L. F. Major. 1979. Aggression in humans correlates with cerebrospinal fluid amine metabolites. *Psychiatry Research.* 1:131–39.

Brown, S. L. 2000. The effect of union type on psychological well-being: Depression among cohabitors versus marrieds. *Journal of Health and Social Behavior.* 41:241–55.

Brunner, E. J., M. G. Marmot, K. Nanchahal, M. J. Shipley, S. A. Stansfeld, M. Juneja, and K. G. M. M. Alberti. 1997. Social inequality in coronary risk: Central obesity and the metabolic syndrome. Evidence from the Whitehall II study. *Diabetologica.* 40:1341–349.

Brunner, E., M. Marmot, K. Nanchahal, M. Shipley, S. Stansfeld, M. Juneja, and K. Alberti. 1997. Social inequality in coronary risk: Central obesity and the metabolic syndrome. Evidence from the Whitehall II study. *Diabetologia.* 40:1341–349.

Bureau of Labor Statistics. 2000. *Traditionally female and male occupations.* http://www.bls.gov.

Bureau of Labor Statistics. 2001. *Women workers, statistics.* http://www.bls.gov.

Burnett, R. 1987. Reflections in personal relationships. In *Accounting for relationships: Explanation, representation, consciousness,* edited by R. Burnett, P. McGhee, and D. Clark. New York: Methuen.

Buunk, B. 1989. Affiliation and helping within organizations: A critical analysis of the role of social support with regard to occupational stress. In *European review of social psychology,* Vol. 1, edited by W. Stroebe and M. Hewstone. Chichester, England: Wiley.

Cacioppo, J. T., W. B. Malarkey, J. K. Kiecolt-Glaser, B. N. Uchino, S. A. Scoutas-Emich, J. F. Sheridan, G. G. Bernston, and R. Glaser. 1995. Heterogeneity in neuroendocrine and immune responses to brief psychological stressors as a function of autonomic cardiac activation. *Psychosomatic Medicine.* 57:154–64.

Cacioppo, J., M. Burleson, K. Poehlmann, W. Malarkey, J. Kiecolt-Glaser, G. Bernston, B. Uchino, and R. Glaser. 2000. Autonomic and neuroendocrine responses to mild psychological stressors: Effects of chronic stress on older women. *Annals of Behavioral Medicine.* 22:140–48.

Campo, A. T., and R. P. Rohner. 1992. Relationships between perceived parental acceptance-rejection, psychological adjustment, and substance abuse among young adults. *Child Abuse and Neglect.* 16:429–40.

Cannon, W. B. 1932. *The wisdom of the body.* New York: Norton.

Capaldi, D. M., L. Crosby, and M. Stoolmiller. 1996. Predicting the timing of first sexual intercourse for at-risk adolescent males. *Child Development.* 67:344–59.

Caporeal, L. R. 1997. The evolution of truly social cognition: The core configuration model. *Personality and Social Psychology Review.* 1:276–98.

Carels, R. A., A. Sherwood, and J. A. Blumenthal. 1998. Psychosocial influences on blood pressure during daily life. *International Journal of Psychophysiology.* 28:117–29.

Carey, B. 2001. Mentors of the mind: Men who wouldn't go anywhere near traditional therapy are more willing to accept short-term career and personal guidance from "coaches." *Los Angeles Times,* pp. S1, S6, 18 June.

Carlson, M., and F. Earls. 1997. Psychological and neuroendocrinological sequelae of early social deprivation in institutionalized children in Romania. *Annals of the New York Academy of Sciences.* 807:419–28.

Carlson, P. 1998. Self-perceived health in East and West Europe: Another European health divide. *Social Science and Medicine.* 46:1355–366.

Carnegie Task Force on Meeting the Needs of Young Children. 1994. *Starting points: Meeting the needs of our youngest children: The report of the Carnegie Task Force on Meeting the Needs of Young Children.* New York: Carnegie Corporation of New York.

Carroll, D., G. Smith, D. Sheffield, M. Shipley, and M. Marmot. 1997. The relationship between socioeconomic status, hostility, and blood pressure reactions to mental stress in men: Data from the Whitehall II study. *Health Psychology.* 16(2):131–36.

Carter, C. S. 1998. Neuroendocrine perspectives on social attachment and love. *Psychoneuroendocrinology.* 23:779–818.

Carter, C. S., A. C. DeVries, and L. L. Getz. 1995. Physiological substrates of mammalian monogamy: The prairie vole model. *Neuroscience and Biobehavioral Reviews.* 19: 303–14.

Carter, C. S., I. I. Lederhendler, and B. Kirkpatrick, eds. 1999. *The integrative neurobiology of affiliation*. Cambridge, Mass.: MIT Press.

Carter, C. S., J. R. Williams, D. M. Witt, and T. R. Insel. 1992. Oxytocin and social bonding. In *Oxytocin in maternal sexual and social behaviors*, edited by C. A. Pedersen, G. F. Jirikowski, J. D. Caldwell, and T. R. Insel. *Annals of the New York Academy of Science*. 652:204–11.

Caspi, A., D. Begg, N. Dickson, J. Langley, T. E. Moffitt, R. McGee, and P. A. Silva. 1995. Identification of personality types at risk for poor health and injury in late adolescence. *Criminal Behavior and Mental Health*. 5:330–50.

Catalano, R., and S. Serxner. 1992. The effect of ambient threats to employment on low birthweight. *Journal of Health and Social Behavior*. 33:363–77.

Chalmers, J., and S. Capewell. 2001. Deprivation, disease, and death in Scotland: Graphical display of survival of a cohort. *British Journal of Medicine*. 323:967–68.

Chen, E., and K. A. Matthews. In press. Cognitive appraisal biases: An approach to understanding the relationship between socioeconomic status and cardiovascular reactivity in children. *Annals of Behavioral Medicine*.

Chen, M., and J. A. Bargh. 1999. Consequences of automatic evaluation: Immediate behavioral predispositions to approach or avoid the stimulus. *Personality and Social Psychology Bulletin*. 25:215–24.

Chiodera, P., C. Salvarani, A. Bacchi-Modena, R. Spailanzani, C. Cigarini, A. Alboni, E. Gardini, and V. Coiro. 1991. Relationship between plasma profiles of oxytocin and adrenocorticotropic hormone during sucking or breast stimulation in women. *Hormone Research*. 35:119–23.

Chorpita, B. F., and D. H. Barlow. 1998. The development of anxiety: The role of control in the early environment. *Psychological Bulletin*. 124:3–21.

Chun, H., and I. Lee. 2001. Why do married men earn more: Productivity or marriage selection? *Economic Inquiry*. 39(2):307.

Cicchetti, D., and V. Carlson, eds. 1989. *Child maltreatment: Theory and research on the causes and consequences of child abuse neglect*. New York: Cambridge.

Clancy, S. M., and S. J. Dollinger. 1993. Photographic description of the self: Gender and age differences in social connectedness. *Sex Roles*. 29:477–95.

Clarke-Stewart, K. A. 1978. A daddy makes three: The father's impact on mother and young child. *Child Development*. 49:466–78.

Clarke-Stewart, K. A., D. L. Vandell, K. McCartney, M. T. Owen, and C. Booth. 2000. Effects of parental separation and divorce on very young children. *Journal of Family Psychology*. 14:304–26.

Clarkson, T. B., S. B. Manuck, and J. R. Kaplan. 1986. Potential role of cardiovascular reactivity in atherogenesis. In K. A. Matthews, S. M. Weiss, T. Detre, T. Dembroski, B. Falkner, S. M. Manuck, and R. B. Williams, eds. *Handbook of stress, reactivity and cardiovascular disease* (pp. 35–48). New York: Wiley-Interscience.

Coccaro, E. F., R. J. Kavoussi, R. L. Trestman, S. M. Gabriel, T. B. Cooper, and L. J. Siever. 1997. Serotonin function in human subjects: Intercorrelations among central 5-HT indices and aggressiveness. *Psychiatric Research*. 73:1–14.

Coccaro, E. F., R. J. Kavoussi, and R. L. Hauger. 1995. Physiological responses to D-fenfluramine and ipsapirone challenge correlate with indices of aggression in males with personality disorders. *International Clinical Psychopharmacology*. 10:177–79.

Cockerham, W. 1997. The social determinants of the decline of life expectancy in Russia and Eastern Europe: A lifestyle explanation. *Journal of Health and Social Behavior*. 38:117–30.

Coe, C. L., and S. Levine. 1983. Biology of aggression. *American Academy of Psychiatry and the Law*. 11:131–48.

Coe, C. L., G. R. Lubach, J. W. Karaszewski, and W. B. Ershler. 1996. Prenatal endocrine activation alters postnatal cellular immunity in infant monkeys. *Brain, Behavior, and Immunity*. 10:221–34.

Coe, C. L., S. P. Mendoza, W. P. Smotherman, and S. Levine. 1978. Mother-infant attachment in the squirrel monkey: Adrenal response to separation. *Behavior and Biology*. 22:256–63.

Coe, C. L., G. R. Lubach, M. L. Schneider, D. J. Dierschke, and W. B. Ershler. 1992. Early rearing conditions alter immune response in the developing infant primate. *Pediatrics*. 90:505–509.

Coe, C. L., S. P. Mendoza, and S. Levine. 1979. Social status constrains the stress response in the squirrel monkey. *Physiology and Behavior*. 23:633–38.

Cohen, P., D. S. Pine, A. Must, S. Kasen, and J. Brook. 1998. Prospective associations between somatic illness and mental illness from childhood to adulthood. *American Journal of Epidemiology*. 147:232–39.

Cohen, S., W. J. Doyle, D. P. Skoner, B. S. Rabin, and J. M. Gwaltney Jr. 1997. Social ties and susceptibility to the common cold. *Journal of the American Medical Association*. 277:1940–944.

Cohen, S., N. Hamrick, M. S. Rodriguez, P. J. Feldman, B. S. Rabin, and S. B. Manuck. 2000. The stability and intercorrelations among cardiovascular, immune, endocrine, and psychological reactivity. *Annals of Behavioral Medicine*. 22:171–79.

Cohen, S., D. A. Tyrrell, and A. P. Smith. 1991. Psychological stress and susceptibility to the common cold. *New England Journal of Medicine*. 325:606–12.

Cole, S. W., B. D. Naliboff, M. E. Kemeny, M. Griswold, J. L. Fahey, and J. A. Zack. 2001. Impaired response to HAART in patients with high autonomic nervous system activity. *Proceedings of the National Academy of Sciences of the USA*. 98:12670–695.

Collins, N. L., C. Dunkel-Schetter, M. Lobel, and S. C. M. Scrimshaw. 1993. Social support in pregnancy: Psychosocial correlates of birth outcomes and post-partum depression. *Journal of Personality and Social Psychology*. 65:1243–58.

Conger, R., and G. Elder. 1994. *Families in troubled times: Adapting to change in rural America*. New York: Aldine de Gruyter.

Conger, R., M. Cui, C. Bryant, and G. Elder Jr. 2000. Competence in early adult romantic relationships: A developmental perspective on family influences. *Journal of Personality and Social Psychology*. 79:224–37.

Conger, R., G. Elder, F. Lorenz, K. Conger, R. Simons, L. Whitbeck, S. Huck, and J. Melby. 1990. Linking economic hardship to marital quality and distress. *Journal of Marriage and the Family*. 52:643–56.

Conger, R., X. Ge, G. Elder, F. Lorenz, and R. Simons. 1994. Economic stress, coercive family process, and developmental problems of adolescents. *Child Development.* 65:541–61.

Conger, R., F. Lorenz, G. Elder, R. Simons, and X. Ge. 1993. Husband and wife differences in response to undesirable life events. *Journal of Health and Social Behavior.* 34:71–88.

Conger, R. D., M. A. Rueter, and G. H. Elder, Jr. 1999. Couple resilience to economic pressure. *Journal of Personality and Social Psychology.* 76(1):54–71.

Copeland, E. P., and R. S. Hess. 1995. Differences in young adolescents' coping strategies based on gender and ethnicity. *Journal of Early Adolescence.* 15:203–19.

Coplan, J. D., M. W. Andrews, L. A. Rosenblum, M. J. Owens, S. Friedman, J. M. Gorman, and C. B. Nemeroff. 1996. Persistent elevations of cerebrospinal fluid concentrations of corticotropin-releasing factor in adult nonhuman primates exposed to early life stressors: Implications for the pathophysiology of mood and anxiety disorders. *Proceedings of the National Academy of Sciences.* 93:1619–623.

Coplan, J. D., R. C. Trost, M. J. Owens, T. B. Cooper, J. M. Gorman, C. B. Nemeroff, and L. A. Rosenblum. 1998. Cerebrospinal fluid concentrations of somatostatin and biogenic amines in grown primates reared by mothers exposed to manipulated foraging conditions. *Archives of General Psychiatry.* 55:473–77.

Corter, C. M., and A. S. Fleming. 1990. Maternal responsiveness in humans: Emotional, cognitive, and biological factors. *Advances in the Study of Behavior.* 19:83–136.

Counts, D. A. 1990a. Domestic violence in Oceania: Introduction. *Pacific Studies.* 13(3):1–5.

Counts, D. A. 1990b. Beaten wife, suicidal woman: Domestic violence in Kaliai, West New Britain. *Pacific Studies.* 13(3):151–69.

Crittenden, A. 2001. *The price of motherhood: why the most important job in the world is still the least valued.* New York: Metropolitan Books.

Crognier, E. 2000. Biological adaptation and social behaviour. *Annals of Human Biology.* 27:221–37.

Cross, S. E., and L. Madson. 1997. Models of the self: Self-construals and gender. *Psychological Bulletin.* 122:5–37.

Cushing, B. S., and C. S. Carter. 1999. Prior exposure to oxytocin mimics the effects of social contact and facilitates sexual behaviour in females. *Journal of Neuroendocrinology.* 11:765–69.

Dabbs, J. 1998. Testosterone and the concept of dominance. *Behavioral and Brain Sciences.* 21:370–71.

Dabbs, J. M., and M. G. Dabbs. 2000. *Heroes, rogues, and lovers: Testosterone and behavior.* New York: McGraw-Hill.

Daly, M., and M. Wilson. 1988. *Homicide.* New York: Aldine de Gruyter.

Daly, M., and M. Wilson. 1996. Violence against stepchildren. *Current Directions in Psychological Science.* 5:77–81.

Damasio, A. R. 1994. *Descartes' error: Emotion, reason, and the human brain.* New York: Avon Books.

Darwin, C. 1871/1952. The descent of man and selection in relation to sex. In *Great Books of the Western World,* Vol. 49, edited by R. M. Hutchins. Chicago: Encyclopaedia Britannica, pp. 253–600.

Davidson, R. J. 1998. Affective style and affective disorders: Perspectives from affective neuroscience. *Cognition and Emotion*. 12:307–30.

Davidson, R. J., K. M. Putnam, and C. L. Larson. 2000. Dysfunction in the neural circuitry of emotion regulation—a possible prelude to violence. *Science*. 289:591–94.

Davies, P. T., and M. E. Cummings. 1995. Children's emotions as organizers of their reactions to interadult anger: A functionalist perspective. *Developmental Psychology*. 31:677–84.

Davis, M. C., K. A. Matthews, and E. W. Twamley. 1999. Is life more difficult on Mars or Venus? A meta-analytic review of sex differences in major and minor life events. *Annals of Behavioral Medicine*. 21:83–97.

Davis, M., K. Matthews, E. Meilahn, and J. Kiss. 1995. Are job characteristics related to fibrinogen levels in middle-aged women? *Health Psychology*. 14(4):310–18.

Davis, M. C., K. A. Matthews, and C. E. McGrath. 2000. Hostile attitudes predict elevated vascular resistance during interpersonal stress in men and women. *Psychosomatic Medicine*. 62:17–25.

Dawkins, R. 1976. *The selfish gene*. Oxford: Oxford University Press.

Dawson, G., D. Hessl, and K. Frey. 1994. Social influences on early developing biological and behavioral systems related to risk for affective disorder. *Development and Psychopathology*. 6:759–79.

de Anda, D. 2001. A qualitative evaluation of a mentor program for at-risk youth: The participants' perspective. *Child and Adolescent Social Work Journal*. 18:97–117.

De Bellis, M. D., A. S. Baum, B. Birmaher, M. S. Keshavan, C. H. Eccard, A. M. Boring, F. J. Jenkins, and N. D. Ryan. 1999. Developmental traumatology: I. Biological stress systems. *Biological Psychiatry*. 45:1259–270.

De Waal, F. 1982. *Chimpanzee politics: Power and sex among apes*. New York: Harper and Row.

De Waal, F. 1991. The social nature of primates: Extreme standpoints and the role of moderates. In *Through the looking glass: Issues of psychological well-being in captive nonhuman primates* (pp. 69–115), edited by M. A. Novak and A. J. Petto. Washington, D.C.: American Psychological Association.

De Waal, F. 1996. *Good natured: The origins of right and wrong in humans and other animals*. Cambridge, Mass.: Harvard University Press.

De Waal, F. 2000. The first kiss: Foundations of conflict resolution research in animals. In *Natural conflict resolution*, edited by F. Aureli and F. B. M. de Waal. Berkeley: University of California Press.

De Waal, F., and M. Berger. 2000. Payment for labour in monkeys. *Nature*. 404:563.

De Waal, F., and D. L. Johanowicz. 1993. Modification of reconciliation behavior through social experience: An experiment with two macaque species. *Child Development*. 64:897–908.

De Waal, F., and F. Lanting. 1997. *Bonobo: The forgotten ape*. Berkeley: University of California Press.

Dehne, K. L., L. Khodakevich, F. F. Hamers, and B. Schwartlander. 1999. The HIV/AIDS epidemic in eastern Europe: Recent patterns and trends and their implications for policy-making. *AIDS*. 13:741–49.

Denton, R. E., and C. M. Kampfe. 1994. The relationship between family variables and adolescent substance abuse: A literature review. *Adolescence*. 29(114):475–95.

DePaulo, B. M. 1992. Nonverbal behavior and self-presentation. *Psychological Bulletin*. 111:203–43.

Dess, N. K. 2001. The nature of monkeys and mothering: Breakthrough research shows how genes and experience form distinct personalities in primates. *Psychology Today*, May/June, p. 32.

Dettwyler, K. A. 1991. Can paleopathology provide evidence for "compassion"? *American Journal of Physical Anthropology*. 84:375–84.

Diamond, J. 1997. *Guns, germs, and steel: The fates of human societies*. New York: W. W. Norton.

Diamond, L. M. 2001. Contributions of psychophysiology to research on adult attachment: Review and recommendations. *Personality and Social Psychology Review*. 5:276–95.

DiBlasio, F. A., and B. B. Benda. 1990. Adolescent sexual behavior: Multivariate analysis of a social learning model. *Journal of Adolescent Research*. 5(4):449–66.

Digest of Education Statistics. 1996. *Table 379: Employment of 12ᵗʰ graders, by selected student characteristics: 1992* [Online]. Available: http://nces.ed.gov/pubs/d96.

Dodge, K. A., G. S. Pettit, and J. E. Bates. 1994. Socialization mediators of the relation between socioeconomic status and child conduct problems. *Child Development*. 65:649–65.

Drago, F., C. A. Pederson, J. D. Caldwell, and A. J. Prange, Jr. 1986. Oxytocin potently enhances novelty-induced grooming behavior in the rat. *Brain Research*. 368:287–95.

Draper, P., and H. Harpending. 1982. Father absence and reproductive strategy: An evolutionary perspective. *Journal of Anthropological Research*. 38:255–73.

Dunbar, R. 1996. *Grooming, gossip, and the evolution of language*. Cambridge, Mass.: Harvard University Press.

Dunbar, R. I. M., and M. Spoors. 1995. Social networks, support cliques, and kinship. *Human Nature*. 6:273–90.

Dunbar, R. I. M. 1998. The social brain hypothesis. *Evolutionary Anthropology*. 6:178–90.

Duncan, S. C., T. E. Duncan, and L. A. Strycker. 2000. Risk and protective factors influencing adolescent problem behavior: A multivariate latent growth curve analysis. *Annals of Behavioral Medicine*. 22:103–109.

Dunkel-Schetter, C. 1998. Maternal stress and prenatal delivery. *Prenatal and Neonatal Medicine*. 3:39–42.

Dunkel-Schetter, C., R. A. R. Gurung, M. Lobel, and P. D. Wadhwa. 2001. Stress processes in pregnancy and birth: Psychological, biological, and sociocultural influences. In *Handbook of health psychology*, edited by A. Baum, T. A. Revenson, and J. Singer. Mahwah, N.J.: Lawrence Erlbaum.

Dunn, J. B., and M. P. Richards. 1977. Observations on the developing relationship between mother and baby in the neonatal period. In *Studies in mother-infant interaction*, edited by H. R. Scaefer. New York: Academic Press.

Dunn, J., J. Brown, and L. Beardsall. 1991. Family talk about feeling states and children's later understanding of others' emotions. *Developmental Psychology*. 27:448–55.

Durkheim, E. [1897] 1951. *Suicide*. Translated by J. A. Spaulding and G. Simpson. New York: Free Press.

Easterbrooks, M. A., E. M. Cummings, and R. N. Emde. 1994. Young children's responses to constructive marital disputes. *Journal of Family Psychology*. 8:160–69.

Eaton, W. W., C. Muntaner, G. Bovasso, and C. Smith. 2001. Socioeconomic status and depressive syndrome: The role of inter- and intra-generational mobility, government assistance, and work environment. *Journal of Health and Social Behavior*. 42:277–94.

Edwards, C. P. 1993. Behavioral sex differences in children of diverse cultures: The case of nurturance to infants. In *Juvenile primates: Life history, development, and behavior*, edited by M. E. Pereira and L. A. Fairbanks. New York: Oxford University Press.

Eisenberg, N., R. A. Fabes, and B. C. Murphy. 1996. Parents' reactions to children's negative emotions: Relations to children's social competence and comforting behavior. *Child Development*. 67:2227–247.

Eisenberg, N., R. A. Fabes, S. A. Shepard, I. K. Guthrie, B. C. Murphy, and M. Reiser. 1999. Parental reactions to children's negative emotions: Longitudinal relations to quality of children's social functioning. *Child Development*. 70:513–34.

Elder, Jr., G. H., and E. C. Clipp. 1988. Wartime losses and social bonding: Influences across forty years in men's lives. *Psychiatry*. 51:177–98.

Ell, K., R. Nishimoto, L. Mediansky, J. Mantell, and M. Hamovitch. 1992. Social relations, social support and survival among patients with cancer. *Journal of Psychosomatic Research*. 36:531–41.

Epel, E. S., B. S. McEwen, and J. R. Ickovics. 1998. Embodying psychological thriving: Physical thriving in response to stress. *Journal of Social Issues*. 54:301–22.

Epel, E. S., B. McEwen, T. Seeman, K. Matthews, G. Castellazzo, K. D. Brownell, J. Bell, and J. R. Ickovics. 2000. Stress and body shape: Stress-induced cortisol secretion is consistently greater among women with central fat. *Psychosomatic Medicine*. 62: 623–32.

Erickson, K., P. Thorsen, G. Chrousos, D. E. Grigoriadis, O. Khongsaly, J. McGregor, and J. Schulkin. 2001. Preterm birth: Associated neuroendocrine, medical, and behavioral risk factors. *The Journal of Clinical Endocrinology and Metabolism*. 86:2544–552.

Erlanger, S. 2000. Birthrate Dips in Ex-Communist Countries. *The New York Times*, May 4, pp. A8(N), A8(L).

Ewart, C. K., C. B. Taylor, H. C. Kraemer, and W. S. Agras. 1991. High blood pressure and marital discord: Not being nasty matters more than being nice. *Health Psychology*. 10:155–63.

Fabes, R. A., N. Eisenberg, S. Jones, M. Smith, I. Guthrie, R. Poulin, S. Shepard, and J. Friedman. 1999. Regulation, emotionality, and preschoolers' socially competent peer interactions. *Child Development*. 70:432–42.

Fahlke, C., J. G. Lorenz, J. Long, M. Champoux, S. J. Suomi, and J. D. Higley. 2000. Rearing experiences and stress-induced plasma cortisol as early risk factors for excessive alcohol consumption in nonhuman primates. *Alcoholism: Clinical and Experimental Research*. 24:644–50.

Fahrbach, S. E., J. I. Morrell, and D. W. Pfaff. 1985. Possible role for endogenous oxytocin in estrogen-facilitated maternal behavior in rats. *Neuroendocrinology*. 40:526–32.

Fairbanks, L. A. 2000. Maternal investment throughout the life span in Old World monkeys. In *Old world monkeys*, edited by P. F. Whitehead and C. J. Jolly. New York: Cambridge University Press.

Fairbanks, L. A. 1996. Individual differences in maternal style: Causes and consequences for mothers and offspring. In *Parental care: Evolution, mechanisms and adaptive significance*, Vol. 25: *Advances in the study of behavior*, edited by J. S. Rosenblatt and C. T. Snowdon. New York: Academic Press, pp. 579–611.

Fairbanks, L. A. 1989. Early experience and cross-generational continuity of mother-infant contact in vervet monkeys. *Developmental Psychobiology*. 22(7):669–81.

Falk, A., B. Hanson, S. Isacsson, and P. Ostergren. 1992. Job strain and mortality in elderly men: Social network, support, and influence as buffers. *American Journal of Public Health*. 82(8):1136–139.

Family Planning and Service Expansion and Technical Support (SEATS) and World Education. 1999. *Vital Connections: Linking Women's Literacy Programs and Reproductive Health Services* [Online]. Available: http://seats.jsi.com/publications/pub25.html.

Farah, M. J., K. D. Wilson, M. Drain, and J. N. Tanaka. 1998. What is "special" about face perception? *Psychological Review*. 105:482–98.

Feeney, B. C., and N. L. Collins. 2001. Predictors of caregiving in adult intimate relationships: An attachment theoretical perspective. *Journal of Personality and Social Psychology*. 80:972–94.

Fehm-Wolfsdorf, G., T. Groth, A. Kaiser, and K. Hahlweg. 1999. Cortisol responses to marital conflict depend on marital interaction quality. *International Journal of Behavioral Medicine*. 6:207–27.

Feldman, P. J., C. Dunkel-Schetter, C. A. Sandman, and P. D. Wadhwa. 2000. Maternal social support predicts birth weight and fetal growth in human pregnancy. *Psychosomatic Medicine*. 62:715–25.

Feldman, R., C. W. Greenbaum, and N. Yirmiya. 1999. Mother-infant affect synchrony as an antecedent of the emergence of self-control. *Developmental Psychology*. 35:223–31.

Felitti, V. J., R. F. Anda, D. Nordenberg, D. F. Williamson, A. M. Spitz, V. Edwards, M. P. Koss, and J. S. Marks. 1998. Relationship of childhood abuse and household dysfunction to many of the leading causes of death in adults. *American Journal of Preventative Medicine*. 14:245–58.

Feminist Majority Foundation. 1995. FMF launches national center for women and policing: More women police, better response to domestic violence are goals of the new center. *Feminist Majority Report*, Vol. 7, no. 1.

Feminist Majority Foundation. 2000. Gender gap in police brutality lawsuits: Men cost more [Online]. Available: http://www.feminist.org/news/pr/pr091800.html [October 15, 2001].

Ferguson, J. N., J. M. Aldag, T. R. Insel, and L. J. Young. 2001. Oxytocin in the medial amygdala is essential for social recognition in the mouse. *The Journal of Neuroscience*. 21:8278–285.

Ferrie, J. E., M. Shipley, M. G. Marmot, S. A. Stansfeld, and G. Davey Smith. 1998. An uncertain future: The health effects of threat to employment security in white collar men and women. *American Journal of Public Health*. 88:1030–1036.

Field, T. M. 2001. Massage therapy facilitates weight gain in preterm infants. *Current Directions in Psychological Science*. 10:51–54.

Field, T. M., R. Woodson, R. Greenberg, D. Cohen. 1982. Discrimination and imitation of facial expressions by neonates. *Science*. 218:179–81.

Fields, R. 2001. 'Married with children' still fading as a model. *Los Angeles Times*, May 15, p. A1.

Fiscella, K., and P. Franks. 1997. Poverty or income inequality as predictor of mortality: Longitudinal cohort study. *British Medical Journal*. 314:1724–728.

Fisher, A. 1998. Success secret: A high emotional IQ. *Fortune*, October 26, pp. 293–98.

Fisher, H. E. 1999. *The first sex: The natural talents of women and how they are changing the world*. New York: Ballantine Books.

Fisher, L., and S. S. Feldman. 1998. Familial antecedents of young adult health risk behavior: A longitudinal study. *Journal of Family Psychology*. 12(1):66–80.

Fleming, A. S., D. Ruble, H. Krieger, and P. Y. Wong. 1997. Hormonal and experiential correlates of maternal responsiveness during pregnancy and the puerperium in human mothers. *Hormones and Behavior*. 31:145–58.

Flinn, M. V., and B. G. England. 1997. Social economics of childhood glucocorticoid stress responses and health. *American Journal of Physical Anthropology*. 102:33–53.

Floeter, M. K., and W. T. Greenough. 1979. Cerebellar plasticity: Modification of purkinje cell structure by differential rearing in monkeys. *Science*. 206:227–29.

Folbre, N. 2001. *The invisible heart: Economics and family values*. New York: New Press.

Fondas, N., and S. Sassalos. 2000. A different voice in the boardroom: How the presence of women directors affects board influence over management. *Global Focus*. 12:13–22.

Fontana, A. M., T. Diegnan, A. Villeneuve, and S. J. Lepore. 1999. Nonevaluative social support reduces cardiovascular reactivity in young women during acutely stressful performance situations. *Journal of Behavioral Medicine*. 22:75–91.

Fossey, D. 1983. *Gorillas in the mist*. Boston: Houghton Mifflin.

Francis, D., J. Diorio, D. Liu, and M. J. Meaney. 1999. Nongenomic transmission across generations of maternal behavior and stress responses in the rat. *Science*. 286:1155–1158.

Frank, R. H., T. Gilovich, and D. T. Regan. 1993. Does studying economics inhibit cooperation? *Journal of Economic Perspectives*. 7:159–71.

Frankenhaeuser, M. 1993. On the psychobiology of working life. International Conference on Work and Health. February 22–25.

Frankenhaeuser, M., U. Lundberg, M. Fredrikson, B. Melin, M. Tuomisto, A. Myrsten, M. Hedman, B. Bergman-Losman, and L. Wallin. 1989. Stress on and off the job as related to sex and occupational status in white-collar workers. *Journal of Organizational Behavior*. 10:321–46.

Frankish, C. J., and W. Linden. 1996. Spouse-pair risk factors and cardiovascular reactivity. *Journal of Psychosomatic Research*. 40:37–51.

Fritsch, J. 2001. A rise in single dads. *The New York Times*, May 20, p. 2.

Garcia-Marques, T., and D. M. Mackie. 2001. The feeling of familiarity as a regulator of persuasive processing. *Social Cognition*. 19:9–34.

Geary, D. C. 1999. Evolution and developmental sex differences. *Current Directions in Psychological Science*. 8:115–20.

Geronimus, A. T. 1996. What teen mothers know. *Human Nature*. 7:323–52.

Gibbs, D. M. 1986. Vasopressin and oxytocin: Hypothalamic modulators of the stress response: A review. *Psychoneuroendocrinology*. 11(2):131–40.

Gingrich, B., Y. Liu, C. Cascio, Z. Wang, and T. R. Insel. 2000. Dopamine D2 receptors in the nucleus accumbens are important for social attachment in female prairie voles (*Microtus ochrogaster*). *Behavioral Neuroscience*. 114:173–83.

Glaser, R., and T. Gottleib-Stematsky. 1982. *Human herpesvirus infections: Clinical aspects*. New York: Marcel Dekker.

Glaser, R., and J. K. Kiecolt-Glaser, eds. 1994. *Handbook of human stress and immunity*. San Diego, Calif.: Academic Press.

Glaser, R., J. K. Kiecolt-Glaser, and R. Bonneau. 1992. Stress-induced modulation of the immune response to recombinant hepatitis B vaccine. *Psychosomatic Medicine*. 54:22–29.

Glaser, R., J. K. Kiecolt-Glaser, C. E. Speicher, and J. E. Holliday. 1985. Stress, loneliness, and changes in herpesvirus latency. *Journal of Behavioral Medicine*. 8:249–60.

Glenn, N. D., and C. N. Weaver. 1981. The contribution of marital happiness to global happiness. *Journal of Marriage and Family*. 43:161–68.

Glenn, N. D., and C. N. Weaver. 1988. The changing relationship of marital status to reported happiness. *Journal of Marriage and the Family*. 46:317–24.

Glenn, N., and K. B. Kramer. 1987. The marriages and divorces of the children of divorce. *Journal of Marriage and the Family*. 49:811–25.

Glynn, L. M., N. Christenfeld, and W. Gerin. 1999. Gender, social support, and cardiovascular responses to stress. *Psychosomatic Medicine*. 61:234–42.

Gold, P. W., F. K. Goodwin, and G. P. Chrousos. 1988a. Clinical and biochemical manifestations of depression: Relation to the neurobiology of stress. *New England Journal of Medicine*. 319:348–53.

Gold, P. W., F. K. Goodwin, and G. P. Chrousos. 1988b. Clinical and biochemical manifestations of depression: Relation to the neurobiology of stress (second of two parts). *New England Journal of Medicine*. 319:413–20.

Goldstein, I. B., D. Shapiro, A. Chicz-DeMet, and D. Guthrie. 1999. Ambulatory blood pressure, heart rate, and neuroendocrine responses in women nurses during work and off work days. *Psychosomatic Medicine*. 61:387–96.

Goleman, D. 1997. *Emotional intelligence*. New York: Bantam Books.

Goodall, J. 1986. *The chimpanzees of Gombe: Patterns of behavior*. Cambridge: Belknap Press of Harvard University Press.

Goodall, J. 1999. *Reason for hope: A spiritual journey*. New York: Warner Books.

Goodman, E., and P. O'Brien. 2000. *I know just what you mean: The power of friendship in women's lives*. New York: Simon & Schuster.

Goodman, L. A., M. P. Koss, L. F. Fitzgerald, N. F. Russo, and G. P. Keita. 1993. Male violence against women: Current research and future directions. *American Psychologist*. 48:1054–1058.

Goodwin, J. S., W. C. Hunt, C. R. Key, and J. M. Samet. 1987. The effect of marital status on stage, treatment, and survival of cancer patients. *Journal of the American Medical Association*. 258:3125–130.

Goodwin, P. J., M. Leszcz, M. Ennis, J. Koopmans, L. Vincent, H. Guther, E. Drysdale, M. Hundleby, H. M. Chochinov, M. Navarro, M. Speca, J. Masterson, L. Dohan, R. Sela, B. Warren, A. Paterson, K. I. Pritchard, A. Arnold, R. Doll, S. E. O'Reilly, G. Quirt, N. Hood, and J. Hunter. 2001. The effect of group psychosocial support on survival in metastatic breast cancer. *New England Journal of Medicine*. 345:1719–26.

Gottlieb, G. 1998. Naturally occurring environmental and behavioral influences on gene activity: From central dogma to probabilistic epigenesis. *Psychological Review*. 105: 792–802.

Gove, W., and C. Zeiss. 1987. Multiple roles and happiness. In *Spouse, parent, worker*, edited by F. Crosby. New Haven, Conn.: Yale University Press.

Gray, J. G. 1959. *The warriors: Reflections on men in battle*. New York: Harper & Row [1970].

Greenberg, E., and L. Grunberg. 1995. Work alienation and problem alcohol behavior. *Journal of Health and Social Behavior*. 36:83–102.

Gunnar, M. R., C. A. Gonzalez, B. L. Goodlin, and S. Levine. 1981. Behavioral and pituitary-adrenal responses during a prolonged separation period in rhesus monkeys. *Psychoneuroimmunology*. 6:65–75.

Gurung, R. A. R., S. E. Taylor, and T. E. Seeman. 2001. Accounting for changes in social support at older ages: Insights from the MacArthur studies of successful aging. Manuscript under review.

Gust, D. A., T. P. Gordon, M. K. Hambright, and M. E. Wilson. 1993. Relationship between social factors and pituitary-adrenocortical activity in female rhesus monkeys (*Macaca mulatta*). *Hormones and Behavior*. 27:318–31.

Gutierres, S., D. Saenz, and B. Green. 1994. Job stress and health outcomes among Anglo and Hispanic employees: A test of the person-environment fit model. In *Job stress in a changing workforce: Investigating gender, diversity, and family issues*, edited by G. Keita and J. J. Hurrell, Jr. Washington, D. C.: American Psychological Association.

Gutner, T. 2001. Do top women execs = stronger IPOs? *Business Week*, February 5, p. 122.

Hagestdad, G. O., and M. A. Smyer. 1982. Dissolving long-term relationships: Patterns of divorcing in middle age. In *Personal relationships: Vol.4 Dissolving relationships*, edited by S. Duck. New York: Academic Press.

Hajdu, P., M. McKee, and F. Bojan. 1995. Changes in premature mortality differentials by marital status in Hungary and in England and Wales. *European Journal of Public Health*. 5:259–64.

Hall, J. A. 1978. Gender effects in decoding nonverbal cues. *Psychological Bulletin*. 85:845–57.

Hamilton, J. A. 1989. *Women's health*. Paper presented at the MacArthur Health and Behavior Network Core Group Meeting, Boston, September.

Hamilton, W. D. 1963. The evolution of altruistic behavior. *The American Naturalist*. 97:354–56.

Hamilton, W. D. 1975. Innate social attitudes of man: An approach from evolutionary genetics. In *Biosocial Anthropology*, edited by R. Fox. New York: Wiley.

Hammar, N., L. Alfredsson, and J. V. Johnson. 1998. Job strain, social support at work, and incidence of myocardial infarction. *Occupational and Environmental Medicine*. 55(8):548–53.

Harlow, H. F., and M. K. Harlow. 1962. Social deprivation in monkeys. *Scientific American*. 207:136–46.

Harris, J. R. 1995. Where is the child's environment? A group socialization theory of development. *Psychological Review*. 102:458–89.

Harris, J. R. 1998. *The nurture assumption: Why children turn out the way they do*. New York: Free Press.

Harvey, J. H., G. L. Wells, and M. D. Alvarez. 1978. Attribution in the context of conflict and separation in close relationships. In *New directions in attribution research*, Vol. 2, edited by J. H. Harvey, W. Ickes, and R. F. Kidd. Hillsdale, N.J.: Erlbaum.

Hazan, C., and L. M. Diamond. 2000. The place of attachment in human mating. *Review of General Psychology*. 4:186–204.

Hazan, C., and P. Shaver. 1987. Romantic love conceptualized as an attachment process. *Journal of Personality and Social Psychology*. 52:511–24.

Heim, C., D. J. Newport, A. H. Miller, and C. B. Nemeroff. 2000. Long-term neuroendocrine effects of childhood maltreatment. *JAMA*, 284:2321.

Heim, C., D. J. Newport, S. Heit, Y. P. Graham, M. Wilcox, R. Bonsall, A. H. Miller, and C. B. Nemeroff. 2000. Pituitary-adrenal and autonomic responses to stress in women after sexual and physical abuse in childhood. *Journal of the American Medical Association*. 284:592–97.

Hellhammer, D. H., W. Hubert, and T. Schurmeyer. 1985. Changes in saliva testosterone after psychological stimulation in men. *Psychoneuroendocrinology*. 10:77–81.

Helmuth, L. 2001. Moral reasoning relies on emotion. *Science*. 293:1971–972.

Helsing, K. J., M. Szklo, and G. W. Comstock. 1981. Factors associated with mortality after widowhood. *American Journal of Public Health*. 71:802–809.

Hennessy, M. B., S. P. Mendoza, and J. N. Kaplan. 1982. Behavior and plasma cortisol following brief peer separation in juvenile squirrel monkeys. *American Journal of Primatology*. 3:143–51.

Hertsgaard, L. G., M. R. Gunnar, M. R. Erickson, and M. Nachmias. 1995. Adrenocortical responses to the strange situation in infants with disorganized/disoriented attachment relationships. *Child Development*. 66:1100–106.

Hertzman, C. 1995. *Environment and health in Central and Eastern Europe*. Washington, D.C.: World Bank.

Higley, J. D., P. T. Mehlman, S. B. Higley, B. Fernald, J. Vickers, S. G. Lindell, D. M. Taub, S. J. Suomi, and M. Linnoila. 1996a. Excessive mortality in young free-ranging male nonhuman primates with low cerebrospinal fluid 5-hydroxyindoleacetic acid concentration. *Archives of General Psychiatry*. 53:537–43.

Higley, J. D., P. T. Mehlman, R. E. Poland, J. V. Taub, S. J. Suomi, and M. Linnoila. 1996b. CSF testosterone and 5-HIAA correlate with different types of aggressive behaviors. *Society of Biological Psychiatry*. 40:1067–1082.

Hobel, C. J., C. Dunkel-Schetter, and S. Roesch. 1998. Maternal stress as a signal to the fetus. *Prenatal and Neonatal Medicine*. 3:116–20.

Hobel, C. J., C. Dunkel-Schetter, S. C. Roesch, L. C. Castro, and C. P. Arora. 1999. Maternal plasma corticotropin-releasing hormone associated with stress at 20 weeks' gestation in pregnancies ending in preterm delivery. *American Journal of Obstetrics and Gynecology.* 180:S257–63.

Hochschild, A. 1989. *The second shift: Working parents and the revolution at home.* New York: Viking Penguin.

Holahan, C., and R. Moos. 1981. Social support and psychological distress: A longitudinal analysis. *Journal of Abnormal Psychology.* 90(4):365–70.

Holden, C. 2000. The violence of the lambs. *Science.* 289:580–81.

Holtzworth-Munroe, A., L. Bates, N. Smutzler, and E. Sandin. 1997. A brief review of the research on husband violence. *Aggression and Violent Behavior.* 2:65–99.

House, J. S., K. R. Landis, and D. Umberson. 1988. Social relationships and health. *Science.* 241:540–45.

House, J. S., C. Robbins, and H. L. Metzner. 1982. The association of social relationships and activities with mortality: Prospective evidence from the Tecumseh Community Health Study. *American Journal of Epidemiology.* 116:123–40.

House, J. S., D. Umberson, and K. R. Landis. 1988. Structures and processes of social support. *American Review of Sociology.* 14:293–318.

House, J., J. Lepkowski, A. Kinney, R. Mero, R. Kessler, and A. Herzog. 1994. The social stratification of aging and health. *Journal of Health and Social Behavior.* 35:213–34.

Hrdy, S. B. 1999. *Mother nature: A history of mothers, infants, and natural selection.* New York: Pantheon Books.

Huber, J., and G. Sitze. 1983. *Sex stratification: Children, housework and jobs.* New York: Academic Press.

Huston, T., G. Geis, and R. Wright. 1976. The angry samaritans. *Psychology Today,* June, pp. 61–65.

Huston, T. L., M. Ruggiero, R. Conner, and G. Geis. 1981. Bystander intervention into crime: A study based on naturally-occurring episodes. *Social Psychology Quarterly.* 44:14–23.

Insel, T. R. 1997. A neurobiological basis of social attachment. *American Journal of Psychiatry.* 154:726–35.

Insel, T. R., and T. J. Hulihan. 1995. A gender specific mechanism for pair bonding: Oxytocin and partner preference formation in monogamous voles. *Behavioral Neuroscience.* 109:782–89.

Insel, T. R., and J. T. Winslow. 1998. Serotonin and neuropeptides in affiliative behaviors. *Biological Psychiatry.* 44:207–19.

Insel, T., J. Winslow, Z. Wang, and L. Young. 1998. Oxytocin, vasopressin, and the neuroendocrine basis of pair bond formation. *Advances in Experimental Medicine and Biology.* 449:215–24.

Istre, G. R., M. A. McCoy, L. Osborn, J. J. Barnard, and A. Bolton. 2001. Deaths and injuries from house fires. *The New England Journal of Medicine.* 344:1911–916.

Izard, C. E., and P. Harris. 1995. Emotional development and developmental psychopathology. In *Developmental Psychopathology,* Vol. 1: *Theory and Methods,* edited by D. Cicchetti and D. J. Cohen. New York: John Wiley & Sons.

Jacobson, N. S., J. M. Bottman, J. Waltz, R. Rushe, J. Bobcock, and A. Holtzworth-Munroe.

1994. Affect, verbal content, and psychophysiology in the arguments of couples with a violent husband. *Journal of Consulting and Clinical Psychology*. 62:982–88.

Jaffe, J. H. 1990. Drug addiction and drug abuse. In *Goodman and Gilman's: The pharmacological basis of therapeutics*, 8th edition, edited by A. G. Gilman, T. W. Rall, A. S. Nies, and P. Taylor. New York: McGraw-Hill.

Jamner, L. D., J. Alberts, H. Leigh, and L. C. Klein. 1998. *Affiliative need and endogenous opioids*. Paper presented to the Society of Behavioral Medicine annual meetings, New Orleans, La., March.

Jensen, P., D. Grogan, S. Xenakis, and M. Bain. 1989. Father absence: Effects on child and maternal psychopathology. *Journal of the American Academy of Child and Adolescent Psychiatry*. 28:171–75.

Jessor, R., and S. L. Jessor. 1977. *Problem Behavior and Psychosocial Development*. New York: Academic Press.

Jezova, D., E. Jurankova, A. Mosnarova, M. Kriska, and I. Skultetyova. 1996. Neuroendocrine response during stress with relation to gender differences. *Acta Neurobiologae Experimentalis*. 56:779–85.

Johnson, J. G., P. Cohen, J. Brown, E. M. Smailes, and D. P. Bernstein. 1999. Childhood maltreatment increases risk for personality disorders during early adulthood. *Archives of General Psychiatry*. 56:600–606.

Johnson, W. B., R. Lall, E. K. Holmes, J. M. Huwe, and M. D. Nordlund. 2001. Mentoring experiences among Navy midshipmen. *Military Medicine*. 166:27–31.

Jonsson, D., A. Rosengren, A. Dotevall, G. Lappas, and L. Wilhelmsen. 1999. Job control, job demands and social support at work in relation to cardiovascular risk factors in MONICA 1995, Goteborg. *Journal of Cardiovascular Risk*. 6(6):379–85.

Justice, B., and R. Justice. 1990. *The abusing family*. New York : Plenum Press.

Kagan, J. 1997. Temperament and reactions to unfamiliarity. *Child Development*. 68:139–43.

Kagan, J., J. Reznick, and N. Snidman. 1988. Bological bases of childhood shyness. *Science*. 240:167–71.

Kagan, J., N. Snidman, and D. M. Arcus. 1992. Initial reactions to unfamiliarity. *Current Directions in Psychological Science*. 1:171–74.

Kalin, N. H., S. E. Shelton, and D. E. Lynn. 1995. Opiate systems in mother and infant primates coordinate intimate contact during reunion. *Psychoneuroendocrinology*. 7:735–42.

Kalin, N., C. Larson, S. Shelton, and R. Davidson. 1998. Asymmetric frontal brain activity, cortisol, and behavior associated with fearful temperament in rhesus monkeys. *Behavioral Neuroscience*. 112:286–92.

Kamarck, T. W., S. B. Manuck, and J. R. Jennings. 1990. Social support reduces cardiovascular reactivity to psychological challenge: A laboratory model. *Psychosomatic Medicine*. 52:42–58.

Kanwisher, N., J. McDermott, and M. M. Chun. 1997. The fusiform face area: A module in human extrastriate cortex specialized for face perception. *The Journal of Neuroscience*. 17:4302–311.

Kaplan, G. A., E. R. Pamuk, J. W. Lynch, R. D. Cohen, and J. L. Balfour. 1996. Inequality in income and mortality in the United States: Analysis of mortality and potential pathways. *British Medical Journal*. 312:999–1003.

Kaplan, H., K. Hill, K. Hawkes, and A. Hurtado. 1984. Food sharing among Ache hunter-gatherers of Eastern Paraguay. *Current Anthropology*. 25:113–15.

Karasek, R. A. 1979. Job demands, job decision latitude, and mental strain: Implications for job redesign. *Administrative Science Quarterly*. 24:285–307.

Karasek, R. A., D. Baker, F. Marxer, A. Ahlbom, and T. Theorell. 1981. Job decision latitude, job demands and cardiovascular disease: A prospective study of Swedish men. *American Journal of Public Health*. 71:694–705.

Karasek, R. A., T. Theorell, J. E. Schwartz, P. L. Schnall, C. F. Pieper, and J. L. Michela. 1988. Job characteristics in relation to the prevalence of myocardial infarction in the US: Health examination survey (HES) and health and nutrition examination survey (HANES). *American Journal of Public Health*. 78:910–19.

Kashima, Y., S. K. Yamaguchi, S. Choi, M. J. Gelfand, and M. Yuki. 1995. Culture, gender, and self: A perspective from the individualism-collectivism research. *Journal of Personality and Social Psychology*. 69:925–37.

Kaufman, J., B. Birmaher, J. Perel, R. E. Dahl, S. Stull, D. Brent, L. Trubnick, M. Al-Shabbout, and N. D. Ryan. 1998. Serotonergic functioning in depressed abused children: Clinical and familial correlates. *Biological Psychiatry*. 44:973–81.

Kaufman, J., P. M. Plotsky, C. B. Nemeroff, and D. S. Charney. 2000. Effects of early adverse experiences on brain structure and function: Clinical implications. *Biological Psychiatry*. 48:778–90.

Kawachi, I., and B. P. Kennedy. 1997. Health and social cohesion: Why care about income inequality? *British Medical Journal*. 314:1037–40.

Kawachi, I., B. Kennedy, V. Gupta, and D. Prothrow-Stith. 1999. Women's status and the health of women and men: A view from the States. *Social Science and Medicine*. 48:21–32.

Kendrick, K. M., and E. B. Keverne. 1989. Effects of intracerebroventricular infusions of naltrexone and phentolamine on central and peripheral oxytocin release and on maternal behaviour induced by vaginocervical stimulation in the ewe. *Brain Research*. 505:329–32.

Kendrick, K. M., E. B. Keverne, and B. A. Baldwin. 1987. Intracerebroventricular oxytocin stimulates maternal behaviour in the sheep. *Neuroendocrinology*. 46:56–61.

Kennedy, B., I. Kawachi, and D. Prothrow-Stith. 1996. Income distribution and mortality: Cross sectional ecological study of the Robin Hood index in the United States. *British Medical Journal*. 312:1004–1007.

Kennell, J., M. Klaus, S. McGrath, S. Robertson, and C. Hinkley. 1991. Continuous emotional support during labor in a U. S. hospital. *Journal of the American Medical Association*. 265:2197–201.

Kessler, R. C., K. A. McGonagle, S. Zhao, C. B. Nelson, M. Hughes, S. Eshleman, H. U. Wittchen, and K. S. Kendler. 1994. Lifetime and 12-month prevalence of DSM-III-R psychiatric disorders in the United States. *Archives of General Psychiatry*. 51:8–19.

Kessler, R. C., and J. D. McLeod. 1985. Social support and mental health in community samples. In *Social Support and Health*, edited by S. Cohen and S. L. Syme. Orlando: Academic Press.

Keverne, E. B., F. L. Martel, and C. M. Nevison. 1996. Primate brain evolution: genetic and functional considerations. *Proceedings of the Royal Society of London*. 262:689–96.

Keverne, E. B., C. M. Nevison, and F. L. Martel. 1999. Early learning and the social bond. In *The integrative neurobiology of affiliation*, edited by C. S. Carter, I. I. Lederhendler, and B. Kirkpatrick. Cambridge, Mass.: MIT Press.

Kiecolt-Glaser, J. K., and T. L. Newton. 2001. Marriage and health: His and hers. *Psychological Bulletin*. 127:472–503.

Kiecolt-Glaser, J. K., L. D. Fisher, P. Ogrocki, J. C. Stout, C. E. Speicher, and R. Glaser. 1987. Marital quality, marital disruption, and immune function. *Psychosomatic Medicine*. 49:13–34.

Kiecolt-Glaser, J. K., R. Glaser, J. T. Cacioppo, R. C. MacCallum, M. A. Snydersmith, K. Cheongtag, and W. B. Malarkey. 1997. Marital conflict in older adults: Endocrinological and immunological correlates. *Psychosomatic Medicine*. 59:339–49.

Kiecolt-Glaser, J. K., R. Glaser, J. T. Cacioppo, and W. B. Malarkey. 1998. Marital stress: Immunologic, neuroendocrine, and autonomic correlates. In *Annals of the New York Academy of Sciences*, Vol. 840: *Neuroimmunomodulation: Molecular aspects, integrative systems, and clinical advances*, edited by S. M. McCann, J. M. Lipton, et al. New York: New York Academy of Sciences, pp. 656–63.

Kiecolt-Glaser, J. K., W. B. Malarkey, M. A. Chee, T. Newton, J. T. Cacioppo, H. Y. Mao, and R. Glaser. 1993. Negative behavior during marital conflict is associated with immunological down-regulation. *Psychosomatic Medicine*. 55:395–409.

Kiecolt-Glaser, J. K., T. Newton, J. T. Cacioppo, R. C. MacCallum, R. Glaser, and W. B. Malarkey. 1996. Marital conflict and endocrine function: Are men really more physiologically affected than women? *Journal of Consulting and Clinical Psychology*. 64:324–32.

King, A., B. Oka, and D. Young. 1994. Ambulatory blood pressure and heart rate responses to stress of work and caregiving in older women. *Journal of Gerontology*. 49:239–45.

King, D. W., L. A. King, D. M. Gudanowski, and D. L. Vreven. 1995. Alternative representations of war zone stressors: Relationships to posttraumatic stress disorder in male and female Vietnam veterans. *Journal of Abnormal Psychology*. 104:184–96.

Kipling, R. [1902] 1994. *Just so stories*. Harmondsworth: Penguin.

Kirschbaum, C., T. Klauer, S. Filipp, and D. H. Hellhammer. 1995. Sex-specific effects of social support on cortisol and subjective responses to acute psychological stress. *Psychosomatic Medicine*. 57:23–31.

Kirschbaum, C., S. Wust, and D. Hellhammer. 1992. Consistent sex differences in cortisol responses to psychological stress. *Psychosomatic Medicine*. 54:648–57.

Klebanov, P. K., J. Brooks-Gunn, and G. J. Duncan. 1994. Does neighborhood and family poverty affect mothers' parenting, mental health, and social support? *Journal of Marriage and the Family*. 56:441–55.

Knopman, D., L. L. Boland, T. Mosley, G. Howard, D. Liao, M. Szklo, P. McGovern, and A. R. Folsom. 2001. Cardiovascular risk factors and cognitive decline in middle-aged adults. *Neurology*. 56:42–48.

Knox, S. S., and K. Uvnas-Moberg. 1998. Social isolation and cardiovascular disease: An atherosclerotic pathway? *Pychoneuroendocrinology*. 23:887–90.

Kobasa, S. C., and M. C. Puccetti. 1983. Personality and social resources in stress resistance. *Journal of Personality and Social Psychology*. 45:839–50.

Koob, G. F., P. P. Sanna, and F. E. Bloom. 1998. Neuroscience of addiction. *Neuron*. 21: 467–76.

Koretz, G. 2001. The young and the disabled: Disturbing signs of declining health. *Business Week*, June 4, p. 30.

Kors, D., W. Linden, and W. Gerin. 1997. Evaluation interferes with social support: Effects on cardiovascular stress reactivity. *Journal of Social and Clinical Psychology*. 16:1–23.

Koskinen, S., and T. Martelin. 1994. Why are socioeconomic mortality differences smaller among women than among men? *Social Science and Medicine*. 38(10):1385–396.

Koss, M. P., L. A. Goodman, A. Browne, L. F. Fitzgerald, L. F. Keita, and N. F. Russo. 1994. *No safe haven: Male violence against women at home, at work, and in the community.* Washington, D.C.: APA Books.

Kraemer, G. W., M. H. Ebert, D. E. Schmidt, and W. T. McKinney. 1989. A longitudinal study of the effect of different social rearing conditions on cerebrospinal fluid norepinephrine and biogenic amine metabolites in rhesus monkeys. *Neuropsychopharmacology*. 2(3):175–89.

Kubzansky, L. D., I. Kawachi, and D. Sparrow. 1999. Socioeconomic status, hostility, and risk factor clustering in the normative aging study: Any help from the concept of allostatic load? *Annals of Behavioral Medicine*. 21(4):330–38.

Kuhn, C. M., J. Pauk, and S. M. Schanberg. 1990. Endocrine responses to mother-infant separation in developing rats. *Developmental Psychobiology*. 23:395–410.

Kupersmidt, J. B., P. C. Griesler, M. E. DeRosier, C. J. Patterson, and P. W. Davis. 1995. Childhood aggression and peer relations in the context of family and neighborhood factors. *Child Development*. 66:360–75.

Ladd, C. O., R. L. Huot, K. V. Thrivikraman, C. B. Nemeroff, M. J. Meaney, and P. M. Plotsky. 2000. Long-term behavioral and neuroendocrine adaptations to adverse early experience. *Progress in Brain Research*. 122:81–103.

Ladd, C. O., M. J. Owens, and C. B. Nemeroff. 1996. Persistent changes in corticotropin-releasing factor neuronal systems induced by maternal deprivation. *Endocrinology*. 137(4):1212–218.

Laireiter, A., and U. Baumann. 1992. Network structures and support functions: Theoretical and empirical analyses. In *The meaning and measurement of social support*, edited by H. O. F. Veiel and U. Baumann. Washington, D.C.: Hemisphere.

Lamb, M. E. 1977. The development of mother-infant and father-infant attachments in the second year of life. *Developmental Psychology*. 13:637–48.

Landsbergis, P., P. Schnall, D. Deitz, R. Friedman, and T. Pickering. 1992. The patterning of psychological attributes and distress by "job strain" and social support in a sample of working men. *Journal of Behavioral Medicine*. 15(4):379.

Larsson, B., K. Svardsudd, L. Welin, L. Wilhelmsen, P. Bjorntorp, and G. Tibblin. 1984. Abdominal adipose tissue distribution, obesity, and risk of cardiovascular disease and death: 13 year follow-up of participants in the study of men born in 1913. *British Medical Journal.* 288:1401–404.

Lauer, R. H., and J. C. Lauer. 2000. *Marriage and family: The quest for intimacy.* Boston: The McGraw-Hill Companies, Inc.

Lavee, Y., H. I. McCubbin, and D. H. Olson. 1987. The effect of stressful life events and transitions on family functioning and well-being. *Journal of Marriage and the Family.* 49:857–73.

Laviola, G., and M. L. Terranova. 1998. The developmental psychobiology of behavioural plasticity in mice: The role of social experiences in the family unit. *Neuroscience and Biobehavioral Reviews.* 23:197–213.

Lavrakas, P. J. 1982. Fear of crime and behavioral restrictions in urban and suburban neighborhoods. *Population and Environment: Behavioral and Social Issues.* 5:242–64.

Le Doux, J. 1996. *The emotional brain: The mysterious underpinnings of emotional life.* New York: Simon & Schuster.

LeFevre, J., and M. K. McClintock. 1991. Isolation accelerates reproductive senescence and alters its predictors in female rats. *Hormones and Behavior.* 25:258–72.

Lemieux, A. M., and C. L. Coe. 1995. Abuse-related posttraumatic stress disorder: Evidence for chronic neuroendocrine activation in women. *Psychosomatic Medicine.* 57:105–15.

Lesch, K-P., D. Bengel, A. Heils, S. Z. Sabol, B. D. Greenberg, S. Petri, J. Benjamin, C. R. Muller, D. H. Hamer, and D. L. Murphy. 1996. Association of anxiety-related traits with a polymorphism in the serotonin transporter gene regulatory region. *Science.* 274:1527–531.

Levenson, R. W., L. L. Carstensen, and J. M. Gottman. 1993. Long-term marriage: Age, gender, and satisfaction. *Psychology and Aging.* 2:301–13.

Levine, J. A., R. Weisell, S. Chevassus, C. D. Martinez, B. Burlingame, and W. A. Coward. 2001. The work burden of women. *Science.* 294:812.

Levine, S., S. G. Wiener, and C. L. Coe. 1993. Temporal and social factors influencing behavioral and hormonal responses to separation in mother and infant squirrel monkeys. *Psychoneuroimmunology.* 18:297–306.

Lewis, B. P., and D. E. Linder. 2000. *Fear and affiliation: Replication and extension of Schachter.* Manuscript in preparation.

Light, K. C., T. E. Smith, J. M. Johns, K. A. Brownley, J. A. Hofheimer, and J. A. Amico. 2000. Oxytocin responsivity in mothers of infants: A preliminary study of relationships with blood pressure during laboratory stress and normal ambulatory activity. *Health Psychology.* 19:560–67.

Lightman, S. L., and W. S. Young III. 1989. Lactation inhibits stress-mediated secretion of cortisosterone and oxytocin and hypothalamic accumulation of corticotropin-releasing factor and enkephalin messenger ribonucleic acids. *Endocrinology.* 124:2358–364.

Liker, J., and G. Elder. 1983. Economic hardship and marital relations in the 1930s. *American Sociological Review.* 48:343–59.

Linnoila, M., M. Virkkunen, M. Scheinin, A. Nuutila, R. Pimon, and F. K. Goodwin. 1983. Low cerebrospinal fluid 5-hydroxyindoleacetic acid concentration differentiates impulsive from nonimpulsive violent behavior. *Life Science.* 33:2609–614.

Litwak, E., and P. Messeri. 1989. Organizational theory, social supports, and mortality rates: A theoretical convergence. *American Sociological Review*. 54:49–66.

Liu, D., J. Diorio, J. C. Day, D. D. Francis, A. Mar, and M. J. Meaney. 2000. Maternal care, hippocampal synaptogenesis and cognitive development in the rat. *Nature*. 3:799–806.

Liu, D., J. Diorio, B. Tannenbaum, C. Caldji, D. Francis, A. Freedman, S. Sharma, D. Pearson, P. M. Plotsky, and M. J. Meaney. 1997. Maternal care, hippocampal glucocorticoid receptors, and hypothalamic-pituitary-adrenal responses to stress. *Science*. 277:1659–662.

Lorenz, K. 1966. *On aggression*. Translated by Marjorie Kerr Wilson. New York: Harcourt, Brace and World.

Loscocco, K., and G. Spitze. 1990. Working conditions, social support, and the well-being of female and male factory workers. *Journal of Health and Social Behavior*. 31:313–27.

Losick, R., and A. L. Sonenshein. 2001. Turning gene regulation on its head. *Science*. 293:2018–2019.

Lubach, G. R., C. L. Coe, and W. B. Ershler. 1995. Effects of early rearing environment on immune responses of infant rhesus monkeys. *Brain, Behavior, and Immunity*. 9:31–46.

Luckow, A., A. Reifman, and D. N. McIntosh. 1998. *Gender differences in coping: A meta-analysis*. Poster presented to the annual meetings of the American Psychological Association, San Francisco, Calif., August.

Lundberg, U., B. Mardberg, and M. Frankenhaeuser. 1994. The total workload of male and female white collar workers as related to age, occupational level, and number of children. *Scandinavian Journal of Psychology*. 35:315–27.

Lundberg, U., and K. Palm. 1989. Workload and catecholamine excretion in parents of preschool children. *Work and Stress*. 3(3):255–60.

Lundy, B. L., N. A. Jones, T. Field, G. Nearing, M. Davalos, P. A. Pietro, S. Schanberg, and C. Kuhn. 1999. Prenatal depression effects on neonates. *Infant Behavior and Development*. 22(1):119–29.

Lynch, J. W., G. A. Kaplan, and S. J. Shema. 1997. Cumulative impact of sustained economic hardship on physical, cognitive, psychological, and social functioning. *New England Journal of Medicine*. 337:1889–895.

Maccoby, E. E. 1998. *The two sexes: Growing up apart, coming together*. Cambridge, Mass.: Harvard University Press.

Maccoby, E. E., and C. H. Jacklin. 1974. *The psychology of sex differences*. Stanford, Calif.: Stanford University Press.

Macintyre, S., S. Maciver, and A. Sooman. 1993. Area, class and health: Should we be focusing on places or people? *Journal of Social Policy*. 22(2):213–34.

Mackenbach, J. P. 2002. Income inequality and population health. *British Medical Journal*. 324:1–2.

Mackenbach, J. P., A. E. Kunst, F. Groenhof, J. K. Borgan, G. Costa, F. Faggiano, P. Jozan, M. Leinsalu, P. Martikainen, J. Rychtarikova, and T. Valkonen. 1999. Socioeconomic inequalities in mortality among women and among men: An international study. *American Journal of Public Health*. 89(12):1800–806.

Maestripieri, D. 1999. The biology of human parenting: Insights from nonhuman primates. *Neuroscience and Biobehavioral Reviews*. 23:411–22.

Malamuth, N. M. 1998. An evolutionary-based model integrating research on the characteristics of sexually coercive men. In *Advances in psychological science*, Vol. 1, edited by J. G. Adair, D. Belanger, and K. L. Dion. New York: Psychology Press Ltd.

Malarkey, W. B., J. K. Kiecolt-Glaser, D. Pearl, and R. Glaser. 1994. Hostile behavior during marital conflict alters pituitary and adrenal hormones. *Psychosomatic Medicine*. 56:41–51.

Malmstrom, M., J. Sundquist, and S. E. Johansson. 1999. Neighborhood environment and self-reported health status: A multilevel analysis. *American Journal of Public Health*. 89:1181–186.

Malyutina, S., M. Bobak, S. Kurilovitch, E. Ryizova, Y. Nikitin, and M. Marmot. 2001. Alcohol consumption and binge drinking in Novosibirsk, Russia, 1985–1995. *Addiction*. 96:987–95.

Manchester, W. 1980. *Goodbye darkness*. Boston: Little, Brown.

Manuck, S. B., J. D. Flory, J. M. McCaffery, K. A. Matthews, J. J. Mann, and M. F. Muldoon. 1998. Aggression, impulsivity, and central nervous system serotonergic responsivity in a nonpatient sample. *Neuropsychopharmacology*. 19(4):287–99.

Manuck, S. B., J. R. Kaplan, M. R. Adams, and T. B. Clarkson. 1988. Studies of psychosocial influences on coronary artery atherogenesis in cynomolgus monkeys. *Health Psychology*. 7:113–24.

Marco, C. A., J. E. Schwartz, J. M. Neale, S. Schiffman, D. Catley, and A. A. Stone. 2000. Impact of gender and having children in the household on ambulatory blood pressure in work and nonwork settings: A partial replication and new findings. *Annals of Behavioral Medicine*. 22:110–15.

Marmot, M. G., and G. Davey Smith. 1997. Socioeconomic differences in health: The contribution of the Whitehall studies. *Journal of Health Psychology*. 2:283–96.

Marmot, M. G., H. Bosma, H. Hemingway, E. Brunner, and S. Stansfeld. 1997. Contribution of job control and other risk factors to social variations in coronary heart disease incidence. *The Lancet*. 350:235–39.

Marmot, M. G., G. Rose, M. Shipley, and P. J. Hamilton. 1978. Employment grade and coronary heart disease in British civil servants. *Journal of Epidemiological Community Health*. 3:244–49.

Martel, F. L., C. M. Nevison, F. D. Rayment, M. J. A. Simpson, and E. B. Keverne. 1993. Opioid receptor blockade reduces maternal affect and social grooming in rhesus monkeys. *Psychoneuroimmunology*. 18:307–21.

Martel, F. L., C. M. Nevison, M. J. A. Simpson, and E. B. Keverne. 1995. Effects of opioid receptor blockade on the social behavior of rhesus monkeys living in large family groups. *Developmental Psychobiology*. 28:71–84.

Martikainen, P. T., and M. G. Marmot. 1999. Socioeconomic differences in weight gain and determinants and consequences of coronary risk factors. *American Journal of Clinical Nutrition*. 69:719–26.

Martin, J. A. 1981. A longitudinal study of the consequences of early mother-infant interaction: A microanalytic approach. *Monographs of the Society for Research in Child Development*. 46: 3, Serial No. 190.

Marwell, G., and R. Ames. 1981. Economists free ride, does anyone else? Experiments on the provision of public goods, IV. *Journal of Public Economics*. 15:295–310.

Mason, W. A., and G. Epple. 1969. Social organization in experimental groups of *Saimiri* and *Callicebus*. *Proceedings of the Second International Congress of Primatology*. 1:59–65.

Matthews, K. A., J. D. Flory, M. F. Muldoon, and S. B. Manuck. 2000. Does socioeconomic status relate to central serotonergic responsivity in healthy adults? *Psychosomatic Medicine*. 62:231–37.

Matthews, K. A., B. B. Gump, and J. F. Owens. 2001. Chronic stress influences cardiovascular and neuroendocrine responses during acute stress and recovery, especially in men. *Health Psychology*. 20:403–10.

Matthews, K. A., K. Raikkonen, S. A. Everson, J. D. Flory, C. A. Marco, J. F. Owens, and C. E. Lloyd. 2000. Do the daily experiences of healthy men and women vary according to occupational prestige and work strain? *Psychosomatic Medicine*. 62:346–53.

Matthews, S., O. Manor, and C. Power. 1999. Social inequalities in health: Are there gender differences? *Social Science and Medicine*. 48:49–60.

Mattiasson, I., F. Lindgarde, J. Nilsson, and T. Theorell. 1990. Threat of unemployment and cardiovascular risk factors: Longitudinal study of quality of sleep and serum cholesterol concentrations in men threatened with redundancy. *British Medical Journal*. 301:461.

Mausner-Dorsch, H., and W. W. Eaton. 2000. Psychosocial work environment and depression: Epidemiological assessment of the demand-control model. *American Journal of Public Health*. 90:1765–770.

Mayer, J. D., and P. Salovey. 1993. The intelligence of emotional intelligence. *Intelligence*. 17:433–42.

Mayer, S. E., and C. C. Jencks. 1989. Growing up in poor neighborhoods: How much does it matter? *Science*. 243:1441–446.

Mayne, T. J., A. O'Leary, B. McCrady, R. Contrada, and E. Labouvie. 1997. The differential effects of acute marital distress on emotional, physiological and immune functions in maritally distressed men and women. *Psychology and Health*. 12:277–88.

Mazur, A., and A. Booth. 1998. Testosterone and dominance in men. *Behavioral and Brain Sciences*. 21:353–97.

McCarthy, M. M. 1995. Estrogen modulation of oxytocin and its relation to behavior. In *Oxytocin: Cellular and molecular approaches in medicine and research*, edited by R. Ivell and J. Russell. New York: Plenum Press.

McCarthy, M. M., and D. Goldman. 1994. An anxiolytic action of oxytocin is enhanced by estrogen in the mouse. *Society for Neuroscience. Abstracts*. 20:441.12.

McCarthy, M. M., S. K. Chung, S. Ogawa, L. Kow, and D. W. Pfaff. 1991. Behavioral effects of oxytocin: Is there a unifying principle? In *Vasopressin*, edited by S. Jard and J. Ramison. Montrouge, France: John Libbey Eurotext.

McCarthy, M. M., C. H. McDonald, P. J. Brooks, and D. Goldman. 1996. An anxiolytic action of oxytocin is enhanced by estrogen in the mouse. *Physiology and Behavior*. 60:1209–215.

McClintock, M. 1998. Personal communication, May 6.

McClintock, M. K. 1971. Menstrual synchrony and suppression. *Nature*. 291:244–45.

McCubbin, J. 1993. Stress and endogenous opioids: Behavioral and circulatory interactions. *Biological Psychology*. 35:91–122.

McDonald, L. M., and K. Korabik. 1991. Sources of stress and ways of coping among male and female managers. *Journal of Social Behavior and Personality*. 6:185–98.

McDonough, P., D. Williams, J. House, and G. Duncan. 1999. Gender and the socioeconomic gradient in mortality. *Journal of Health and Social Behavior*. 40:17–31.

McEwen, B. S. 1999. Stress and the aging hippocampus. *Frontiers in Neuroendocrinology*. 20:49–70.

McEwen, B. S., and E. Stellar. 1993. Stress and the individual. Mechanisms leading to disease. *Archives of Internal Medicine*. 27:2093–101.

McEwen, B. S. 1998. Protective and damaging effects of stress mediators. *New England Journal of Medicine*. 338:171–79.

McEwen, B. S. 2002. Protective and damaging effects of the mediators of stress and adaptation: Allostasis and allostatic load. In *Homeostatic and allostatic regulation in physiological systems*, edited by J. Schulkin. New York: Cambridge University Press.

McEwen, B. S., and T. Seeman. 1999. Protective and damaging effects of mediators of stress: Elaborating and testing the concepts of allostasis and allostatic load. In *Socioeconomic status and health in industrial nations: Social, psychological, and biological pathways*, Vol. 896, edited by N. E. Adler and M. Marmot. New York: Annals of the New York Academy of Sciences.

McEwen, B. S., M. J. de Leon, S. J. Lupien, and M. J. Meaney. 1999. Corticosteroids, the aging brain and cognition. *Trends in Endocrinology and Metabolism*. 10:92–96.

McFarlane, A. H., K. A. Neale, G. R. Norman, R. G. Roy, and D. L. Streiner. 1981. Methodological issues in developing a scale to measure social support. *Schizophrenia Bulletin*. 7:90–100.

McGaugh, J. L., L. Cahill, and B. Roozendaal. 1996. Involvement of the amygdala in memory storage: Interaction with other brain systems. *Proceedings of the National Academy of Sciences of the United States of America*. 93:13508–514.

McGuffin, P., B. Riley, and R. Plomin. 2001. Toward behavioral genomics. *Science*. 291:1232–249.

McKendy, J. P. 1997. The class politics of domestic violence. *Journal of Sociology and Social Welfare*. XXIV:135–55.

McKenna, J. J. 1981. The primate infant caregiving behavior: Origins, consequences and variability with emphasis on the common Indian Langur monkey. In *Parental care in mammals*, edited by D. J. Gubernick and P. H. Klopfer. New York: Plenum.

McLoyd, V. C. 1998. Socioeconomic disadvantage and child development. *American Psychologist*. 53:185–204.

Meaney, M. J., J. Diorio, D. Francis, J. Widdowson, P. LaPlante, C. Caldji, S. Sharma, J. R. Seckl, and P. M. Plotsky. 1996. Early environmental regulation of forebrain glucocorticoid receptor gene expression: Implications for adrenocortical response to stress. *Developmental Neuroscience*. 18:49–72.

Medrich, E. A., J. A. Roizen, V. Rubin, and S. Buckley. 1982. *The serious business of growing up: A study of children's lives outside school*. Berkeley: University of California Press.

Mehlman, P. T., J. D. Higley, I. Faucher, A. A. Lilly, D. M. Taub, J. Vickers, S. J. Suomi, and M. Linnoila. 1995. Correlation of CSF 5-HIAA concentration with sociality and the timing of emigration in free-ranging primates. *American Journal of Psychiatry*. 152:907–13.

Mehren, E. 1994. Study finds most child care lacking. *Los Angeles Times*, April 8, p. E5.

Meijer, A. 1985. Child psychiatric sequelae of maternal war stress. *Acta Psychiatrica Scandinavia*. 72:505–11.

Meltzoff, A. N., and M. K. Moore. 1977. Imitation of facial and manual gestures by human neonates. *Science*. 198:75–78.

Mendoza, S. P., C. L. Coe, W. P. Smotherman, J. Kaplan, and S. Levine. 1980. Functional consequences of attachment: A comparison of two species. In *Maternal influences and early behavior*, edited by R. W. Bell and W. P. Smotherman. New York: Spectrum.

Mendoza, S. P., W. P. Smotherman, M. Miner, J. Kaplan, and S. Levine. 1978. Pituitary-adrenal response to separation in mother and infant squirrel monkeys. *Developmental Psychology*. 11:169–75.

Meyer, L., and H. Kurtz. 1982. 71 feared dead as plane hits bridge, smashes cars, plunges into Potomac. *The Washington Post*, January 14, pp. A1, A6.

Mikulincer, M., and P. R. Shaver. 2001. Attachment theory and intergroup bias: Evidence that priming the secure base schema attenuates negative reactions to out-groups. *Journal of Personality and Social Psychology*. 81:97–115.

Miller, D. T. 1999. The norm of self-interest. *American Psychologist*. 54:1053–1060.

Miller, D. T., and R. K. Ratner. 1998. The disparity between the actual and assumed power of self-interest. *Journal of Personality and Social Psychology*. 74:53–62.

Miller, K. S., R. Forehand, and B. A. Kotchick. 1999. Adolescent sexual behavior in two ethnic minority samples: The role of family variables. *Journal of Marriage and the Family*. 61:85–98.

Minde, K. M. 1980. Bonding of parents to premature infants: Theory and practice. In *Parent-Infant Relationships*, edited by P. M. Taylor. New York: Grune and Stratton.

Mitchell, W. E. 1990. Why Wape men don't beat their wives: Constraints toward domestic tranquility in a New Guinea society. *Pacific Studies*. 13(3):141–50.

Mittag, W., and R. Schwarzer. 1993. Interaction of employment status and self-efficacy on alcohol consumption: A two-wave study on stressful life transitions. *Psychology and Health*. 8:77–87.

Moen, P., J. Robison, and V. Fields. 1994. Women's work and caregiving roles: A life course approach. *Journal of Gerontology*. 49:176–86.

Montgomery, S. M., M. J. Bartley, and R. G. Wilkinson. 1997. Family conflict and slow growth. *Archives of Disease in Childhood*. 77:326–30.

Moore, P. D. 2001. Crowd trouble for predators. *Nature*. 413:265.

Morell, J. A., and R. F. Apple. 1990. Affect expression, marital satisfaction, and stress reactivity among premenopausal women during a conflictual marital discussion. *Psychology of Women Quarterly*. 14:387–402.

Morris, D. 1967. *The naked ape*. New York: Dell Publishing Company.

Moss, H. B., M. Vanyukov, J. K. Yao, and G. P. Kirillova. 1999. Salivary cortisol responses in prepubertal boys: The effects of parental substance abuse and association with drug use behavior during adolescence. *Biological Psychiatry*. 45:1293–299.

Mota, M. T., and M. B. C. Sousa. 2000. Prolactin levels of fathers and helpers related to alloparental care in common marmosets, *Callithrix jacchus*. *Folia Primatologica*. 71:22–26.

Muirhead, J. 1986. *Those who fall*. New York: Random House.

Murphy, Y., and R. F. Murphy. 1985. *Women of the forest*. 2nd ed. New York: Columbia University Press.

Nash, J. 1990. Factors relating to infrequent domestic violence among the Nagovisi. *Pacific Studies*. 13(3):127–40.

National Center for Health Statistics. 1998. Suicide as a Leading Cause of Death, by Age, Race, and Sex [Online]. Available: www.cdc.gov/nchs [December 10, 2001].

Nelson, E. E., and J. Panksepp. 1998. Brain substrates of infant-mother attachment: Contributions of opioids, oxytocin, and norepinephrine. *Neuroscience and Biobehavioral Reviews*. 22:437–52.

New England Research Institutes. 1997. Gender differences in social supports: Data from the Massachusetts Male Aging Study and the Massachusetts Women's Health Study. *Network*, Spring/Summer, p. 12.

Newcomb, M. D., E. Maddahian, and P. M. Bentler. 1986. Risk factors for drug use among adolescents: Concurrent and longitudinal analyses. *American Journal of Public Health*. 76(5):525–31.

Newman, K. 1999. *No shame in my game: The working poor in the inner city*. New York: Alfred Knopf/Russell Sage Foundation.

Niedenthal, P. M., and D. R. Beike. 1997. Interrelated and isolated self-concepts. *Personality and Social Psychology Review*. 1:106–28.

O'Connor, T. G., K. Deater-Deckard, D. Fulker, M. Rutter, and R. Plomin. 1998. Genotype-environment correlations in late childhood and early adolescence: Antisocial behavioral problems and coercive parenting. *Developmental Psychology*. 5:970–81.

O'Reilly, B. 2000. Meet the future: It's your kids. *Fortune*, July 24, pp. 145–65.

Oakley, A., L. Rajan, and A. Grant. 1990. Social support and pregnancy outcome. *British Journal of Obstetrics and Gynaecology*. 97:155–62.

Odell, P. M., K. O. Korgen, P. Schumacher, and M. Delucchi. 2000. Internet use among female and male college students. *CyberPsychology and Behavior*. 3:855–62.

Ogus, E. D., E. R. Greenglass, and R. J. Burke. 1990. Gender-role differences, work stress and depersonalization. *Journal of Social Behavior and Personality*. 5:387–98.

Ohman, A., D. Lundqvist, and F. Esteves. 2001. The face in the crowd revisited: A threat advantage with schematic stimuli. *Journal of Personality and Social Psychology*. 80: 381–96.

Olds, D., C. R. Henderson Jr., R. Cole, J. Eckenrode, H. Kitzman, D. Luckey, L. Pettitt, K. Sidora, P. Morris, and J. Powers. 1998. Long-term effects of nurse home visitation on children's criminal and antisocial behavior: 15-year follow-up of a randomized controlled trial. *Journal of the American Medical Association*. 280:1238–244.

Olweus, D., A. Mattsson, D. Schalling, and H. Low. 1980. Testosterone, aggression, physical, and personality dimensions in normal adolescent males. *Psychosomatic Medicine*. 42:253–69.

Panksepp, J. 1998. *Affective neuroscience*. London: Oxford University Press.

Panksepp, J., E. Nelson, and M. Bekkedal. 1999. Brain systems for the mediation of social separation distress and social-reward: Evolutionary antecedents and neuropeptide intermediaries. In *The integrative neurobiology of affiliation*, edited by C. S. Carter, I. I. Lederhendler, and B. Kirkpatrick. Cambridge, Mass.: MIT Press.

Parish, A. R. 1996. Female relationships in Bonobos (*Pan paniscus*): Evidence for bonding, cooperation, and female dominance in male-philopatric species. *Human Nature*. 7:61–96.

Parish, A. R., and F. B. M. De Waal. 2000. The other "closest living relative": How bonobos (*Pan paniscus*) challenge traditional assumptions about females, dominance, intra- and intersexual interactions, and hominid evolution. In *Evolutionary perspectives on human reproductive behavior*, Vol. 907, edited by D. LeCroy and P. Moller. New York: Annals of the New York Academy of Sciences, pp. 97–113.

Patterson, G. R. 1986. Performance models for antisocial boys. *American Psychologist*. 41:432–44.

Pedersen, F. A. 1980. *The father-infant relationship: Observational studies in the family setting*. New York: Praeger.

Pedersen, F. A., J. L. Rubenstein, and L. J. Yarrow. 1979. Infant development in father-absent families. *The Journal of Genetic Psychology*. 135:51–61.

Pellis, S. M., and A. N. Iwaniuk. 2000. Comparative analysis of the role of postnatal development on the expression of play fighting. *Developmental Psychobiology*. 36:136–47.

Pellis, S. M., and V. C. Pellis. 1996. On knowing it's only play: The role of play signals in play fighting. *Aggression and Violent Behavior*. 1:249–68.

Pellis, S. M., and V. C. Pellis. 1998a. Play fighting of rats in comparative perspective: A schema for neurobehavioral analyses. *Neuroscience and Biobehavioral Reviews*. 23: 87–101.

Perry, B. D., and R. Pollard. 1998. Homeostasis, stress, trauma, and adaptation: A neurodevelopmental view of childhood trauma. *Child and Adolescent Psychiatric Clinics of North America*. 7:33–51.

Phillipson, C. 1997. Social relationships in later life: A review of the research literature. *International Journal of Geriatric Psychiatry*. 12:505–12.

Pihoker, C., M. J. Owens, C. M. Kuhn, S. M. Schanberg, and C. B. Nemeroff. 1993. Maternal separation in neonatal rats elicits activation of the hypothalamic-pituitary-adrenocortical axis: A putative role for corticotropin-releasing factor. *Psychoneuroendocrinology*. 18:485–93.

Pine, D. S., J. D. Coplan, G. A. Wasserman, L. S. Miller, J. E. Fried, M. Davies, T. B. Cooper, L. Greenhill, D. Shaffer, and B. Parsons. 1997. Neuroendocrine response to fenfluramine challenge in boys: Associations with aggressive behavior and adverse rearing. *Archives of General Psychiatry*. 54:839–46.

Pitkow, L. J., C. A. Sharer, R. Xianglin, T. R. Insel, E. F. Terwilliger, and L. J. Young. 2001. Facilitation of affiliation and pair-bond formation by vasopressin receptor gene transfer into the ventral forebrain of a monogamous vole. *The Journal of Neuroscience*. 21:7392–396.

Pitman, R. K., S. P. Orr, and N. B. Lasko. 1993. Effects of intranasal vasopressin and oxytocin on physiologic responding during personal combat imagery in Vietnam veterans with posttraumatic stress disorder. *Psychiatry Research*. 48:107–17.

Plomin, R., J. C. DeFries, G. E. McClearn, and M. Rutter. 1997. *Behavioral Genetics*, 3rd ed. New York: Freeman.

Popik, P., J. Vetulani, and J. M. Van Ree. 1992. Low doses of oxytocin facilitate social recognition in rats. *Psychopharmacology*. 106:71–74.

Preuschoft, S., and C. P. van Schaik. 2000. Dominance and communication: Conflict management in various social settings. In *Natural conflict resolution*, edited by F. Aureli and F. B. M. de Waal. Berkeley, Calif.: University of California Press, pp. 77–105.

Prevosto, P. 2001. The effect of "mentored" relationships on satisfaction and intent to stay of company-grade U.S. Army Reserve nurses. *Military Medicine*. 166:21–26.

Ptacek, J. T., R. E. Smith, and J. Zanas. 1992. Gender, appraisal, and coping: A longitudinal analysis. *Journal of Personality*. 60:747–70.

Putnam, R. D. 2000. *Bowling alone: The collapse and revival of American community*. New York: Simon & Schuster.

Raine, A., P. Brennan, B. Mednick, and S. A. Mednick. 1996. High rates of violence, crime, academic problems, and behavioral problems in males with both early neuromotor deficits and unstable family environments. *Archives of General Psychiatry*. 53:544–49.

Raine, A., P. Brennan, and S. A. Mednick. 1994. Birth complications combined with maternal rejection at one year predispose to violent crime at age 18 years. *Archives of General Psychiatry*. 51:984–88.

Raleigh, M. J., M. T. McGuire, G. L. Brammer, D. B. Pollack, and A. Yuwiler. 1991. Serotonergic mechanisms promote dominance acquisition in adult male vervet monkeys. *Brain Research*. 559:181–90.

Rands, M. 1988. Changes in social networks following marital separation and divorce. In *Families and social networks*, edited by R. M. Milardo. Newbury Park, Calif.: Sage Publications, pp. 127–46.

Reite, M., T. Short, C. Seiler, and J. D. Pauley. 1981. Attachment, loss, and depression. *Journal of Child Psychology and Psychiatry*. 22:141–69.

Repetti, R. 1989. Effects of daily workload on subsequent behavior during marital interactions: The roles of social withdrawal and spouse support. *Journal of Personality and Social Psychology*. 57:651–59.

Repetti, R. 1993. The effects of workload and the social environment at work on health. In *Handbook of stress*, edited by L. Goldberger and S. Breznitz. New York: The Free Press, pp. 368–85.

Repetti, R. L. 1997. *The effects of daily job stress on parent behavior with preadolescents*. Paper presented to the biennial meeting of the Society for Research in Child Development, Washington, D.C., April.

Repetti, R. L. 2000. *The differential impact of chronic job stress on mothers' and fathers' behavior with children*. Manuscript in preparation.

Repetti, R. L., and J. Wood. 1997. Effects of daily stress at work on mothers' interactions with preschoolers. *Journal of Family Psychology*. 11:90–108.

Repetti, R. L., S. E. Taylor, and T. E. Seeman. 2002. Risky families: Family social environments and the mental and physical health of offspring. *Psychological Bulletin*. 128(2).

Reyes, T. M., and C. L. Coe. 1997. Prenatal manipulations reduce the proinflammatory response to a cytokine challenge in juvenile monkeys. *Brain Research.* 769:29–35.

Reynolds, P., and G. A. Kaplan. 1990. Social connections and risk for cancer: Prospective evidence from the Alameda County study. *Behavioral Medicine.* 16:101–10.

Ribeiro, E. B., R. L. Bettiker, M. Bogdanov, and R. J. Wurtman. 1993. Effects of systemic nicotine on serotonin release in rat brain. *Brain Research.* 621:311–18.

Rodin, J., and J. Ickovics. 1990. Women's health: Review and research agenda as we approach the 21st century. *American Psychologist.* 45(9):1018–1034.

Rohner, R. 1975. Parental acceptance-rejection and personality: A universalistic approach to behavioral science. In *Cross cultural perspectives on learning,* edited by R. Brislin et al. New York: Halsted.

Rosenblatt, J. S. 1990. Landmarks in the physiological study of maternal behavior with special reference to the rat. In *Mammalian parenting: Biochemical, neurobiological, and behavioral determinants,* edited by N. A. Krasnegor, R. S. Bridges, et al. New York: Oxford University Press, pp. 40–60.

Rosenblum, L. A., and G. S. Paully. 1984. The effects of varying environmental demands on maternal and infant behavior. *Child Development.* 55:305–14.

Ross, C. E., and J. Mirowsky. 2001. Neighborhood disadvantage, disorder, and health. *Journal of Health and Social Behavior.* 42:258–76.

Ross, C. E., J. Mirowsky, and K. Goldsteen. 1990. The impact of the family on health: The decade in review. *Journal of Marriage and the Family.* 52:1059–1078.

Ross, M., and D. Holmberg. 1990. Recounting the past: Gender differences in the recall of events in the history of a closer relationship. In *Self-inference processes: The Ontario Symposium,* Vol. 6, edited by J. M. Olson and M. P. Zanna. Hillsdale, N.J.: Erlbaum.

Ross, P. 1994. Inequality. *Forbes,* January 31, p. 84.

Rothschild, E. 2001. Who's going to pay for all this? An economist examines the problems in modern caregiving. *The New York Times Book Review,* July 1, p. 8.

Roughton, E., M. Schneider, L. Bromley, and C. Coe. 1998. Maternal endocrine activation during pregnancy alters neurobehavioral state in primate infants. *American Journal of Occupational Therapy.* 52(2):90–98.

Roy, M. P., A. Steptoe, and C. Kirschbaum. 1988. Life events and social support as moderators of individual differences in cardiovascular and cortisol reactivity. *Journal of Personality and Social Psychology.* 75:1273–281.

Ruppenthal, G. C., G. A. Arling, H. F. Harlow, G. P. Sackett, and S. J. Suomi. 1976. A ten-year perspective of motherless mother monkey behavior. *Journal of Abnormal Psychology.* 85:341–48.

Ruppenthal, G. C., M. K. Harlow, C. D. Eisele, H. F. Harlow, and S. F. Suomi. 1974. Development of peer interactions of monkeys reared in a nuclear family environment. *Child Development.* 45:670–82.

Russek, L. G., and G. E. Schwartz. 1997. Feelings of parental caring can predict health status in midlife: A 35-year follow-up of the Harvard Mastery of Stress study. *Journal of Behavioral Medicine.* 20:1–13.

Russell, J. A., and G. Leng. 1998. Sex, parturition and motherhood without oxytocin? *Journal of Endocrinology.* 157:343–59.

Saltzman, W., S. P. Mendoza, and W. A. Mason. 1991. Sociophysiology of relationships in squirrel monkeys. I. Formation of female dyads. *Physiology and Behavior*. 50:271–80.

Sampson, R. J., S. W. Raudenbush, and F. Earls. 1997. Neighborhoods and violent crime: A multilevel study of collective efficacy. *Science*. 277:918–24.

Sanders, B., and M. Gray. 1997. Early environmental influences can attenuate the blood pressure response to acute stress in borderline hypertensive rats. *Physiology and Behavior*. 61:749–54.

Sandman, C. A., P. D. Wadhwa, A. Chicz-DeMet, C. Dunkel-Schetter, and M. Porto. 1997. Maternal stress, HPA activity, and fetal/infant outcome. *Annals of the New York Academy of Sciences*. 814:266–75.

Sapolsky, R. M. 1990. Adrenocortical function, social rank, and personality among wild baboons. *Biological Psychiatry*. 28:862–78.

Sapolsky, R. M. 1992a. *Stress, the aging brain, and the mechanisms of neuron death*. Cambridge, Mass.: MIT Press.

Sapolsky, R. M. 1992b. Cortisol concentrations and the social significance of rank instability among wild baboons. *Psychoneuroendocrinology*. 17:701–9.

Sapolsky, R. M. 1998. *Why zebras don't get ulcers: An updated guide to stress, stress-related disease, and coping*. New York: W. H. Freeman.

Sapolsky, R. M. 2001. *A primate's memoir: A neuroscientist's unconventional life among the baboons*. New York: Scribner.

Sapolsky, R. M., and J. C. Ray. 1989. Styles of dominance and their endocrine correlates among wild olive baboons (*Papio anubis*). *American Journal of Primatology*. 18:1–13.

Sapolsky, R. M., and T. M. Donnelly. 1985. Vulnerability to stress-induced tumor growth increases with age in rats: Role of glucocorticoids. *Endocrinology*. 117:662–66.

Schachter, S. 1959. *The psychology of affiliation*. Stanford, Calif.: Stanford University Press.

Schino, G., and A. Troisi. 1992. Opiate receptor blockade in juvenile macaques: effect on affiliative interactions with their mothers and group companions. *Brain Research*. 576:125–30.

Schlussel, Y. R., P. L. Schnall, M. Zimbler, K. Warren, and T. G. Pickering. 1990. The effect of work environments on blood pressure: Evidence from seven New York organizations. *Journal of Hypertension*. 8:679–85.

Schmidt, L. A. 1999. Frontal brain electrical activity in shyness and sociability. *Psychological Science*. 10:316–20.

Schmitt, E. 2001. For first time, nuclear families drop below 25 percent of households. *The New York Times*, May 15, pp. A1, A18.

Schnall, P. L., C. Pieper, J. E. Schwartz, R. Karasek, Y. Schlussel, R. Devereux, M. Alderman, K. Warren, and T. Pickering. 1990. The relationship between "job strain," workplace diastolic blood pressure, and left ventricular mass index. *Journal of the American Medical Association*. 263:1929–935.

Schnall, P. L., J. E. Schwartz, P. A. Landsbergis, K. Warren, and T. G. Pickering. 1992. Relation between job strain, alcohol, and ambulatory blood pressure. *Hypertension*. 19(5):488–94.

Schneider, M., and C. Coe. 1993. Repeated social stress during pregnancy impairs neuromotor development of the primate infant. *Journal of Development and Behavioral Pediatrics*. 14(2):81–87.

Schneider, M. L., C. L. Coe, and G. R. Lubach. 1992. Endocrine activation mimics the adverse effects of prenatal stress on the neuromotor development of the infant primate. *Developmental Psychobiology*. 25(6):427–39.

Schreibner, H. L., R. W. Bell, M. Kufner, and R. Villescas. 1977. Maternal behavior: A determinant of amphetamine toxicity in rats. *Psychopharmacology*. 52:173–76.

Schulz, R., and S. Beach. 2000. Caregiving as a risk factor for mortality: The caregiver health effects study. *Journal of the American Medical Association*. 282:2215–219.

Schwarzer, R., A. Hahn, and H. Schroder. 1994. Social integration and social support in a life crisis: Effects of macrosocial change in East Germany. *American Journal of Community Psychology*. 22:685–706.

Sears, D. O., and C. L. Funk. 1991. The role of self-interest in social and political attitudes. In *Advances in experimental social psychology*, vol. 24, edited by M. P. Zanna. San Diego, Calif.: Academic Press, pp. 1–91.

Seeman, T. E. 1996. Social ties and health: The benefits of social integration. *Annals of Epidemiology*. 6:442–51.

Seeman, T. E., and B. S. McEwen. 1996. Impact of social environment characteristics on neuroendocrine regulation. *Psychosomatic Medicine*. 58:459–71.

Seeman, T. E., L. F. Berkman, D. Blazer, and J. W. Rowe. 1994. Social ties and support and the neuroendocrine function: The MacArthur studies of successful aging. *Annals of Behavioral Medicine*. 16:95–106.

Seeman, T. E., B. S. McEwen, J. W. Rowe, and B. H. Singer. 2001. Allostatic load as a marker of cumulative biological risk: MacArthur studies of successful aging. *Proceedings of the National Academy of Sciences of the United States of America*. 98:4770–775.

Seeman, T. E., B. H. Singer, J. W. Rowe, R. I. Horwitz, and B. S. McEwen. 1997. Price of adaptation—allostatic load and its health consequences. *Archives of Internal Medicine*. 157:2259–268.

Segerstrom, S. C., S. E. Taylor, M. E. Kemeny, and J. L. Fahey. 1998. Optimism is associated with mood, coping, and immune change in response to stress. *Journal of Personality and Social Psychology*. 74(6):1646–655.

Seligman, D. 1994. The Carnegie solution, yet again. *Fortune*, May 16, p. 154.

Selye, H. 1956. *The stress of life*. New York: McGraw-Hill.

Sephton, S. E., R. M. Sapolsky, H. C. Kraemer, and D. Spiegel. 2000. Diurnal cortisol rhythm as a predictor of breast cancer survival. *Journal of the National Cancer Institute*. 92:994–1000.

Sharpe, R. 2000. As leaders, women rule. *Business Week*, November 20, pp. 75–84.

Shedler, J., and J. Block. 1990. Adolescent drug use and psychological health: A longitudinal inquiry. *American Psychologist*. 45:612–30.

Shi, L., B. Starfield, B. Kennedy, and I. Kawachi. 1999. Income inequality, primary care, and health indicators. *The Journal of Family Practice*. 48(4):275–84.

Sicher, P., O. Lewis, J. Sargent, M. Chaffin, W. N. Friedrich, N. Cunningham, R. Thomas, P. Thomas, and V. S. Villani. 2000. Developing child abuse prevention, identification, and treatment systems in Eastern Europe. *Journal of the American Academy of Child and Adolescent Psychiatry*. 39:660–67.

Silk, J. B. 2000. Ties that bond: The role of kinship in primate societies. In *New directions in anthropological kinship*, edited by L. Stone. Boulder, Colo.: Rowman and Littlefield.

Silk, J. B. 1992. The origins of caregiving behavior. *American Journal of Physical Anthropology*. 87:227–29.

Silk, J. B., R. M. Seyfarth, and D. L. Cheney. 1999. The structure of social relationships among female savanna baboons in Moremi Reserve, Botswana. *Behaviour*. 136:679–703.

Simon, N. G., A. Cologer-Clifford, S. Lu, S. E. McKenna, and S. Hu. 1998. Testosterone and its metabolites modulate $5HT_{1A}$ and $5HT_{1B}$ agonist effects on intermale aggression. *Neuroscience and Biobehavioral Reviews*. 23:325–36.

Simpura, J., B. Levin, and H. Mustonen. 1997. Russian drinking in the 1990s: Patterns and trends in international comparison. In *Demystifying Russian drinking. Comparative studies from the 1990s*, edited by J. Simpura and B. Levin. Helsinki: STAKES, pp. 79–107.

Slotow, R., G. van Dyk, J. Poole, B. Page, and A. Klocke. 2000. Older bull elephants control young males. *Nature*. 408:425–26.

Small, S. A., and T. Luster. 1994. Adolescent sexual activity: An ecological, risk-factor approach. *Journal of Marriage and the Family*. 56:181–92.

Smith, T., and K. Allred. 1989. Blood pressure responses during social interaction in high and low cynically hostile males. *Journal of Behavioral Medicine*. 12:135–43.

Smith, T., L. C. Gallo, L. Goble, L. Q. Ngu, and K. A. Stark. 1998. Agency, communion, and cardiovascular reactivity during marital interaction. *Health Psychology*. 17:537–45.

Smuts, B. B., and R. W. Smuts. 1993. Male aggression and sexual coercion of females in nonhuman primates and other mammals: Evidence and theoretical implications. *Advances in the Study of Behavior*. 22:1–63.

Smuts, B. B. 1987. Gender, aggression, and influence. In *Primate societies*, edited by B. B. Smuts et al. Chicago: University of Chicago Press, pp. 400–12.

Snydersmith, M. A., and J. T. Cacioppo. 1992. Parsing complex social factors to determine component effects: I. Autonomic activity and reactivity as a function of human association. *Journal of Social and Clinical Psychology*. 11:263–78.

Sorenson, G., P. Pirie, A. Folsom, R. Luepker, D. Jacobs, and R. Gillum. 1985. Sex differences in the relationship between work and health: The Minnesota heart survey. *Journal of Health and Social Behavior*. 26:379–94.

Sosa, R., J. Kennell, M. Klaus, S. Robertson, and J. Urrutia. 1980. The effect of a supportive companion on perinatal problems, length of labor, and mother-infant interaction. *New England Journal of Medicine*. 303:597–600.

Spanier, G. B., and L. J. Thompson. 1984. *Parting: The aftermath of separation and divorce*. Beverly Hills, Calif.: Sage.

Spear, L. P. 2000. Neurobehavioral changes in adolescence. *Current Directions in Psychological Science*. 9:111–14.

Spear, L. P. 2000. The adolescent brain and age-related behavioral manifestations. *Neuroscience and Biobehavioral Reviews*. 24:417–63.

Spelke, E., P. Zelazo, J. Kagan, and M. Kotelchuck. 1973. Father interaction and separation protest. *Developmental Psychology*. 9:83–90.

Spiegel, D., and J. R. Bloom. 1983. Group therapy and hypnosis reduce metastatic breast carcinoma pain. *Psychosomatic Medicine*. 45:333–39.

Spiegel, D., J. R. Bloom, H. C. Kraemer, and E. Gottheil. 1989. Effect of psychosocial treatment on survival of patients with metastatic breast cancer. *The Lancet*. 14:888–91.

Spigelman, A., G. Spigelman, and I. Englesson. 1994. The effects of divorce on children: Post-divorce adaptation of Swedish children to the family breakup: Assessed by interview data and Rorschach responses. *Journal of Divorce and Remarriage*. 21(3):171–90.

Spitz, R. A., and K. M. Wolff. 1946. Anaclitic depression: An inquiry into the genesis of psychiatric conditions in early childhood, II. In *The psychoanalytic study of the child*, Vol. II, edited by A. Freud et al. New York: International Universities Press, pp. 313–42.

Spitze, G., J. Logan, G. Joseph, and E. Lee. 1994. Middle generation roles and the well-being of men and women. *Journal of Gerontology*. 49:107–16.

Spoth, R., C. Redmond, C. Hockaday, and S. Yoo. 1996. Protective factors and young adolescent tendency to abstain from alcohol use: A model using two waves of intervention study data. *American Journal of Community Psychology*. 24(6):749–70.

Stack, C. 1975. *All our kin*. New York: Harper and Row.

Stahl, S. M. 1996. *Essential psychopharmacology: Neuroscientific basis and practical applications*. Cambridge, Mass.: Cambridge University Press.

Stanford, M. S., K. W. Greve, and T. J. Dickens. 1995. Irritability and impulsiveness: Relationship to self-reported impulsive aggression. *Personality and Individual Differences*. 23:961–66.

Stansfeld, S. A., J. Head, and M. G. Marmot. 1998. Explaining social class differences in depression and well-being. *Social Psychiatry and Psychiatric Epidemiology*. 33:1–9.

Stansfeld, S. A., H. Bosma, H. Hemingway, and M. G. Marmot. 1998. Psychosocial work characteristics and social support as predictors of SF-36 health functioning: The Whitehall II study. *Psychosomatic Medicine*. 60:247–55.

Stanton, M. E., Y. R. Gutierrez, and S. Levine. 1988. Maternal deprivation potentiates pituitary-adrenal stress responses in infant rats. *Behavioral Neuroscience*. 102:692–700.

Stegmayr, B., T. Vinogradova, S. Malyutina, M. Peltonen, Y. Nikitin, and K. Asplund. 2000. Widening gap of stroke between East and West: Eight-year trends in occurrence and risk factors in Russia and Sweden. *Stroke*. 31:2–8.

Stephens, M., M. Franks, and A. Townsend. 1994. Stress and rewards in women's multiple roles: The case of women in the middle. *Psychology and Aging*. 9:45–52.

Stern, D. N. 1983. The goal and structure of mother-infant play. *Psychiatrie de l'Enfant*. 1:193–216.

Stern, K., and M. K. McClintock. 1998. Regulation of ovulation by human pheromones. *Nature*. 392:177–79.

Stets, J. E. 1995. Job autonomy and control over one's spouse: A compensatory process. *Journal of Health and Behavior*. 36:244–58.

Stone, R. 2000. Stress: The invisible hand in eastern Europe's death rates. *Science*. 288:1732–733.

Storey, A. E., C. J. Walsh, R. L. Quinton, and K. E. Wynne-Edwards. 2000. Hormonal correlates of paternal responsiveness in new and expectant fathers. *Evolution and Human Behavior*. 21:79–95.

Storr, C., A. Trinkoff, and J. Anthony. 1999. Job strain and non-medical drug use. *Drug and Alcohol Dependence*. 55(1–2):45–51.

Strasser, T. 1998. Hypertension: The East European experience. *American Journal of Hypertension*. 11:746–58.

Straus, M. A., and R. J. Gelles. 1986. Societal change and change in family violence from 1975 to 1985 as revealed by two national surveys. *Journal of Marriage and the Family*. 48:465–79.

Straus, M. A., R. J. Gelles, and S. Steinmetz. 1980. *Behind closed doors: Violence in the American family*. Garden City, N.Y.: Doubleday/Anchor Press.

Stribley, J. M., and C. S. Carter. 1999. Developmental exposure to vasopressin increases aggression in adult prairie voles. *Proceedings of the National Academy of Sciences*. 96:12601–604.

Stroebe, M. S., and W. Stroebe. 1983. Who suffers more? Sex differences in health risks of the widowed. *Psychological Bulletin*. 93:279–301.

Stronks, K., H. van de Mheen, J. Van Den Bos, J. P. Mackenback. 1995. Smaller socio-economic inequalities in health among women: The role of employment status. *International Journal of Epidemiology*. 24(3):559–68.

Suchecki, D., P. Rosenfeld, and S. Levine. 1993. Maternal regulation of the hypothalamic-pituitary-adrenal axis in the infant rat: The roles of feeding and stroking. *Developmental Brain Research*. 75:185–92.

Sugiyama, Y. 1988. Grooming interactions among adult chimpanzees at Bossou, Guinea, with special reference to social structure. *International Journal of Primatology*. 9:393–408.

Suh, B. Y., J. H. Liu, D. D. Rasmussen, D. M. Gibbs, J. Steinberg, and S. S. C. Yen. 1986. Role of oxytocin in the modulation of ACTH release in women. *Neuroendocrinology*. 44:309–13.

Suomi, S. J. 2000. A biobehavioral perspective on developmental psychopathology: Excessive aggression and serotonergic dysfunction in monkeys. In *Handbook of developmental psychopathology*, 2nd ed., edited by A. J. Sameroff, M. Lewis, and S. Miller. New York: Plenum Press.

Suomi, S. J. 1997. Early determinants of behaviour: Evidence from primate studies. *British Medical Bulletin*. 53:170–84.

Suomi, S. J. 1987. Genetic and maternal contributions to individual differences in rhesus monkey biobehavioral development. In *Perinatal development: A psychobiological perspective*, edited by N. A. Krasnagor, E. M. Blass, M. A. Hofer, and W. P. Smotherman. New York: Academic Press, pp. 397–420.

Suomi, S. J. 1977. Adult male-infant interactions among monkeys living in nuclear families. *Child Development*. 48:1255–270.

Szalai, A., ed. 1972. *The use of time: Daily activities of urban and suburban populations in twelve countries*. Hawthorne, N.Y.: Mouton de Gruyter Press.

Tannen, D. 1990. *You just don't understand: Women and men in conversation*. New York: Morrow.

Tapscott, D., D. Ticoll, and A. Lowy. 2000. Relationships rule: Business webs are creating relationship capital, shifting control away from marketers, and forming new marketing rules. *Business 2.0*, May, pp. 300–19.

Taylor, J., and R. J. Turner. 2001. A longitudinal study of the role of significance of mattering to others for depressive symptoms. *Journal of Health and Social Behavior.* 42:310–25.

Taylor, S. E. 1991. The asymmetrical impact of positive and negative events: The mobilization-minimization hypothesis. *Psychological Bulletin.* 110:67–85.

Taylor, S. E. 1989. *Positive illusions: Creative self-deception and the healthy mind.* New York: Basic Books.

Taylor, S. E. 1999. *Health psychology,* 4th ed. New York: McGraw-Hill.

Taylor, S. E., S. S. Dickerson, and L. C. Klein. 2001. Toward a biology of social support. In *Handbook of positive psychology,* edited by C. R. Snyder and S. J. Lopez. London: Oxford University Press.

Taylor, S. E., L. C. Klein, B. P. Lewis, T. L. Gruenewald, R. A. R. Gurung, and J. A. Updegraff. 2000. Biobehavioral responses to stress in females: Tend-and-befriend, not fight-or-flight. *Psychological Review.* 107:411–29.

Taylor, S. E., L. A. Peplau, and D. O. Sears. 1999. *Social psychology,* 10th ed. Englewood Cliffs, N.J.: Prentice-Hall.

Taylor, S. E., R. L. Repetti, and T. E. Seeman. 1997. Health psychology: What is an unhealthy environment and how does it get under the skin? *Annual Review of Psychology.* 48:411–47.

Taylor, S. E., R. M. Sage, and J. S. Lerner. 2002. Pathways from early family environment to stress regulatory systems and subjective health. Manuscript under review.

Terkel, S. 1997. *Working.* New York: The New Press.

The Economist. 1994. Living, and dying, in a barren land. *The Economist,* April 23, p. 54.

The Economist. 1996. Tomorrow's second sex. *The Economist,* September 28, pp. 23–26.

Thomsen, D. G., and D. G. Gilbert. 1998. Factors characterizing marital conflict states and traits: Physiological, affective, behavioral and neurotic variable contributions to marital conflict and satisfaction. *Personality and Individual Differences.* 25:833–55.

Thorsteinsson, E. B., J. E. James, and M. E. Gregg. 1998. Effects of video-relayed social support on hemodynamic reactivity and salivary cortisol during laboratory-based behavioral challenge. *Health Psychology.* 17:436–44.

Tiger, L. 1970. *Men in groups.* New York: Vintage Books.

Tooby, J., and I. DeVore. 1987. The reconstruction of hominid behavioral evolution through strategic modeling. In *The evolution of human behavior,* edited by W. G. Kinzey. New York: State University of New York Press.

Tremblay, R. E., B. Schaal, B. Boulerice, L. Arseneault, R. G. Soussignan, D. Paquette, and D. Laurent. 1998. Testosterone, physical aggression, dominance, and physical development in early adolescence. *International Journal of Behavioral Development.* 22:753–77.

Trevarthen, C., and K. J. Aitken. 1994. Brain development, infant communication, and empathy disorders: Intrinsic factors in child mental health. *Development and Psychopathology.* 6:597–633.

Trivers, R. L. 1971. The evolution of reciprocal altruism. *Quarterly Review of Biology.* 46:35–37.

Troutt, D. D. 1993. *The thin red line: How the poor still pay more.* San Francisco, Calif.: West Coast Regional Office.

Trull, T. J., K. J. Sher, C. Minks-Brown, J. Durbin, and R. Burr. 2000. Borderline personality disorder and substance use disorders: A review and integration. *Clinical Psychology Review*. 20:235–53.

Tucker, J. S., H. S. Friedman, J. E. Schwartz, M. H. Criqui, C. Tomlinson-Keasey, D. L. Wingard, and L. R. Martin. 1997. Parental divorce: Effects on individual behavior and longevity. *Journal of Personality and Social Psychology*. 73:381–91.

Tucker, J. S., and J. S. Mueller. 2000. Spouses' social control of health behaviors: Use and effectiveness of specific strategies. *Personality and Social Psychology Bulletin*. 26(9): 1120–130.

Turner, J. B., R. C. Kessler, and J. S. House. 1991. Factors facilitating adjustment to unemployment: Implications for intervention. *American Journal of Community Psychology*. 19:521–42.

Turner, R. A., C. E. Irwin Jr., J. M. Tschann, and S. G. Millstein. 1993. Autonomy, relatedness, and the initiation of health risk behaviors in early adolescence. *Health Psychology*. 12:200–208.

Turner-Cobb, J., S. Sephton, C. Koopman, J. Blake-Mortimer, and D. Spiegel. 2000. Social support and salivary cortisol in women with metastatic breast cancer. *Psychosomatic Medicine*. 62:337–45.

Twenge, J. M. 2000. The age of anxiety? Birth cohort change in anxiety and neuroticism, 1952–1993. *Journal of Personality and Social Psychology*. 79:1007–1021.

U. S. Department of Health and Human Service. 1999. *Child Maltreatment 1997: Reports from the States to the National Child Abuse and Neglect Data System*. Washington, D.C.: U. S. Government Printing Office.

U. S. Department of Justice. 1992. *Crime and neighborhoods*. www.usdoj.gov.

U. S. Department of Justice. 1997. *Domestic violence*. www.usdoj.gov/domesticviolence.htm.

Uchino, B. N., J. T. Cacioppo, W. Malarkey, R. Glaser, and J. K. Kiecolt-Glaser. 1995. Appraisal support predicts age-related differences in cardiovascular function in women. *Health Psychology*. 14:556–62.

Uchino, B. N., J. Holt-Lunstad, D. Uno, R. Betancourt, and T. S. Garvey. 1999. Social support and age-related differences in cardiovascular function: An examination of potential mediators. *Annals of Behavioral Medicine*. 21:135–42.

Uchino, B., J. Cacioppo, J. Kiecolt-Glaser. 1996. The relationship between social support and physiological processes: A review with emphasis on underlying mechanisms and implications for health. *Psychological Bulletin*. 119:488–531.

Umberson, D. 1992. Gender, marital status and the social control of health behavior. *Social Science and Medicine*. 24:907–17.

Umberson, D. 1987. Family status and health behaviors: Social control as a dimension of social integration. *Journal of Health and Social Behavior*. 28:306–19.

Umberson, D., C. B. Wortman, and R. C. Kessler. 1992. Widowhood and depression: Explaining long-term gender differences in vulnerability. *Journal of Health and Social Behavior*. 33:10–24.

UNICEF. 2001. *The State of the World's Children* [Online]. Available: http://www.unicef.org [November 16, 2001].

Uno, H., S. Eisele, A. Sakai, S. Shelton, E. Baker, O. DeJesus, and J. Holden. 1994. Neurotoxicity of glucocorticoids in the primate brain. *Hormones and Behavior*. 28: 336–48.

Uvnas-Moberg, K. 1996. Neuroendocrinology of the mother-child interaction. *Trends in Endocrinology and Metabolism*. 7:126–31.

Uvnas-Moberg, K. 1998. Oxytocin may still mediate the benefits of positive social interaction and emotions. *Psychoneuroendocrinology*. 23:819–35.

Uvnas-Moberg, K. 1999. Physiological and endocrine effects of social contact. In *The integrative neurobiology of affiliation*, edited by C. S. Carter, I. I. Lederhendler, and B. Kirkpatrick. Cambridge, Mass.: MIT Press.

Uvnas-Moberg, K. 1997. Oxytocin linked antistress effects—the relaxation and growth response. *Acta Psychologica Scandinavica*. 640(Suppl.):38–42.

Valenzuela, C. F., and R. A. Harris. 1997. Alcohol: Neurobiology. In *Substance abuse: A comprehensive textbook*, 7th ed., edited by J. H. Lowinson, P. Ruiz, R. B. Millman, and J. G. Langrod. Baltimore, Md.: Williams and Wilkins.

van den Berg, C. L., T. Hol, J. M. Van Ree, B. M. Spruijt, H. Everts, and J. M. Koolhaas. 1999. Play is indispensible for an adequate development of coping with social challenges in the rat. *Developmental Psychobiology*. 34:129–38.

Van Schaik, C. P., and R. I. M. Dunbar. 1990. The evolution of monogamy in large primates: A new hypothesis and some crucial tests. *Behaviour*. 115:30–62.

Vanhanen, M., and H. Soininen. 1998. Glucose intolerance, cognitive impairment and Alzheimer's disease. *Current Opinion in Neurology*. 11:673–77.

Vazquez, D. M., J. F. Lopez, H. Van Hoers, S. J. Watson, and S. Levine. 2000. Maternal deprivation regulates serotonin 1A and 2A receptors in the infant rat. *Brain Research*. 855:76–82.

Veroff, J., R. Kulka, and E. Douvan. 1981. *Mental health in America: Patterns of help-seeking from 1957 to 1976*. New York: Basic Books.

Verrier, R. L., and D. B. Carr. 1991. Stress, opioid peptides and cardiac arrhythmias. In *Stress, neuropeptides, and systematic disease*, edited by J. A. McCubbin, P. G. Faufmann, and C. B. Nemeroff. San Diego, Calif.: Academic Press.

Wacquant, L. J. D., and W. J. Wilson. 1989. The cost of racial and class exclusion in the inner city. *Annals of the American Academy of Political and Social Science*. 501:8–25.

Wadhwa, P. D., J. F. Culhane, V. Rauh, and S. S. Barve. 2001. Stress and preterm birth: Neuroendocrine, immune/inflammatory, and vascular mechanisms. *Maternal and Child Health Journal*. 5:119–25.

Walker, E. A., A. Gelfand, W. J. Katon, M. P. Koss, M. Von Korff, D. Bernstein, and J. Russo. 1999. Adult health status of women with histories of childhood abuse and neglect. *American Journal of Medicine*. 107:332–39.

Wallace, J. E. 2001. The benefits of mentoring for female lawyers. *Journal of Vocational Behavior*. 58:366–91.

Wallace, R., and D. Wallace. 1990. Origins of public health collapse in New York City: The dynamics of planned shrinkage, contagious urban decay and social disintegration. *Bulletin of the New York Academy of Medicine*. 66:391–434.

Wandersman, A., and M. Nation. 1998. Urban neighborhoods and mental health. *American Psychologist*. 53:647–56.

Wang, S., J. V. Bartolome, and S. M. Schanberg. 1996. Neonatal deprivation of maternal touch may suppress ornithine decarboxylase via downregulation of the proto-oncogenes c- myc and max. *Journal of Neuroscience*. 16:836–42.

Watson, P. 1995. Explaining rising mortality among men in Eastern Europe. *Social Science and Medicine*. 41(7):923–34.

Watters, E. 2001. In my tribe. *The New York Times Magazine*, October 14, pp. 25–26.

Weidner, G. 1998. Gender gap in health decline in East Europe. *Nature*. 395:835.

Weidner, G. 2000. Why do men get more heart disease than women? An international perspective. *Journal of American College Health*. 48:291–94.

Weiser, E. B. 2000. Gender differences in Internet use patterns and Internet application preferences: A two-sample comparison. *CyberPsychology and Behavior*. 3:167–77.

Weiss, R. S. 1975. *Marital separation*. New York: Basic.

Welbourne, T. M. In press. Wall Street likes its women: An examination of women in the top management teams of initial public offerings. *Center for Advanced Human Resource Studies: Working Paper Series*. Working Paper 99-07.

Wethington, E., J. D. McLeod, and R. C. Kessler. 1987. The importance of life events for explaining sex differences in psychological distress. In *Gender and stress*, edited by R. C. Barnett, L. Biener, and G. K. Baruch. New York: The Free Press.

Wheeler, L., S. Reis, and J. Nezlek. 1983. Loneliness, social interaction, and sex roles. *Journal of Personality and Social Psychology*. 45:943–53.

Whiting, B., and J. Whiting. 1975. *Children of six cultures*. Cambridge, Mass.: Harvard University Press.

Wickrama, K., R. D. Conger, and F. O. Lorenz. 1995. Work, marriage, lifestyle, and changes in men's physical health. *Journal of Behavioral Medicine*. 18:97–111.

Widdowson, E. M. 1951. Mental contentment and physical growth. *The Lancet*. 260: 1316–318.

Wiklund, I., A. Oden, H. Sanne, G. Ulvenstam, C. Wilhelmsson, and L. Wilhelmsen. 1988. Prognostic importance of somatic and psychosocial variables after a first myocardial infarction. *American Journal of Epidemiology*. 128:786–95.

Wilkinson, R. G. 1996. *Unhealthy societies: The afflictions of inequality*. London: Routledge.

Williams, D. R., and C. Collins. 1995. U. S. socioeconomic and racial differences in health. *Annual Review of Sociology*. 21:349–86.

Williams, K., J. Suls, G. Alliger, S. Learner, and C. Wan. 1991. Multiple role juggling and daily mood states in working mothers: An experience sampling study. *Journal of Applied Psychology*. 76(5):664–74.

Williams, R. B. 1998. Lower socioeconomic status and increased mortality: Early childhood roots and the potential for successful interventions. *Journal of the American Medical Association*. 279:1745–746.

Williams, R. B., J. Barefoot, and R. Shekelle. 1985. The health consequences of hostility. In *Anger and hostility in cardiovascular and behavioral disorders*, edited by M. Chesney and R. Rosenman. Washington, D.C.: Hemisphere.

Wills, T. A., and S. D. Cleary. 1996. How are social support effects mediated? A test with parental support and adolescent substance use. *Journal of Personality and Social Psychology*. 71:937–52.

Wilson, E. O. 1998. *Consilience: The unity of knowledge*. New York: Knopf.

Windle, R. J., N. Shanks, S. L. Lightman, and C. D. Ingram. 1997. Central oxytocin administration reduces stress-induced corticosterone release and anxiety behavior in rats. *Endocrinology*. 138:2829–834.

Winslow, J. T., N. Hastings, C. S. Carter, C. R. Harbaugh, and T. R. Insel. 1993. A role for central vasopressin in pair bonding in monogamous prairie voles. *Nature*. 365:545–48.

Witt, D. M., and T. R. Insel. 1991. A selective oxytocin antagonist attenuates progesterone facilitation of female sexual behavior. *Endocrinology*. 128:3269–276.

Witt, D. M., C. S. Carter, and D. Walton. 1990. Central and peripheral effects of oxytocin administration in prairie voles (*Microtus ochrogaster*). *Pharmacology, Biochemistry, and Behavior*. 37:63–69.

Witt, D. M., J. T. Winslow, and T. R. Insel. 1992. Enhanced social interactions in rats following chronic, centrally infused oxytocin. *Pharmacology, Biochemistry, and Behavior*. 43:855–86.

Wolf, M. 1975. Women and suicide in China. In *Women in Chinese society*, edited by M. Wolf and R. Witke. Stanford: Stanford University Press.

Women's Justice Center. Women in Policing [Online]. Available: *http://www.justice-women.com/police_women.html* [October 15, 2001].

Woodall, K. L., and K. A. Matthews. 1989. Familial environment associated with type A behaviors and psychophysiological responses to stress in children. *Health Psychology*. 8:403–26.

Wrangham, R. W. 1980. An ecological model of female-bonded primate groups. *Behaviour*. 75:262–300.

Wright, R. J., S. Cohen, V. Carey, S. T. Weiss, and D. R. Gold. In press. Parental stress as a predictor of wheezing in infancy: A prospective birth-cohort study. *The American Journal of Respiratory and Critical Care Medicine*.

Wu, H., J. Wang, J. T. Cacioppo, R. Glaser, J. K. Kiecolt-Glaser, and W. B. Malarkey. 1999. Chronic stress associated with spousal caregiving of patients with Alzheimer's dementia is associated with downregulation of B-lymphocyte GH mRNA. *Journal of Gerontology. Series A, Biological Sciences and Medical Sciences*. 54:M212–15.

Wynne-Edwards, K. E. 2001. Hormonal changes in mammalian fathers. *Hormones and Behavior*. 40:139–45.

Yogman, M. W. 1990. Male parental behavior in humans and nonhuman primates. In *Mammalian parenting: Biochemical, neurobiological, and behavioral determinants*, edited by N. A. Krasnegor and R. S. Bridges. New York: Oxford University Press, pp. 461–81.

Young, M., and P. Willmott. 1957. *Family and kinship in East London*. London: Routledge and Kegan Paul.

Yu, Y., and D. R. Williams. 1999. Socioeconomic status and mental health. In *Handbook of the sociology of mental health*, edited by C. S. Aneshensel and J. C. Phelan. New York: Kluwer Academic/Plenum Publishers.

Zajonc, R. B. 1965. Social facilitation. *Science*. 149:269–74.

Zajonc, R. B. 1968. Attitudinal effects of mere exposure. *Journal of Personality and Social Psychology* (Monograph Suppl., Pt. 2). 1–29.

Zajonc, R. B. 2001. Mere exposure: A gateway to the subliminal. *Current Directions in Psychological Science*. 10:224–28.

Zeskind, P. S., and V. Collins. 1987. The pitch of infant crying and caregiver responses in a natural setting. *Infant Behavior and Development*. 10:501–504.

Ziegler, T. E., and C. T. Snowdon. 2000. Preparental hormone levels and parenting experience in male cotton-top Tamarins, Saguinus Oedipus. *Hormones and Behavior*. 38:159–67.

Zimmerman, S. L. 1994. The role of the state in family life: States' AFDC payments and divorce rates in the United States. *International Journal of Sociology and Social Policy*. 14:4–23.

Index

rhesus monkeys, 156
 with genetic risk of impulsive aggression,
  61–62
risky family life, lifetime impacts of, 52–58,
  198
 adolescent behavior, 62–65
 interventions to moderate, 189–93
 on physical and mental health, 53, 54–58,
  65–69
 preexisting vulnerabilities and, 58, 69
 stress response and, 56–67, 64–66
Rock, Chris, 176
Romanian orphans, 44–45, 82
Rosenblum, Leonard, 169–70
Ross, Michael, 117
Russia:
 alcoholism among men of, 127
 life expectancy, gender differences in, 126

Sanders, Brian, 14
Sapolsky, Robert, 166–67
Schachter, Stanley, 105–6
Schulz, Richard, 153
Sears, David, 183
Seeman, Teresa, 195
self-interest as motivation for human behavior,
  181–84, 193
"selfish gene," 159
Selfish Gene, The (Dawkins), 9
serotonin:
 maternal behavior and, 27
 mood problems and, 64–65
 social confidence and, 83
 studies of monkeys and levels of, 61–62,
  139–40
sewing and mending circles, 91
sexual abuse, 55
sexual assault, 186
 protection against, 101–2
 social class and victims of rape, 175
sexuality:
 adolescent, 63, 64, 65
 female, maternal-infant bond and, 121–23
 male, 123
sexually transmitted diseases, risky family life
  and, 55
shyness, 59–60, 69
sick, caring for the, 40
skin cancer, 68
Skutnik, Lenny, 146–47
sleep, 115
Slowtow, Rob, 135

smoking:
 by adolescents, 63, 65
 married men and, 115
 risky family life and, 57, 68
 social class and, 164
"social capital," building, 191
social class and health, 160–80, 191
 African Americans, high income and well
  educated, 177–78
 crime victims, 175–76, 177
 dominance hierarchies and tending,
  165–68
 friends and family, social support from, 179
 health habits, 164–65
 muting the impact of gap between rich and
  poor, 184–85
 neighborhood and social life, 175–77
 tending and, 168–80
 women, high income and well educated,
  177–78
 work and, 170–75
social support, 13
 in childhood, *see* children; fathering;
  mother-child relationship
 community support, 75–76, 185, 191
 friendships, *see* friendships
 health and, 76–77, 80–81, 84–86
 the human brain and, 36–45
 under intense stress, 11, 77–79, 157–58
 "invisible," 85
 of men's groups, 140–45
 social isolation and health problems, 76
 with strangers, *see* strangers, ties to
 weakening of, 193
sociobiology, competitive, aggressive view of
  human social relationships of, 2
South Africa, elephant problem in Pilanesberg
  region of, 134–35, 138
Spiegel, David, 80–81
squirrel monkeys, studies of female bonding
  with, 92, 96–97
status and altruism, 156–57
strangers, ties to, 13, 77–81, 157–58
 mentoring, 192–93
stress:
 bonding engendered by intense, 11, 77–79,
  157–58
 chronic, *see* chronic stress
 female friendships as buffer against, 92–112
 poor parenting and, 169–70
 response to, *see* stress response
 at work, 22–23

About the Author

SHELLEY E. TAYLOR is a Professor of Psychology at UCLA. A world-renowned expert on stress and health, Taylor is the author of more than 200 papers in the fields of psychology and medicine. Her work on the "tend and befriend" theory was profiled in newspapers, magazines, and television shows throughout the world. She is a recipient of the Distinguished Scientific Contribution Award in Health Psychology, the Donald Campbell Award in Social Psychology, Yale University's Wilbur Lucius Cross Medal, and the prestigious Distinguished Scientific Contribution Award of the American Psychological Association. Taylor lives in Los Angeles.